Josiah Williams

Life in the Soudan

Adventures amongst the Tribes, and Travels in Egypt, in 1881 and 1882

Josiah Williams

Life in the Soudan
Adventures amongst the Tribes, and Travels in Egypt, in 1881 and 1882

ISBN/EAN: 9783337177560

Printed in Europe, USA, Canada, Australia, Japan

Cover: Foto ©ninafisch / pixelio.de

More available books at **www.hansebooks.com**

LIFE IN THE SOUDAN:

ADVENTURES AMONGST THE TRIBES, AND TRAVELS

IN EGYPT, IN 1881 AND 1882.

BY

Dr. JOSIAH WILLIAMS, F.R.G.S.

(Surgeon-Major, Imperial Ottoman Army, 1876-1877).

ILLUSTRATED.

LONDON:
REMINGTON & CO., PUBLISHERS,
HENRIETTA STREET, COVENT GARDEN.
1884.
[*All Rights Reserved.*]

To

SIR SAMUEL WHITE BAKER, F.R.G.S.,

I DEDICATE, WITH HIS PERMISSION,

THIS BOOK,

CONTAINING AN ACCOUNT OF

TRAVELS IN THE SOUDAN

AND EXPLORATION IN THE

BASÉ OR KUNAMA COUNTRY IN 1882.

ILLUSTRATIONS.

THE AUTHOR ...	*Frontispiece.*
SOUÂKIN ...	... 97
HADENDOWAH ARAB CAMEL-MEN ...	... 128
KASSALA MOUNTAIN ...	... 160
THE AUTHOR ATTENDING TO ARAB AILMENTS ...	... 248
MOUNTAIN PASS NEAR SANHÎT ...	... 304
THE CAUSEWAY AT MASSAWAH ...	... 312

CONTENTS.

CHAPTER I.
PAGE

Leave England for Paris—Drugs and Clothing Required—A "Sleeby" German—Turin ... ... 5—12

CHAPTER II.

Milan—The Cathedral—Galleria Vittorio Emmanuele—Piazza d'Armi—Palazzo de Brera—Lake of Como—Bologna—Its Ancient History—Leaning Towers—The Certosa—Teatro Communale—Brindisi ... 13—23

CHAPTER III.

P. and O. Steamer *Tanjore*—Arrival of the Mail and Passengers—Ancient Brindisi—Brindisi to Alexandria—Alexandria Past and Present—Its Trade ... ... 24—37

CHAPTER IV.

The Fertilizing Rivers of Egypt — Leave 'Alexandria — Incidents *en route*—Shepheard's Hotel—Ancient and Modern Cairo—The Donkey-boys—Arab Patients—Dancing Dervishes—The House where Joseph, Mary, and the Infant Saviour Lived in Old Cairo—The Boulac Museum—The Petrified Forest—Mokattam Hills—Tombs of the Caliphs and Citadel—Cairo by Sunset ... ... 38—66

CHAPTER V.

A Young American at Shepheard's Hotel—Drive to the Pyramids of Gizeh—Ascent and Exploration of the Pyramid of Cheops—The Sphinx ... ... 67—80

CHAPTER VI.

Heliopolis—The Shoubra Road—Bedrashyn—Mitrahenny—Memphis—Sakhara—Apis Mausoleum——Worship of the Bull Apis—Tomb of King Phta—Meet the Khedive—Engage Servants for the Soudan 81—91

CONTENTS.

CHAPTER VII.
PAGE

The Land of Goshen—Ancient Canals—Suez—Howling Dervishes—Eclipse of the Moon and Strange Behaviour of Natives—Leave Suez—Where the Israelites Crossed the Red Sea—Pass Mount Sinai—Coral Reefs Abundant ... ... 92—97

CHAPTER VIII.
Arrival at Souâkin—The Soudan—Bedouin Arab Prisoners in the Square, Not "on the Square"—Ivory—Engage Camels—Sheik Moussa—Souâkin Slaves—Tragic End of a Doctor—Hadendowah Arabs—An Ill-fated Missionary Enterprise ... ... 98—110

CHAPTER IX.
The Start Across the Desert—My Camel Serves me a Scurvy Trick—The Camel, its Habits and Training ... ... 111—118

CHAPTER X.
Our First Camp—Torrents of Rain—Jules Bardet—Camel-drivers Behave Badly—Suleiman in Trouble—Camel-drivers get Upset—The Desert—Two of Us Lose our Way—Jules Suffers from Dysentery—Sand-storm—A Pilgrim Dies on the Road; Another in the Camp—Jules' Illness—Camp Split Up—Lose Our Way—Encamp Several Days in the Desert—Arab Huts—The Mirage—A Lion ... 119—143

CHAPTER XI.
Arrive at Kassala—Description of Kassala—We buy Camels and Horses—The Mudir gives a Dinner—Jules' Death and Burial—Hyænas—Arab Patients—Mahoom's History—Demetrius Mosconas on Slavery—Menagerie at Kassala ... ... 144—153

CHAPTER XII.
Camels from the Atbara—The Mudir—Gordon Pasha's Character in the Soudan—Fertility of the Soudan ... ... 154—159

CHAPTER XIII.
Leave Kassala—Character of the Country—Meet Beni-Amir Arabs on the River-bed—The Baobob Tree ... ... 160—164

CHAPTER XIV.
Encamp at Heikota—Sheik Ahmed—Herr Schumann and His Zareeba—We Make a Zareeba—The Mahdi—Excitement in the Village—Horrible Tragedy—Sheik Ahmed Dines with us—The Magic Lantern—Lions Visit Us ... ... 165—177

CHAPTER XV.
Patients at Heikota—Leave Heikota—Game in the Basé Country—See our First Lion—A Lion Interviews the Author—Tétel, Nellut, and other Game Killed on the March ... ... 178—183

CONTENTS.

CHAPTER XVI.

We Arrive at the Basé or Kunama Country—The Village of Sarcella—Murder of Mr. Powell and Party—My Camel and I Unceremoniously Part Company—The First Basó We See—Encamp at Koolookoo—Our First Interview with Basó—They make "Aman" with Us—Their Appearance—Description of Koolookoo and the Basé People—Their Habits and Customs ... ... 184—200

CHAPTER XVII.

We leave Koolookoo, Accompanied by a Number of the Basé—The Magic Lantern—See Buffalo and Giraffe for the First Time—Two Buffalos Killed—A Basé Feast—Curious Basé Dance—They Dry their Meat on Lines in the Sun—A Wounded Buffalo—Hoodoo, Chief Sheik of the Basé, Visits Us—A Column of Sand—A Leper—The Basé Squabble over the Meat—We Arrive at Abyssinia ... ... 201—214

CHAPTER XVIII.

The Dembelas Attack Us, Mahomet Wounded, Narrow Escape of two of our Party—Activity in Camp, We Make a Zareeba and Fire the Country—Hold a Council of War—Our Silent and Dangerous Ride—Hoodoo's Sagacity—Arrival in Camp of Mahomet, Wounded—We Retreat—Mahomet's Death and Burial ... ... 215—229

CHAPTER XIX.

Messrs. James and Phillipps Start on a Visit to Rasalulu—Curious Way of Shaving Children's Heads—A Disgusting Basé—The Camel-drivers become Mutinous—Intended Attack by Basé—We Fire the Country and Make a Zareeba—Encamp at Woamma—Trouble Again with Camel-men—Lions Disturb Us—Arrival at Heikota—A Tale of Blood and Slavery ... ... 230—243

CHAPTER XX.

Patients Arrive from all Parts—Rough Journeys—Arrive at the Hamran Settite—Mahomet Sali Deceives us—Crocodiles, Turtle, and Fish—We Move on to Boorkattan, in Abyssinia—Next Day we Move off as Abyssinians Approach—We Catch Enormous Quantities of Fish with the Net—Narrow Escape from a Wounded Buffalo—The Coorbatch Administered—Scorpions and Snakes—Hamrans Visit Us—Hamran mode of Hunting and Snaring—Hamran and Basó—The Hamrans Threaten to Fire on Us—Again Return to the Hamran Settite—Encamp at Omhagger ... ... 244—263

CHAPTER XXI.

A Boa-constrictor Visits Us—The Burton Boat—Moussa's Behaviour Entails a Thrashing and His Discharge—Great Heat—A Fine Hippopotamus Killed—Hamran Feast—The White Ants—Another

CONTENTS.

PAGE

Hippopotamus Killed—Mahomet Sali Brings Supplies—Native Music in the Night—Delicate Hints Conveyed to the Performer—A Remarkably Fine Nellut Shot—Arab and Egyptian Taxation—Baboons—A Hamran Story—Ali Stung by a Scorpion—On the March Once More—Rough Journeys ... ... 264—278

CHAPTER XXII.

Encamp at Lakatakoora Without the Caravan—Description of Village—Basó Ladies Visit Me ere I Get Out of Bed—They Receive Presents and are very Amusing—Enormous Numbers of Doves and Sand-grouse—Aboosalal to Sogoda—Boa-constrictor Killed—An Unpleasant Journey, We all Get Separated—Arrive at Heikota Again   279—284

CHAPTER XXIII.

An Abyssinian Improvisatore and His Little Slave—Prepare for a March to Massawa—A Strange Basé Breakfast—Patients—Arrive at Toodloak—Beni-Amirs Encamped on the Gash—Lions and Leopards are Shot—Our Monkeys in Camp—Baboon Mode of Attacking Leopards—Crafty Baboons—Lions Abound—Hyæna Method of Attacking a Lion—Hyæna Interviews Mr. Colvin—Arrival at Amadeb—Departure from Amadeb—Bareas Attempt an Attack on the Caravan—Beni-Amirs Watering their Flocks and Herds—We Meet with a young Elephant—Leopard and Hyæna Shot at Khor-Baraker   ...   . 285—297

CHAPTER XXIV.

A Lion Near the Camp—The Monks of Chardamba—We Meet Ali Dheen Pasha, Governor-General of the Soudan—Arrival at Keren, or Sanhit—The Priests at Keren—Account of Keren—Merissa—Dra, a Domestic Slave, Made Free—Descent from Sanhit to the Anseba Valley—The Birds There—Along the River-bed of the Labak—A Big March—Massawa—Farewell to Camels—Massawa to Souâkin—Take in Cargo—Farewell to the Soudan—Arrival at Suez ... 298—314

CHAPTER XXV.

Suez to Cairo—Alexandria—On Board the *Mongolia*—Passengers on Board—Hibernian Humour—Venice—The Piazza of St. Mark—The Campanile—The Piazetta—The Zecca, or Mint—The Palace of the Doges—St. Mark's—The Arsenal ...   . 315—330

CHAPTER XXVI.

We Hear of the Murder of Lord Frederick Cavendish and Mr. Burke—A Grand Serenade on the Grand Canal—My Journey from Venice to England   ...   . 331—338

PREFACE.

THE SOUDAN, two years ago, was a name unknown to the million, and I will venture to say that at that time not one in fifty knew anything about it. Only those who could afford to obtain Sir Samuel Baker's interesting and instructive work, "The Nile Sources of Abyssinia," would be acquainted with the locality and other particulars.

The literature extant on Egypt proper would probably amount to tons, but that on the Soudan would occupy a very small space indeed on the library shelf, for the simple reason that so very few have travelled through it.

In November, 1881, I left England to accompany six gentlemen on an exploring expedition in the Soudan, and, in view of passing events in Egypt and that locality, I indulged in the hope that an account of my journey will not be unacceptable to the public. I held the post of medical officer to the expedition, partly on account of my experience in the Turkish war, where I was continually brought face to face with dysentery, ague, and other tropical diseases, which are so easily recognised without any extraneous assistance, medical or lay, but which are troublesome to treat, especially when hampered by an ignorant and fussy interference. Doubtless many faults of omission and commission may be found in my book; but I trust that those who criticise it will do so leniently, and remember that it has been written during spare hours, when the exigencies of practice would allow of my seeking recreation by the use of my pen. "Oh, that mine enemy would write a book!" was the heartfelt expression of a vindictive old gentleman, well known for his great patience. My enemies, I trust, are few; those I have shall be gratified, though I hope I shall not find any who are utterly callous, but will use me in a gentlemanly fashion.

I have ventured to describe not only my travels in the Soudan, but the journey from England and home again, extracted from my journal, which is most accurate, as I kept it religiously day by day. Much of the old-world history has been culled from various sources of information. The Illustrations of Soudan scenery, natives, and objects of interest are from rude sketches of my own, elaborated by Mr. Fanshawe, a perfect master in the art. The frontispiece is from a photograph taken by Messrs. Lombardi and Co., of Pall Mall.

Although I am aware of the fact that Mr. F. L. James has published a book on the Soudan, I have carefully refrained from reading it, fearing I might inadvertently use any of his expressions, and also feeling sure that in *some* matters we may materially differ in opinion.

Although I have, on some occasions, written for the medical journals, I am quite aware that there may be many faults of style and finish in this my first effort at a book; such shortcomings I would ask the reader to overlook. It is but a plain, unvarnished account of a journey through a territory hitherto but little known, and as such I trust it may be of interest to the majority of my readers.

CHAPTER I.

LEAVE ENGLAND FOR PARIS—DRUGS AND CLOTHING REQUIRED—A "SLEEBY" GERMAN—TURIN.

I WAS bound for the Soudan, and had arranged to meet my party at Brindisi on the 21st of November, 1881. I therefore sent on all my heavy baggage by Peninsular and Oriental steamer to Suez; included in this was a good-sized medicine chest, well stocked with drugs for the relief or cure of nearly all the ills that flesh is heir to.

I am an old campaigner, having served as a surgeon-major in the Turkish Army in 1876 and '77, consequently had a very good idea of what drugs would be most necessary and useful. Knowing also that we were going to a very hot part of the globe, I took as few liquids, such as tinctures, &c., as possible.

Everything that I could have made in the form of

pills I got Messrs. Richardson and Co., of Leicester, to do ; their coated pills stood the journey splendidly, and could always be depended on.

It will not be necessary to enumerate all the contents of the medicine-chest; but I think it might be useful to those who take a similar journey if I mention a few things that ought certainly to be taken, and they are the following : A good stock of quinine, oil of male-fern, as tape-worm is by no means uncommon ; ipecacuanha, for that formidable complaint, dysentery ; castor oil, opium, Dover's powder, iodoform, chlorodyne, calomel, blue pill, and various other mercurial preparations, much required for complaints in the Soudan ; iodide of potash, carbonate of soda, powdered alum, sulphate of zinc, sugar of lead, solution of atropine, solution of ammonia, Epsom salts, a large bottle of purgative pills, nitrate of silver (lunar caustic), carbolic acid, lint, a few dozen bandages, and plaster in a tin. Ointments are useless, as they soon become quite liquid in such a hot climate, and run all over the medicine chest, making a great mess.

Clothing.—Of course every gentleman will be provided with the ordinary European clothing for use in civilized parts, but such things as nicely-polished boots, collars, neckties, and so forth, may be easily dispensed with in the Soudan. The most necessary articles are two or three dozen pairs summer socks, half-a-dozen thin flannel shirts, three or four silk shirts, three pairs of *brown* leather lace-up boots, and a comfortable pair of slippers, three or four suits of thin light clothing, a strong jean coat and trousers, that will not be easily torn by the thorns whilst hunting, and a pith helmet.

Soldiers cannot march without easy boots, and travellers cannot travel with comfort unless they have suitable braces. This may seem a small matter to talk about, but I have often heard strong language poured forth at the secession of a trouser-button; and I know from past experience what a nuisance it is to be obliged to sew on one's trouser-buttons. A long time is spent in searching for a needle and thread, and a much longer time, by the unpractised one, in sewing on the button. Now, fortunately, these annoyances are things of the past, since the invention of what is known as "the traveller's patent buttonless brace."

It is simplicity itself. Instead of buttons on the trousers, there are eyelet holes, through which a little bar attached to the brace—instead of a loop—is slipped, and there is an end for ever of the nuisance of buttons coming off.

A good supply of soap for washing clothes should be taken, also plenty for personal use. Pear's

Soap, I think, is an excellent one in every respect. Some of our party took thick woollen pads with them, which they wore over the spine. I did not, neither do I think them at all necessary.

As I was not due at Brindisi until the 21st November, I decided to have a ramble through parts of Italy which I had not before visited. Accordingly, I left England in the early part of the month.

On my way to Paris I made the acquaintance of a German residing in London. We soon got on conversational terms, and ere long he informed me that he had not been well lately, and was much concerned about himself, that one afternoon, feeling rather tired, he lay down on the sofa, intending to have a nap. He was so unhappy or unwise as to sleep for a whole week without once awaking. To sink into this blissful state of oblivion may have its advantages, also its disadvantages. On another occasion he performed the same feat, but indulged in this lethargic propensity for a much longer period. If I remember rightly, he observed this condition during a fortnight. However, I pointed out to him what an immense advantage this was, as he would not have his mind worried by the Income Tax, Poor Rate, and other objectionable collectors; also what a saving in eating and drinking would be effected by this *somnia similima mortis* habit of his, and that balmy sleep was kind nature's sweet restorer. Strange to say, my arguments were ineffective, as he replied that "Sleeb vas all very vell in its way, but I would rater not sleeb so much as dat, as I have my business to attend to, for vich I must be wide-avake."

We were glad to get off the boat that took us from Dover to Calais, as both of us suffered from that miserable complaint, *mal-de-mer*, to some extent. We reached la belle Paris in the evening, very glad of a rest. After spending two days very pleasantly and agreeably in Paris, I took train at 9 p.m. from the Gare de Lyon for Turin. Fortunately, a French gentleman and I were the only two occupants of the carriage during the night. We turned up the arm-rests, each occupied a side of the carriage, and slept soundly all night. At Maćon we had breakfast, wash and brush up, then resumed our journey. Passing through grand mountain scenery, and quite close to the railway, we passed a beautiful lake some miles in extent, the name of which I forget. When we reached Chambery I lost my agreeable French companion. In the afternoon we ran through the Mont Cenis tunnel, the time occupied being just thirty-eight minutes. The gradient became somewhat steep, and the lovely Alpine scenery glorious and lonely, now winding through deep gorges, anon running downwards for miles along the very edge of a fearful precipice.

I reached Turin in the evening succeeding my departure from Paris. The station is situated in the Piazza Carlo Felice, and is a fine, spacious building. When my luggage had been duly inspected by Custom House officials, I was permitted to transport myself and my belongings to an omnibus from the Hotel Trambetta, whither I was driven just in time for *table d'hôte*. Immediately after leaving the station the driver was stopped by an official, who opened the door, asked if I had any complaint to make, and looked round to see if there were any provisions, as the octroi duties prevail in Italy. I had no complaint; the door was shut, and off we went.

As I did not intend to remain long in Turin, I was up the following morning in good time, determined to see as much of the place as I could in a short time. The streets are clean and well laid out, the houses large and handsome generally, and the town comparatively modern, although it was originally founded by a tribe called the Taurini, was the capital of Piedmont during the 14th century, and the capital of Italy until 1865. The population is about 208,000, and the University perhaps the most important in Italy, there being over 1,500 students.

I should liked to have spent a week in exploring Turin and the neighbourhood, but had to be content with the short time at my disposal. I took a walk down the Via Lagrange, and soon reached the Palazzo Madama (Piazza Castello). This Palace was used for the sittings of the Italian Senate when Turin was the seat of government (1865). In the early part of last century the mother of King Amadeus lived in and embellished it. Opposite this is the Sardinian monument, presented to the city by the Milanese in 1859, just after the war, on which, *in relievo*, is the figure of Victor Emmanuel—*Il re galuntuomo*—at the head of his troops. Just beyond the Palazzo Madama is the Palazzo Reale (Royal Palace). The exterior is nothing to look at, being plain and heavy, but the interior is magnificent. From here I extended my walk to the Giardino Reale (Royal Gardens), then the Cathedral of Turin, Santa Giovanni Battista, which was erected in the latter part of the 15th century by Pintelli. In the chapel of St. Sudorio, just behind the high altar, is a small portion of linen cloth in a glass case. This is a valuable relic, for it is said to be a portion of the cloth in which the body of the Saviour was embalmed. This may, or may not, be true; belief in the matter is optional. One really gets so accustomed in Italy to seeing the bones of deceased saints, a bit of the true cross, a nail of it, and so on, that the probability is nine out of ten are sceptical.

CHAPTER II.

MILAN—THE CATHEDRAL—GALLERIA VITTORIO EMMANUELE
—PIAZZA D'ARMI—PALAZZO DE BRERA—LAKE OF COMO
BOLOGNA—ITS ANCIENT HISTORY—LEANING TOWERS—
THE CERTOSA—TEATRO COMMUNALE—BRINDISI.

FROM Turin I went by train to Milan. I ought to have gone direct past Magenta, but by some mistake I found myself making quite a round-about journey, viâ Piacenza and Lodi; however, all's well that ends well. I arrived at the hotel in Milan in time for *table d'hôte*. Now, although I am writing a book principally on travels and adventures in Egypt and the Soudan, I dare say my readers will excuse me if I attempt a description of my travels out and home. All the places I visited were extremely interesting to me, and I cannot forbear a little gossip and relating what I know respecting them. Those who have not visited these places will perhaps be pleased to read my description, and those who have will be able to compare notes and see if they are correct. I had been told that the best time to visit Il Duomo —the Cathedral—was at eight or nine o'clock in the morning, on account of the splendid view obtainable from the roof; this I did on the morning following my arrival, and was richly rewarded for my trouble. Il Duomo is certainly a magnificent structure, inferior in magnitude to St. Peter's at Rome, but in some respects not an unworthy rival. It is built of white marble, and is one of the most impressive ecclesiastical edifices in the world. In its present form it was commenced in 1387, and is not yet entirely completed. Its form is that of a Latin cross, divided into five naves, terminated by an octagonal apsis, and supported by fifty-two octagonal pilasters of uniform size, except four, which, having to bear the cupola, are larger.

Around the exterior are 4,500 niches, of which above 3,000 are already occupied by statues. In the interior everything is of the most imposing and gorgeous description. I said everything, but I should except an image of wax of the Virgin Mary, with the infant Saviour in her arms. The waxen face and arms looked very dirty, her attire was very commonplace-looking stuff, and I did not think her rather dirty-looking neck was much improved by a bit of paltry-looking green ribbon encircling it. This image would certainly be more suitable at Madame Tussaud's than in this beautiful cathedral. But I will finish with the exterior. The roof is a perfect forest of marble pinnacles, nearly all crammed with most valuable marble statues. The celebrated marble flower-bed contains several thousand flowers, each distinct and each different in design. I leave the roof and ascend the tower, from which I obtain a magnificent view of the Alpine range, Mont Blanc, Monte Rosa, the St. Bernard and Matterhorn right away to the Superga and Mont Cenis.

In the interior we notice the rich stained-glass windows of the choir, comprising about 350 subjects of Biblical history, the Gothic decorations of the sacristy, the candelabra in front of the altar shaped like a tree, and decorated with jewels, then the Chapel of St. Borromeo, which is a subterranean chapel of a most gorgeous and costly character, as it is one mass of jewels. The shrine and walls are silver, all inlaid with gold and precious stones. If I remember rightly, I paid a franc extra for my visit here, and had the gratification of seeing the embalmed body of St. Borromeo, with the valuable rings of office still on his fingers. A golden crown (presented by the unfortunate Maria Teresa) is suspended over his head, and a large crucifix of splendid emeralds lies on his chest—this, I am told, was given by the Empress of Austria.

Of course, in Milan, as in all large towns in Italy, there are any number of beautiful and remarkable churches. Among the most remarkable edifices are the church of Sant' Ambrogio, founded by St. Ambrose in 387, the churches of Sant' Eustargio, San Lorenzo, Santa Maria delle Grazie, with a cupola and sacristy by Bramante, and the celebrated Last Supper by Leonardo da Vinci; Santa Maria della Passione, a majestic edifice, with excellent paintings and a magnificent mausoleum; San Paolo, San Carlo Borromeo, &c.

Immediately adjoining the Cathedral is a magnificent square, which was finished on the occasion of the Austrian Emperor's visit to Milan in 1875. This is called the Piazza del Duomo. From this square I pass through the Galleria Vittorio Emmanuele, a very fine glass-roofed arcade, or gallery, connecting the Piazza del Duomo with the Scala Theatre; the cost of this was about £320,000. It was commenced in 1865 and opened in 1867. The glass canopy is illuminated by 2,000 jets of gas, and when these and the beautiful and brilliant shops are lighted the effect is charming. The length of this kind of covered street is 320 yards. La Scala

Theatre was not open for performances when I was there, but by the judicious disposition of a franc or so I obtained admission just to see it. It is, I understand, capable of accommodating 3,600 spectators. I next strolled on to the Piazza d'Armi, which occupies an immense space, obtained by the demolition of the citadel and its outworks. Part of it has been converted into an amphitheatre, 800 feet long by 400 feet broad, used in summer for races and shows, and capable of containing 30,000 spectators. The castle, now a barrack, fronts the Piazza d'Armi on one side; at the opposite side is the Porta Sempione, with the fine Arco Sempione, or Arco della Pace. This is a lofty gateway, with three passages, built of blocks of white marble, adorned with reliefs and statues, and bearing inscriptions commemorating the emancipation of Italy. My next visit was to the Palazzo di Brera, or Delle Scienze Lettere ed Arte, containing the Pinacoteca, or picture-gallery, with a very valuable collection of paintings and statuary, and containing also the library of the Academy (170,000 volumes). Besides this library, Milan possesses the Ambrosian library, the earliest and still one of the most valuable public libraries in Europe. There is also a valuable museum of natural history, a conservatory of music, a military college, a theological seminary, and a veterinary school.

Though Milan is one of the most ancient towns in Lombardy, it has so often been partially destroyed and rebuilt that few antiquities remain. It is entered by eleven gates, several of which are magnificent. Its foundation is attributed to the Insubrian Gauls; but the first distinct notice of it occurs B.C. 221, when it was subdued by the Romans, under whom it acquired so much importance that in the division of the empire attributed to Constantine the Great it ranks as the second city of Italy. In the middle of the fifth century it was sacked by the Huns, under Attila, and again in the following century by the Goths; but greater horrors yet awaited it, for the Goths, who had been driven out by Belisarius, having regained possession by the aid of the Burgundians, gave it up to the flames, and put almost all its inhabitants to the sword. The most important manufactures are tobacco, silks, cottons, lace, carpets, hats, earthenware, white-lead, jewelry, and articles in gold and silver. The spinning and throwing of silk employs a large number of hands, and furnish the staple article of trade. The other principal articles are corn, rice, cheese, and wines.

In the evening of the second day (whilst engaged in the purchase of everything Milanese in the way of photographs) I met with a Milan gentleman, who had lived some years in America, and who could speak English remarkably well. He was a genial, good-hearted looking kind of fellow, and we soon got into an animated conversation. I was surprised to find how well up he was in English politics, and as for the Irish question, he could hold his own with any Englishman; he was, too, a great admirer of Lord Beaconsfield. When we had had about an hour's chat I was about to return to my hotel; he then asked me how long I was going to remain in Milan. I told him I intended leaving next day for Bologna.

" Have you seen the lake of Como?" said he.

" No," I replied. " I should like to do so very much, but fear I cannot spare the time, as I have to be at Brindisi on the 21st."

" But you must not leave," said he, " until you have been there; it is only a run of thirty miles to Como by rail. I live there. Come to-morrow and visit me, and I will put you in the way of seeing Bologna in half the time that you would do it in without assistance."

This very kind offer I accepted, and spent next day a very agreeable time with my new acquaintance, who was most hospitable and friendly. We parted with mutual protestations of goodwill, and

I took train for Bologna, which is several hours' ride from Milan.

Bologna (anciently Bonovia) is one of the oldest, largest, and richest cities of Italy. It lies at the foot of the Apennines, between the Rivers Reno and Savena, 190 miles N.N.W. from Rome. It is five or six miles in circumference, and is surrounded by an unfortified wall of brick; it has extensive manufactures of silk goods, velvet, artificial flowers, &c. It struck me as being a quaint old city. All the houses, or nearly so, are built out over the shops and pavement, supported by large pillars, and forming a covered way nearly all over the city which affords shade and shelter to the foot-passengers.

Bologna was long renowned for its university, founded, according to tradition, by Theodosias, the younger, in 425, and restored by Charlemagne, which, in the centuries of barbarism, spread the light of knowledge all over Europe. It once had 10,000 students, but the number now averages only 300. The university formerly possessed so much influence, that even the coins of the city bore its motto—*Bonovia docet*. During 1400 years every new discovery in science and the arts found patrons here. The medical school is celebrated for having introduced the dissection of human bodies, and the scientific journals prove that the love of investigation is still awake in Bologna. The chief square in the city, Piazza Maggiore, the forum in the Middle Ages, is adorned by several venerable buildings. Among them are the Palazzo Pubblico, which contains some magnificent halls, adorned with statues and paintings; Palazzo del Padesta, chiefly remarkable as having been the prison of Eugenis, King of Sardinia, and son of the Emperor Frederick II. who was captured and kept here by the Bolognese for more than twenty years, till his death; and the church or Ansilica of St. Petronio, which was commenced in 1390, and is not yet finished. The palaces and churches are too numerous to make any remarks on. The leaning towers, Degli Asmilli and Garisenda, dating from the twelfth century, are among the most remarkable objects in Bologna. The former is square, and of massive brick-work, built in three portions, and diminishing in diameter to the top. Its height is 321 feet, and its inclination from the perpendicular 6ft. 10in. The Garisenda is 161 feet high, and inclines a little more than 8 feet. Bologna has always been famous for cheap living, and has been chosen as a residence by many literary men. Gourmands praise it as the native country of excellent maccaroni, sausages, liquors, and preserved fruits. The pilgrimage to the Madonna di S. Lucca, whose church is situated at the foot of the Apennines, half a league distant from Bologna, and to which an arcade of 640 arches leads, annually attracts a great number of people from all parts of Italy. Bologna was founded by the Etruscans under the name of *Felsina*, before the foundation of Rome. In 189 B.C. it was made a Roman colony, and called *Bonovia*.

I had been told that the Certosa, or burying ground, was well worth a visit. It is about $2\frac{1}{2}$ miles outside the city by the Porta St. Isaia, so I took a cab and was well rewarded for my trouble, for this burying ground is the most beautiful and remarkable in Italy. Here we can walk for hours under cover between rows of statues and marble tablets of the greatest beauty. When I returned to my hotel I found dinner waiting, and afterwards it struck me that I must seek some more exhilarating mode of amusement after my visit to the Certosa. I accordingly made my way to the Teatro Communale, one of the three best theatres in Italy, San Carlos at Naples and La Scala in Milan taking precedence. The opera was "Mefistofele," splendidly mounted and well supported by artistes. The orchestra was large and all that could be desired by the most fastidious critics, and there are plenty of them in a Bolognese audience. Boxes are in *every* tier in the house, and the effect is very pretty.

As I had to start for Brindisi at 3 a.m. on Sunday, November 20th, I had not much time for sleep, notwithstanding which I got between the sheets until then, when I was conveyed to the station and finished my nap in the train.

CHAPTER III.

P. AND O. STEAMER "TANJORE"—ARRIVAL OF THE MAIL AND PASSENGERS—ANCIENT BRINDISI—BRINDISI TO ALEXANDRIA—ALEXANDRIA PAST AND PRESENT—ITS TRADE.

I ARRIVED at Brindisi at 10 p.m. and was straightway driven off to the quay, was soon on board the P. and O. steamship *Tanjore*, commanded by Captain Briscœ, and not many minutes afterwards in my berth and fast asleep. My slumber was disturbed at 6 a.m. by the arrival of the Indian mail and a large number of passengers, who produced a great commotion over-head quite incompatible with sleep. I therefore turned out, and was soon on deck watching the busy scene. Some little time after I had breakfasted I discovered two of the party which I was to accompany, Messrs. F. L. James and E. L. Phillipps. We were to meet three more at Cairo, and one at Suez, to complete the party.

No one would care to remain very long in Brindisi, as it is a most uninteresting place notwithstanding its antiquity. I remember once, in 1877, spending a few hours there, and was then very glad when my train left for Naples. Brindisi (ancient *Brundusium*) was, if I remember rightly, the birth-place of Virgil. It is a sea-port and fortified town 45 miles from Taranto. In ancient times it was one of the most important cities of Calabria. It is said by Strabo to have been governed by its own kings at the time of the foundation of Tarentum. It was one of the chief cities of the Sallentines, and the excellence of its port and commanding situation in the Adriatic were among the chief inducements of the Romans to attack them. The Romans made it a naval station, and frequently directed their operations from it. It was the scene of important operations in the war between Cæsar and Pompey. On the fall of the Western Empire it declined in importance. In the eleventh century it fell into the possession of the Normans, and became one of the chief ports of embarkation for the Crusades. Its importance as a sea-port was subsequently completely lost, and its harbour blocked. In 1870 the Peninsular and Oriental Steam Navigation Company put on a weekly line of steamers between Brindisi and Alexandria for the conveyance of Her Majesty's eastern mails, and at the same time made it a post of transit for goods brought from India by these steamers to be forwarded to the north of Italy by rail. From this cause the imports of Brindisi have suddenly risen in importance.

About 12 mid-day on the 21st November, we got under way with 110 first-class passengers on board, the weather was fine, much warmer than in Turin and Milan, and the sea smooth, which I was thankful for; 22nd the same; 23rd fine and sea smooth until about 4 p.m., when the sea became rough, and I very uncomfortable, undesirous of dinner and very desirous of being quietly settled in my berth, which I sought without loss of time, knowing by a past bitter and sour experience that I should ere long present a pitiable spectacle. During the night the sea became so rough that the port-holes of the cabins had to be closed, so that in addition to feeling excessively sick I was almost suffocated, as the weather was very warm. On the morning of the 24th, at 10 o'clock, we landed at the far-famed city of Alexandria.

Even in sunny Italy I had felt the weather, in the neighbourhood of Turin, Milan, and Bologna, cold and frosty enough in the morning for an overcoat. At Brindisi it was not so cold, but as we neared the African coast the sky grew warmer and warmer, and tinged, so to speak, with a reflection of the Libyan desert, a soft purple hue, rather than the deep blue of Italy. Only those who have witnessed sunset in Africa can form any conception of the beautiful tints reflected from the rocks and sands; there you see the soft purple, lovely crimson, pale gold, rose and violet colours all shading off into one another in the most charming manner. I have never seen anywhere such glorious sunsets as in Africa.

Having but a short time to stay in Alexandria, I made good use of it in exploring the place. Through what strange vicissitudes has this ancient city passed. Alexandria was founded by Alexander the Great, B.C. 332, on the site of a village called Rakôtis, or Racoudah. Its founder wished to make it the centre of commerce between the east and west, and we know how fully his aspirations have been realized. It stood a little to the south of the present town, was 15 miles in circumference, and had a population of 300,000 free inhabitants, and at least an equal number of slaves. So distinguished was it for its magnificence, that the Romans ranked it next to their own capital, and when captured by Amru, general of the Caliph Omar (A.D. 641), it contained 4,000 palaces, 4,000 baths, 400 theatres.

or places of amusement, 12,000 shops for the sale of vegetables, and 40,000 tributary Jews. But we are getting on a little too fast. As I said before, it was founded B.C. 332, by Alexander the Great, who is said to have traced the plan of the new city himself, and his architect, Dinarchus or Dinocrates (the builder of the temple of Diana at Ephesus) directed its execution. The city was regularly built, and traversed by two principal streets, each 100 feet wide, and one of them four miles long. Campbell says: "He designed the shape of the whole after that of a Macedonian cloak, and his soldiers strewed meal to mark the line where its walls were to rise. These, when finished, enclosed a compass of 80 furlongs filled with comfortable abodes, and interspersed with palaces, temples, and obelisks of marble porphyry, that fatigued the eye with admiration. The main streets crossed each other at right angles, from wall to wall, with beautiful breadth, and to the length (if it may be credited) of nearly nine miles. At their extremities the gates looked out on the gilded barges of the Nile, of fleets at sea under full sail, on a harbour that sheltered navies, and on a lighthouse that was the mariner's star and the wonder of the world."

One-fourth of the area upon which it was built was covered with temples, palaces, and public buildings. Conspicuous upon its little isle was the famous lighthouse of Pharos, the islet being connected with the city by a mole. Under the Cæsars, Alexandria attained extraordinary prosperity; large merchant fleets carried on a reciprocal commerce with India and Ethiopia, and its industrial population were chiefly employed in the weaving of linen, and the manufacture of glass and papyrus.

The Alexandrians were turbulent, and several times revolted under the Ptolemies and the Romans. Cæsar was obliged, in B.C. 47, to put down a terrible insurrection in this city. Under the emperors, Alexandria suffered a series of massacres, which gradually depopulated it. In 611, Chosroës, King of Persia, seized it, but his son restored it to the emperors. In 641, Amru—whom I spoke of just now—took it by storm, after a siege of 14 months, and a loss of 23,000 men. The Turks captured it in 868 and 1517.

So from time to time Alexandria has been the scene of the greatest splendour, adorned by marble palaces, temples, and obelisks, also of great squalor, and covered with mud huts; passing under the sway of Persian, Greek, Roman, and Turk, and at the time I am writing this (March, 1884) I think I may safely say under the *sway* of Great Britain, although not belonging to this country.

In the early part of this century, under the vigorous, but most unscrupulous, rule of Mehemet Ali (who was appointed Pasha of Alexandria, and afterwards of all Egypt), Alexandria became again a thriving and important place.

It is said that in the character of the population, at least, there still remains a strong resemblance to the ancient city of the Ptolemies. Sullen-looking Copts replace the exclusive old Egyptians, their reputed ancestors. Greeks and Jews, too, swarm as before, both possibly changed a little for the worse. The mass of Levantines and (with, of course, honourable exceptions) Franks, who make up the sum of the population, may, I think, without any exaggeration, be designated as the off-scourings of their respective countries. The streets swarm with Turks in many-coloured robes, half-naked, brown-skinned Arabs, glossy negroes in loose white dresses and vermilion turbans, sordid, shabby-looking Israelites in greasy black, smart, jaunty, rakish Greeks, heavy-browed Armenians, unkempt, unmasked Maltese ragamuffins, Albanians and Europeans of every shade of respectability, from lordly consuls down to refugee quacks, swindlers, and criminals, who here get whitewashed and established anew. Here you see a Frank lady in the last Parisian bonnet, there Egyptian women enveloped to the eyes in shapeless black wrappers, while dirty Christian monks, sallow Moslem dervishes, sore-eyed beggars, and naked children covered with flies, present a shifting and everlasting kaleidoscope of the most undignified phases of Eastern and Western existence.

The great square, or Grande Place, is the chief place of business and resort. It is a quarter of a mile long, and 150 feet wide, paved on each side, with a railed garden in the centre, planted with lime-trees, and having a fountain at each end. Here are the principal shops and hotels, the English consulate and church, banks, offices of companies, &c. The buildings are all in the Italian style, spacious and handsome, or, rather, were when I visited it. Most of the ancient landmarks are fast disappearing. The site of Cleopatra's Palace is now occupied by a railway station for the line to Ramleh, seven miles distant, over-looking the bay of Abaukir, the scene of Nelson's victory over the French fleet in 1798. Of course, I could not be in Alexandria without paying a visit to Pompey's pillar, or, more properly, Diocletian's pillar. It is a grand column, and occupies an eminence 1,800 feet to the south of the present walls; its total height is 98 feet 9 inches. It is a single block of red granite on the mounds overlooking the lake Mareotis and the modern city.

An account of the ancient and modern history of Alexandria would fill a volume of the most stirring interest. I, however, will be content with giving to my readers a very small portion of a volume on Alexandria, as I shall have a good deal yet to say on Cairo and neighbourhood, and still more to say on the Soudan.

It was to Alexandria that science, fostered by the munificence of the Ptolemies, retired from her ancient seat at Heliopolis. "The sages of the Museum, who lodged in that part of the palace of the Lagides, might there be said to live as the priests of the Muses, taking the word in its wide sense, as the patronesses of knowledge. They had gardens, and alleys, and galleries where they walked and conversed, a common hall where they made their repasts, and public rooms where they gave instruction to the youth who crowded from all parts of the world to hear their lectures." This museum, a unique establishment in literary history, was founded by Ptolemy Soter, King of Egypt, who died B.C. 283, and was greatly enlarged by his son Ptolemy Philadelphus and the succeeding Ptolemies. In connection with the museum was the Alexandrian

Library, the most famous and the largest collections of books in the world, and the glory of Alexandria. Demetrius Phalereus, after his banishment from Athens, is said to have been its first superintendent, when the number of volumes, or rolls, amounted to 50,000.

If the other Ptolemies were as unscrupulous in obtaining books as Energetes is said to have been, it is no wonder that the library increased in magnitude or value. We are told that he refused to sell corn to the Athenians during a famine unless he received in pledge the original manuscripts of Aschylus, Sophocles, and Euripides. These were carefully copied, and the copies returned to the owners, while the King retained the originals. Various accounts are given of the number of books contained in the library at its most flourishing period, when Zenodotus, Callimachus, the poet Eratosthenes, of Cyrene, and Appolinius Rhodius were its librarians. Seneca states the number at 400,000; Aulus Gellius makes it 700,000. Some reconcile the discrepancy by making the statements refer to different periods, while others believe that the larger figure includes more than one collection. That there were more than one collection is known. The original, or Alexandrian library *par excellence*, was situated in the *Brucheion*, a quarter of the city in which the royal palace stood; and besides this there was a large collection in the Serapeion, or temple of Jupiter Serapis, but when or by whom this was founded we do not know. The former was accidentally burned during the Julius Cæsar's siege of the city, but was replaced by the library of Pergamus, which was sent by Antony as a present to Cleopatra. The Serapeion library, which probably included the Pergamean collection, existed to the time of the Emperor Theodosius the Great. At the general destruction of the heathen temples, which took place under this emperor, the splendid temple of Jupiter Serapis was set upon and gutted (A.D. 391) by a fanatical crowd of Christians at the instigation of the Archbishop Theophilus, when its literary treasures were destroyed or scattered. The historian Orosius relates that in the beginning of the fifth century only the empty shelves were to be seen.

A valuable collection was again accumulated in Alexandria, but was doomed to suffer the same fate, being burned by the Arabs when they captured the city under the Caliph Omar in 641. Amru, the captain of the Caliph's army, would have been willing to spare the library, but the fanatical Omar disposed of the matter in the famous words:—
"If these writings of the Greeks agree with the

Koran, there could be no need of them; if they disagree, they are pernicious, and ought to be destroyed;" and they were accordingly used for heating the 4,000 baths in the city. Just before the time of Mehemet Ali, Alexandria was a miserable place of a few thousand inhabitants, cut off from the valley of the Nile by the ruin of the ancient canal. Under his rule it greatly revived in political and commercial importance, and the re-opening of its canal has restored to its harbour all the trade of Egypt.

The principal articles of export are cotton, beans, peas, rice, wheat, barley, gums, flax, hides, lentils, linseed, mother-of-pearl, sesamum, senna, ostrich feathers, &c.

Those who are not given to pedestrian exercise can easily avail themselves of a cab or donkey, and they will find the streets, which are spacious and handsome, very pleasant to traverse, as they are all well paved in the city; but the dust outside the walls covers the ground from four to six inches deep, and in combination with the intense glare of the sun, and the wretched hovels of the natives, produces the ophthalmia so common, especially among the Arabs. Owing to the want of proper drainage, what would otherwise be a salubrious site is subject to malarious disease and the plague.

I have spoken of the Alexandrian library; quite as much may be said of the Alexandrian school; combined, they may be justly considered the first academy of arts and sciences.

The grammarians and poets are the most important among the scholars of Alexandria. These grammarians were philologists and literati, who explained things as well as words, and may be considered a sort of encyclopedists. Such were Zenodotus the Ephesian, who established the first grammar school in Alexandria; Eratosthenes, of Cyrene; Aristophanes, of Byzantium; Aristarchus, of Samothrace; Crates, of Mallus; Dionysius the Thracian; Appolonius the sophist; and Zoilus. To the poets belong Appolonius the Rhodian, Lycophron, Aratus, Nicander, Emphorion, Callimachus, Theocritus, Philetas, Phanocles, Timon the Philasian, Scymnus, Dionysius, and seven tragic poets, who were called *Alexandrian Pleiads*.

The most violent religious controversies disturbed the Alexandrian church until the orthodox tenets were established in it by Athanasius, in the controversy with the Arians.

Among the scholars are to be found great mathematicians, as Euclid, the father of scientific geometry, and whose work, I distinctly recollect, was a great bore to me in my younger days;

Appolonius, of Perga, in Pamphylia, whose work on conic sections still exists; Nichomachus, the first scientific arithmetician; astronomers, who employed the Egyptian hieroglyphics for marking the northern hemisphere, and fixed the images and names (still in use) of the Constellations, who left astronomical writings (*e.g.*, the *Phænomena* of Aratus, a didactic poem; the *Spherica* of Menelaus; the anatomical works of Eratosthenes, and especially the *Magna Syntaxis* of the geographer Ptolemy), and made improvements in the theory of the calendar, which were afterwards adopted into the Julian calendar; natural philosophers, anatomists, as Herophilus and Erasistratus; physicians and surgeons, as Demosthenes Philalethes, who wrote the first work on diseases of the eye; Zopyrus and Cratenas, who improved the art of pharmacy and invented antidotes; instructors in the art of medicine, to whom Asclepiades, Loranus, and Galen owed their education; medical theorists and empirics, of the sect founded by Philinus. All these belonged to the numerous association of scholars continuing under the Roman dominion and favoured by the Roman emperors, which rendered Alexandria one of the most renowned and influential seats of science in antiquity. With this passing glance at Alexandria, we will journey on to Cairo.

CHAPTER IV.

THE FERTILIZING RIVERS OF EGYPT—LEAVE ALEXANDRIA—INCIDENTS EN ROUTE—SHEPHEARD'S HOTEL—ANCIENT AND MODERN CAIRO—THE DONKEY BOYS — ARAB PATIENTS—DANCING DERVISHES—THE HOUSE WHERE JOSEPH, MARY, AND THE INFANT SAVIOUR LIVED IN OLD CAIRO—THE BAULAC MUSEUM—THE PETRIFIED FOREST—MOKATTAM HILLS — TOMBS OF THE CALIPHS AND CITADEL—CAIRO AT SUNSET.

IN former times, before the introduction of railways, the traveller to Cairo had to go by canal, hire a boat, servant; procure a carpet, mattress, and bedding; lay in a store of provisions, and a variety of minor articles that would fill a page or two to mention. Now we can go comfortably by rail in a few hours, the distance being something like 120 miles, I think.

We pass, *en route*, Lake Mareotis and the

Mohmoudieh Canal, cultivated land near Alexandria, then a good deal uncultivated and desert; but as we approach Cairo, we see large tracts of cultivated land, all accomplished by irrigation, and I am told that as much as two or three crops in the year can be obtained off these lands without very great labour. A hot sun can always be depended on. The agricultural labourer has not to go through the laborious work of ploughing and manuring as in England. All he has to do is to scratch the ground, and put in the seed in the fertilizing alluvium which has been brought down from the rich lands of Meroe and portions of Abyssinia by the Athara river and its tributaries, the Salaam, Augrab, and the greater stream, Tacazze or Settite. All these rivers cut through a large area of deep soil, through which, in the course of ages, they have excavated valleys of great depth, and in some places of more than two miles in width. The contents of these enormous cuttings have been delivered upon the low lands of Egypt at the period of the inundations. The Athara is the greatest mud-carrier, then the Blue Nile, which effects a junction with the White Nile at Khartoum.

The White Nile is of lacustrine origin, and conveys no mud, but an excess of vegetable matter, suspended in the finest particles, and exhibiting beneath the microscope minute globules of green matter, which have the appearance of germs. When the two rivers meet at the Khartoum junction, the water of the Blue Nile, which contains lime, appears to coagulate the alluminous matter in that of the White Nile, which is then precipitated, and forms a deposit; after which the true Nile, formed by a combination of the two rivers, becomes wholesome, and remains comparatively clear, until it meets the muddy Athara. The Sobat river is a most important tributary, supposed to have its sources in the southern portion of the Galla country.

For the foregoing information on these rivers I am indebted to an article of Sir Samuel Baker's, which I read with great interest in the *Contemporary Review;* and I daresay many of my readers will thank me for reproducing it.

After this slight digression, I will continue my journey to Cairo. At the stations were numbers of women and children with refreshments for the traveller in this land, where the sun always shines with a burning heat; women with goolehs of water to sell; children naked, or nearly so, with sugar-cane, melons, oranges, dates, fresh sugar-cane, figs, &c. Vast numbers of these poor creatures were afflicted with ophthalmia, their eyelids covered with flies, which they take no notice of whatever, many of them blind, or partially so, blind beggars; one and all, whether they can sell anything or not, continually uttering the cry of "Backsheesh, backsheesh, howaga," which comes faintly on my ears as the train leaves the station. As we journey on there is much to be noticed. Now we pass a camp of Bedouins in the desert; next a large grove of date-palms (the owner of which has to pay a tax on every tree). Here the domestic buffalo walks round and round a circle; he is working the sakia or water-wheel, which winds up the water for irrigation. This is also taxed. Scattered all over the country are innumerable shadoofs, another mode, and the most ancient, of obtaining water; there the stately-looking camel strides along, looking intensely unconcerned. Trotting past him on his little donkey is an Arab in loose, white, flowing robes, and turbaned head. At one time we pass squalid, wretched-looking mud-huts; anon Nubians, as black as coal, working in the fields. We arrived at Cairo in the evening about seven, and were at once driven off to the well-knewn Shepheard's Hotel. The *cuisine* is all that could be desired, and every attention is paid to insure the comfort of visitors. Mr. Grose, the manager, is a particularly obliging and attentive gentleman.

Cairo (in Arabic, *Kahira*, which signifies *victorious*) is the capital city of Egypt. It lies on the east bank of the Nile, in a sandy plain, and contains old Cairo, Boulac (*the harbour*), and new Cairo, which are, to a considerable degree, distinct from each other. The city itself, separate from the gardens and plantations which surround it, is about 10 miles in circuit, has 31 gates, and 240 irregular unpaved streets, which during the night are, or were, closed at the end of the quarter, to prevent disturbances. The houses are for the most part built of brick, with flat roofs, and the interior of many of them is very sumptuous. The chief square of Cario, El-Esbekiah, has a magnificent area, the centre of which is laid out as a garden, and is annually inundated by the overflowing of the Nile. It is surrounded by the finest palaces. There is in it a monument to General Kleber. The inhabitants of the city and suburbs, in 1871 353,851, are Arabs or Mahomedans, Coptish Christians, Mamelukes, Greeks, Syrians, Armenians, Jews, and natives of various countries of Europe. The castle, or citadel, situated on a rock, containing Joseph's Well, 276 feet deep, is the residence of the Pasha. There are 80 public baths, 400 mosques, two Greek, 12 Coptish, one Armenian, and one English church, 36 synagogues, and many silk, camlet, tapestry, gunpowder, leather, linen, and cotton factories. Among the mosques, which, though many of them are in ruins, form the most conspicuous edifices of the city, the most remarkable is that of Sultan Hassan, which is built of blocks of polished marble, obtained from the outer casing of the pyramids, or pyramid rather, for, if my memory serves me right, they are from the great pyramid of Cheops at Gizeh. It has a beautifully ornamented porch, richly corniced walls, and many tall minarets. Here is also a Mahomendan high school, a printing office and 25,000 volumes. The largest convent of dervishes is at Cairo. It was built in 1174. The traffic of Cairo is very great, since it is the centre of communication between Europe, the Mediterranean Sea, Asia, and the North of Africa, and is upon the railway from Alexandria to Suez. The principal bazaars are the Ghoreah and Khan Khalel. Goods are disposed of there by public auction, and the different bazaars exhibit different kinds of merchandise. Ibrahim Pasha commenced a public library in 1830, and in 1842 a European Society, called the Egyptian Literary Association, was established. Mehemet Ali introduced schools for elementary education, and the Church of England Missionary Society has two schools.

Cairo was founded by Jauhar, general of the

Caliph Moez, in the year of the Hegira 368, or A.D. 969, on the site of the Egyptian Babylon. Moez afterwards made it his capital, which distinction it retained until the overthrow of the Mamelukes by Sultan Selim in 1517. Saladin extended and fortified it in 1176. It was repeatedly attacked by the Crusaders, particularly by St. Louis in 1249. It was occupied by the French from 1798 to 1801, when it was recovered by the Turks with the assistance of the English. A great fire occurred there in February, 1863; advantage was taken of it to improve the town.

Our military occupation of Egypt (or shall I say that it is simply a " measure of police ? "), and events that are now transpiring there, are a sufficient excuse (if one were required) for dealing shortly with the ancient history of Cairo and the neighbourhood.

Soon after our arrival at Shepheard's Hotel, when we had restored ourselves to our personal comfort, our host provided us with a good dinner, to which we did ample justice, and as the weather (although the end of November) was like a summer's evening in England, we enjoyed the usual after-dinner cigarettes in the balcony, which is a very pleasant lounge, even in the day time, as it is quite sheltered from the blazing sun. I soon strolled off to bed with the idea of obtaining a good night's rest, so that I should awake refreshed and fit for a pilgrimage to the various shrines of intense interest with which Cairo and its neighbourhood abounds. I have visited and seen all that was interesting in Rome, once the mistress of the world—Corinth, once the seat of learning and the abode of a most polished people; Ephesus; have stood on the ancient Acropolis of Athens, the plains of Troy, celebrated by Virgil; explored Misenum, Pateoli, Baiæ, Pompeii, and Herculaneum, all rich in historical associations; but compared with the remains of ancient cities near Cairo these places were of yesterday's growth, and were not even thought of until ages after the glory and high civilization of the people in the land of the Pharaohs had passed away. When Abraham entered the Delta from Canaan with his countrymen, moving about in tents and waggons, the Egyptians were living in cities enjoying all the advantages of a settled government and established laws; had already cultivated agriculture, parcelled out their valley into farms, and reverenced a landmark as a god.

While Abraham knew of no property but herds and movables, they had invented records and wrote their kings' names and actions on the massive temples which they raised. They had invented hieroglyphics and improved them into syllabic writing, and almost into an alphabet. The history of Greece *begins* with the Trojan war, but *before* the time of David and *before* the time of the Trojan war, the power and glory of Thebes had already passed away. About 1,000 years B.C. Shishak the conqueror of Rehoboam, son of Solomon, governed all Egypt; at his death it was torn to pieces by civil wars. After a time the kings of Ethiopia reigned in Thebes, and helped the Israelites to fight against their Assyrian masters. This unsettled state of things lasted nearly 300 years, during which, as the Prophet Isaiah foretold, " Egyptians fought against Egyptians, brother against brother, city against city, and kingdom against kingdom." At last the city of Sais put an end to this state of things and under the Sais kings Egypt enjoyed again a high degree of prosperity. They were more despotic than the kings of Thebes, and struggled with the Babylonians for the dominion of Judæa.

Probably many of my readers are aware that M. Ferdinand de Lesseps was not the originator of a canal to the Red Sea, for Pharaoh Necho, one of the Sais kings, began it from the Nile. His sailors, circumnavigated Africa; he conquered Jerusalem, and when the Chaldees afterwards drove back the Egyptian army the remnant of Judah, with the Prophet Jeremiah, retreated into Egypt to seek a refuge with King Hophra.

523 B.C. the Persians became masters of Egypt, and behaved with great tyranny. Cambyses plundered the tombs and temples, broke the statues, and scourged the priests. They ruled for 200 years; then the Greeks, B.C. 332, the Romans, B.C. 30, and on the division of the Roman Empire, A.D. 337, Egypt fell to the lot of Constantinople. In A.D. 640, just 670 years after the Roman conquest, Egypt was conquered by the followers of Mahomet, and now, in this year of grace, A.D. 1884, we are rather upsetting the late order of things, but whether for good or evil time will show.

In this age of progress, it may seem strange to say so, but Egyptian landlords had much the same tastes 3,000 years ago as English landlords have now. They were much addicted to field-sports. Not only does history tell us so, but I have seen often in their sculptures and paintings that this was so. Even on the tomb and chapel of King Phty at Sakkara, which is said to be over 5,000 years old, I saw scenes of fowling, fishing, hunting, running down the gazelle, spearing the hippopotamus, of coursing and netting hares, of shooting wild cattle with arrows, and catching them with the lasso. They had fish ponds, game preserves, and game laws, they were fond of horses and dogs, kept good tables, gave morning and evening parties, amused themselves with games of skill and chance, were proud of their ancestors, built fine houses and furnished them handsomely, and paid great attention to horticulture and arboriculture.

This certainly reads like contemporary history; but I will go further. To use a well-known expression, "would you be surprised to hear" that the tenants paid the same proportionate rent as the British farmer of to-day? The average gross produce of a farm here was £8 an acre, average rent about 32s. an acre—just one-fifth—the exact rent paid by the tenants of Potiphar, Captain of the Guard, and of Potipherah, Priest of On, Joseph's father-in-law, and the same was paid to Pharaoh himself by his tenants. At that time the whole acreage of the country was divided into rectangular estates. One-third belonged to the king, two-thirds in equal proportions to the priestly and military castes; and these were cultivated by another order of men, who, for the use of the land, paid rent—one-fifth of the gross produce—to the owner.

Altogether I spent nearly a fortnight in Cairo, and feeling a great interest in the historical associations of this ancient place and the neighbourhood, I resolved to see and learn as much as I could of them during my short stay. In the morning, after early breakfast, I amused myself for a short time by sitting in the shade of the extensive balcony in front of Shepheard's Hotel, which overlooks the street, and is contiguous to it. The scene which presented itself to my gaze was truly Oriental in character. Now I see a few camels stalking silently, slowly, and sedately on, variously laden—some with baskets of large stones for building purposes, others with long pieces of timber on each side, others with skins of water and so on; then an Arab lady on donkey-back, riding after the manner of men, and covered from head to foot in unsightly black wrappers, having just a slit in them, through which can be seen a large pair of lustrous dark eyes, and down the bridge of her nose are some brass-looking ornaments, resembling as much as anything a row of thimbles inserted in one another. A Turkish lady's dress and yashmack (covering worn over the face) is much more becoming, and her nose is not ornamented by the addition of the thimble arrangement. The Turkish ladies wear (in Constantinople) quite a thin white muslin yashmack over their faces. This does not conceal very much of the features, which, as a rule, are very beautiful. The Egyptian ladies wear a black yashmack, which conceals all except the eyes. Report says they are ugly; if so, they are quite right to do so. Next I see a carriage driven along preceded by two sais, or runners, to clear the way, and it is surprising what a pace they go at with a long, swinging trot. They are picturesquely and gorgeously dressed, each bearing a long wand, and wearing a tarboosh (Turkish fez), the long thick blue tassel of which floats gracefully over the shoulders, and not at all unlike what some of the ladies in Athens wear, except that their tassels are black. Then we see blind, or partially blind, beggars, of whom there are vast numbers, Coptic and Mahomedan women and children, girls with baskets of flowers and lovely roses, sweet-meat, fly-whisp, water, and fruit-sellers, conjurers, snake-charmers, one and all soliciting "backsheesh," dusky, brown-skinned Arabs clad in loose-flowing robes and white turbans, coal-black Nubians, Jews, Greeks, Armenians, and Europeans of all shades of colour, religion, and politics. Here, in fact, in this city of Saladin and of the "Arabian Nights Entertainments" creations (which once seemed to be so fanciful and visionary) kindle into life and reality as I look upon everything around me.

The apartments of an Arab house of the well-to-do are decorated with Arabesque lattices, instead of glass windows. Inside are luxurious divans heaped with soft cushions, instead of sofas and chairs; and instead of the rattling of cabs, carts, and tramcars we hear the wild, shrill, trilling note of the Arabian women indicating some occasion of joy or sorrow, or hear the equally peculiar long drawn-out note of the muezzin from some minaret calling the faithful to prayer.

Very near to our hotel, on the opposite side, are always to be found a number of donkeys ready for hire, and very good little donkeys they are. I can see the head, legs, and tail of a donkey; the remaining portion of him is almost concealed by a great padded saddle, to which is attached a very inconvenient pair of stirrups, into which you *may* get the tips of your toes, and sometimes a portion of the foot, but if the foot is not small, or is so unfortunate as to possess a respectably-sized bunion, you must be content if you can get the tips of your toes only in the stirrup; this, again, slips down to the right or left, according as you put more pressure on one side or the other. There are no girths, but one long strap placed around the saddle and donkey very insecurely fixes the former. If my reader has not been accustomed to circus-riding, I assure him he would experience some difficulty at first in exhibiting his powers of equitation before the Egyptian public under these circumstances, and I have seen more than one individual come into ignominous contact with mother earth; fortunately he has not far to go ere he humbles and tumbles himself in the dust.

My first experience was this: as soon as I was seated and had rammed the tip of my boot into the stirrup, the donkey-boy shouts, "Ha—ha." This warning note the donkey knows full well, and off he goes at a kind of running trot, which is all right. Soon these ha-ha's increase in frequency, and ere long I can fancy myself a second Mezeppa. The imp behind now accompanies his peculiar yell with a sharp prog of a pointed stick, and the donkey takes a very pointed cognisance of it, for now "He urges on his wild career." In the wide, open streets this rapid mode of progression has an exhilarating tendency, but in the narrow streets of the bazaars unguarded human beings fly to the right of me, unguarded human beings fly to the left of me, and imprecations, not loud, but deep, in an unknown tongue, fall on my untutored ear as my donkey indiscriminately cannons on to the unobservant. A few words about these donkeys, and donkey-boys so called. Most of the latter are not boys at all, but full-grown men, notwithstanding which they are always called donkey-boys. These and their donkeys are quite an institution in the East. The donkeys own all kinds of popular English names, and of course (if the owner may be believed) are possessed of every good quality. Most of the donkey-boys have picked up more or less English, and in expatiating on the good qualities of their beasts are accustomed to interlard their speech with the strong language of the West, and you would be surprised to hear how promptly they will consign a fellow donkey-boy to an inhospitable and much-warmer region than Cairo, and to the care of a much blacker individual than themselves. The reader is here called upon to exercise his or her imagination. I had myself derived considerable amusement when watching an intending pilgrim securing one of these donkeys. To be forewarned is to be forearmed; I flattered myself that by making my selection sure before I got amongst them, my tactics would be most successful, but as the sequel will show, I was grossly deceived, having reckoned without my host, or hosts I ought to say. First intending pilgrim. He descends the steps of Shepheard's Hotel, and moves towards the donkeys—a fatal movement. Instantly the air is thick with donkeys and donkey-boys. The latter yell frantically a chorus of praises concerning the useful quadrupeds, which are most adroitly and with surprising dexterity brought one after the other under his very nose, whilst the poor victim is jostled about in the most bewildering and unpleasant manner. I have been both a spectator of and an actor in this performance, and I can safely say the spectator derives by far the greatest amusement.

I resolved to pay a visit to the bazaars and some of the mosques of note. Having, as I thought, gained some experience by observing the misfortunes of others, I executed a strategic movement which I fondly imagined would turn out successful. I had, from a distance selected my donkey; then cunningly walked up and down the pavement smoking a cigarette, apparently with no object in view. Suddenly I darted on to the enemy, but alas! I found myself in an absolute whirlwind of donkeys and their troublesome two-legged attendants, who yelled into my ears and bumped me about until I was quite unable to recognise the donkey I had selected. Beauties were here represented, such as Mrs. Cornwallis West, and Mrs. Langtry; national names, such as John Bull, and Yankee-doodle; mythical names, such as Jim Crow and Billy Barlow. One donkey rejoiced in the name of Dr. Tanner, another in that of Madame Rachel; others, again, had been honoured with the names of statesmen, such as Prince Bismarck, John Bright, Sir Stafford Northcote, Lord Randolph Churchill, Mr. Gladstone, Mr. Parnell, Lord Beaconsfield, and others. "Dr. Tanner, he debbil to go—he berry good donkey indeed, hakeem," said the owner. However, I declined him, as he was said to be a FAST one (excuse the joke), and as this was entirely an Eastern question, I could not help thinking that Lord Beaconsfield would certainly be the most likely to carry me safely through. I therefore selected him, and had every reason to be satisfied with him and his secretary, Lord Rowton *alias* Ibrahim, the donkey-boy, whom I employed on several subsequent occasions. He proved a very good conductor, for he took me through the various bazaars, Tunis, Algiers, Turkish, Persian, and Arab, &c., pointing out all places of note and interest *en route*. Ibrahim soon got to know that I was a doctor, and so indeed did all the attendant Arabs about the hotel. He, like hundreds of his countrymen, suffered from ophthalmia, and when I was out with him he said—

"Hakeem, what I do with my eyes? They very bad sometimes."

"Oh!" said I, "you bring me a bottle to-morrow morning, and I will give you something for them," little thinking of the consequences. The lotion did his eyes a great deal of good, and two days afterwards a great many of his friends called, to all of whom I gave lotion. During my stay here, and some months afterwards on returning from the Soudan, I was, every morning, employed after breakfast at my medicine chest preparing eye lotions for my Arab friends, invocations for the blessings of Allah being my recompense. The poor fellows appeared to be grateful, and I dare say it was genuine, not like a canting old Irish vagrant woman, who, if you give a hunk of bread and cheese to, will exclaim —

"Thank yer honour kindly!" and as long as she is in hearing keep muttering, "Och! sure now, there's a kind jintleman for ye, me darlint. Sure now he is intirely an illigant jintleman; only for him I would not have a bite this morning, that's sure for ye. May Heaven guide him and the blessed Virgin protect him!" Then out of hearing it is, "Och! the dirty spalpeen! What will I do wid this? May the curse of Cromwell light on ye for a murthering Sassenach. What will I do honey? and I not had a sup of gin this blessed day to keep the cowld out of me poor thrimbling ould body!"

But I am digressing. One day I took a donkey ride to old Cairo, and with others from the hotel visited the dancing dervishes, and the house said to have been inhabited by our Saviour. Old Cairo is about two miles distant from Grand Cairo. It was at old Cairo that the child Jesus, with Joseph and Mary, lived for a time, having fled from the bloody, persecuting Herod. The place said to have been His exile home is now a small Greek church. The steps to the room are very much worn, but great care is taken of every part of it; silver lamps, hung from the ceiling, are burning night and day, and no one is allowed to enter without the presence of a Greek priest. It certainly is not difficult to believe that, considering the mild Syrian atmosphere, and the absence of rain, the building may be much more than 1,800 years old.

The dancing dervishes next engaged our attention. When in Constantinople I visited the dancing dervishes at Pera and the howling dervishes on the other side of the Bosphorus at Scutari. The dancing dervishes wear a dress of greyish material, which reaches a little below the knee, and is confined by a girdle round the waist. When they spin round like Teetotums this looks like an open umbrella. The head is covered by a curious-looking, tall, conical felt hat without any brim.

The word itself, Dervish, or Dervise, is of Persian origin, and signifies poor. It denotes the same amongst Mahomedans as *monk* with Christians. The observance of strict forms, fasting and acts of piety, give them a character of sanctity amongst the people. They live partly together in monasteries partly alone, and from their number the Imams (priests) are generally chosen. Throughout Turkey they are freely received, even at the tables of persons of the highest rank. Among the Hindus they are called *fakirs*. There are throughout Asia multitudes of these devotees, monastic and ascetic, not only among the Mahomedans, but also among the followers of Brahma. There are no less than thirty-two religious orders now existing in the Turkish Empire, many of whom are scarcely known beyond its limits; but others, such as the Nasksh-bendies and Mevlevies, are common in Persia and India. All these communities are properly stationary, though some of them send out a portion of their members to collect alms. The regularly itinerant dervishes in Turkey are all foreigners or outcasts, who, though expelled from their orders for misconduct, find their profession too agreeable and profitable to be abandoned, and therefore set up for themselves, and, under colour of sanctity, fleece honest people. All these orders, except the Nakshbendies are considered as living in seclusion from the world; but that order is composed entirely of persons who, without quitting the world, bind themselves to a strict observance of certain forms of devotion, and meet once a week to perform them together. Each order has its peculiar-statutes, exercises, and habits. Most of them impose a novitiate, the length of which depends upon the spiritual state of the candidate, who is sometimes kept for a whole year under this kind of discipline. In the order of the Mevlevies, the novice perfects his spiritual knowledge in the kitchen of the convent. The numerous orders of dervishes are all divided into two great classes, the dancing and the howling dervishes. The former are the Mevlevies, and are held in much higher estimation than the other class, and are the wealthiest of all the religious bodies of the Turkish Empire. Their principal monastery is at Konieh, but they have another at Pera, a suburb of Constantinople, where they may be seen engaged in their exercises every Wednesday and Thursday. These are performed in a round chamber, in the centre of which sits their chief or sheik, the hem of whose garment each dervish reverently kisses on entering the chamber, after which they go and range themselves round the chamber with their legs tucked under them. When all the dervishes have entered and saluted the sheik, they all rise together and go in procession three times round the room, the sheik at their head. Each time they do obeisance to the empty seat of the sheik on coming to a certain part of the room. The procession ended, the sheik again takes his place in the centre, and all the others begin dancing round him, turning on themselves at the same time that they move round the room. The arms are extended, the palm of the right turned upward and the palm of the left downward, to indicate that what they receive from heaven with the right they give away to the poor with the left, while sounds of music are heard from a neighbouring gallery. The movement at first is slow, but as the dervishes become excited they become more animated, and revolve so quickly that they look like tops spinning round; at last they sink exhausted on the floor. After a while they renew their exertions, and repeat it several times. The whole is concluded by a sermon.

The howling dervishes do not confine themselves in their exercises to the dancing just described. They accompany them with loud vociferations of the name of Allah, and violent contortions of the body such as are seen in persons seized with epileptic fits. And even these extravagances are not so bad as those which were formerly practised, when the dervishes, after working themselves into a frenzy, used to cut and torture themselves in various ways with apparent delight. The sheiks of all orders have the credit of possessing miraculous powers. The interpretation of dreams, the cure of diseases, and the removal of barrenness, are the gifts for which the dervishes are most in repute. Had I to live in such a hot climate as Cairo, I should feel thankful that our religion does not necessitate such violent bodily exertion as that which these dervishes indulge in. The road to old Cairo was very, very dusty, and the weather excessively hot, as it always is in the day time. We left the dancing dervishes after remaining about half-an-hour, and rode back to our hotel in the afternoon too late for any further explorations that day. On the following day I spent some hours in a very enjoyable and also instructive manner, namely in inspecting the priceless articles in the Baulac Museum. This museum, I suppose, contains some of the most ancient things in this world, and I regret very much that I could not devote a week to inspecting the contents of it instead of a few hours. I should have seen the treasures contained here, and known very little concerning them (as there was no catalogue), had I not been so fortunate as to get into conversation with Brusch Bey, the curator, a most intelligent and obliging gentleman, whose heart is enthusiastically in his work. He was kind enough to spend about two or three hours with me and enlighten me on very many things which would have been a sealed book to me but for him. There lay before us one grand discovery of 32 kings and queens, who had ruled Egypt in the dim distant ages long ago. The gilding on the inner coffins was as perfect and untarnished as it was the week they were executed, although thousands of years have rolled by since the handy craftsman was engaged on them. They were covered with information that none but an Egyptologist could decipher. In this museum was pointed out to me a picture said to be the most ancient in the world, it was a painted picture of Egyptian geese, as well done, I should imagine, as any ordinary painter of the present day could do it. There were bronzes and polished marble statuary as perfect in appearance as when they left the workmen's hands, and, as far as I could judge, as well finished as they would be by workmen of the present day, although 2,000 or 3,000 years old. An ingenious and strong little cabinet engaged my attention some time; the doors of hard wood were well carved and the joints as exquisitely dove-tailed in as any man of the present day could make them. In a glass case I saw basket-work, a chair, rope, twine, seals, rings, javelins, slings, food and seeds as they were found in an ancient tomb, the mason's mallet cut out of a solid piece of wood, precisely the same shape and size as those in use here at the present time, jewellery well-finished and solid-looking, and many other things too numerous to mention. On carefully examining this valuable and interesting collection, some of which were 3,000, 4,000, or 5,000 years old, I could not help thinking that they served well to illustrate the highly civilized condition of the people at so remote a period.

To give details of all the interesting things in this museum would occupy too much time to the exclusion of other matter, but there are two things that call for notice on account of their very great antiquity. One is a wooden statue, which has been carved out of a solid block of very hard wood, and is that of a man about 5ft. 7in. in height. As one stands in front of that wooden statue gazing for a short time, he almost appears to be endowed with a soul and the power of speech, so excellent is the execution of the figure, and so expressive the face; no one can doubt for a moment that he was the creation of a high civilization. It was found in a tomb at Sakhara and belongs to one of the early dynasties of the old primæval monarchy, and is absolutely untarnished by the thousands of years it has been reposing in that tomb; there is actually no sign of decay. The antiquity of that statue astonishes me, and I dare say it will my readers. Brusch Bey told me that it was supposed to be 5,400 years old, and that probably it was older than that. The other statue, that of Chephren, the builder of the second Pyramid, with his name inscribed upon it, is in Diorite, one of the hardest kind of stones, carefully executed and beautifully polished. These Egyptians were evidently people of considerable forethought, and when they wanted their names and deeds to live long after them engraved on tablets of stone, they selected the most durable they could, and it is more than probable that had they contemplated building such houses of Parliament as we have built in London, they would have selected a hard, not a soft stone, that continually requires patching up. Well, the features of Chephren's statue are uninjured, and Brusch Bey and I gazed on them just as they were seen by Chephren and his court 5,000 years ago. It was discovered by Mariette Bey, at the bottom of a well, which supplied the water used for sacred purposes in the sepulchral temple attached to Chephren's Pyramid. It was no doubt originally erected in the temple, and was probably thrown into the well by the barbarous Hyksos or iconoclastic Persians.

During the late military operations, or " police measures," grave apprehensions for the safety of the Baulac Museum arose, but fortunately it escaped the violence of the mob. The greater part of one day was occupied by a visit with my familiar

Ibrahim to the mosques of note, the citadel, tombs of the Caliphs and Mamelukes. Another day I got a companion from the hotel to accompany me to the petrified forest, some miles out in the desert. It covers an area of about 15 miles. All this space is pretty thickly strewed over with what appears to be trunks and branches of trees. I took hold of what appeared exactly like the wooden branch of a tree, and so it had once been, but for ages it had lain here, a solid piece of very hard stone. The place is an absolutely desolate one in the desert, with not a sign of vegetation in sight. Whether these had been washed here during the flood or had once grown in the neighbourhood or not, or how they came there, I never could ascertain, although I have sought for information on the subject in all directions. No one seems to be able to tell me anything about the origin of this petrified forest, and I have not hitherto found a book containing any allusion to it. We returned to Cairo by the Mokhottam hills behind the citadel somewhat late in the afternoon, consequently had to urge on our donkeys so that we should see Cairo by sunset. We were here just in time to do so, as there is scarcely any twilight in the East; the transition from day to night does not occupy very many minutes. The picturesque panorama that opened out to our view well repaid

F

us for our trouble. There before and beneath us lay Cairo with its innumerable mosques and minarets, the Nile with the peculiar Nile boats called dahabeahs floating peacefully on its surface. Here and there the stately camel strides silently on, veiled women and turbaned Arabs in loose flowing robes, groves of palm trees, while nearer to us we see the half-ruined tombs of the Caliphs and Mamelukes, the citadel and the beautiful mosque of Mehemet Ali full of carved columns of alabaster. To the late burning heat which we encountered in the desert succeeds a soft, balmy, dry air, and the beautiful and varied hues of the setting sun is reflected from the glittering mosques and minarets, rocks and sands, presenting a picture which will not soon fade from my memory, and which requires the poetry, eloquence, and pen of a Byron to adequately describe. In striking contrast to the beautiful scene we had just enjoyed was the wretched-looking houses of the Arabs, the squalor, dirt and miserable pathways on the hill-side which we encountered immediately afterwards as we pursued our homeward journey.

CHAPTER V.

A YOUNG AMERICAN AT SHEPHEARD'S HOTEL—DRIVE TO THE
PYRAMIDS OF GIZEH—ASCENT AND EXPLORATION OF THE
PYRAMID OF CHEOPS—THE SPHINX.

WE arrived at our hotel rather tired, and felt it quite a relief to stretch our legs out straight after having them cramped up so long whilst on our donkeys. Having partaken of a good dinner, I adjourned to the balcony with a cigarette, sank into an easy lounge, and communed with my own thoughts. I had not been here long before I discovered sitting near me an individual, apparently about 23 years of age, whose nether extremities rested on the back of a chair, his feet being parallel with his chin. He was dressed in a somewhat *outré* manner, the lower limbs being encased in check prolongations; the body in a brown coat, something like a sack in shape; the throat was surrounded by a loose, turn-down collar, and loose neckerchief, whilst the summit of this curious specimen of humanity was crowned by a huge felt hat, with an enormous brim. The clouds of smoke which he emitted from his mouth rivalled a young volcano; he was smoking a cigar, and did not forget to expectorate in a most profuse and dangerous manner, so much so that, feeling in somewhat dangerous proximity to the fire of his artillery, I got up with the intention of escaping any little salivary accidents; but my silent companion had his eye on me, and thus suddenly addressed me in the decidedly nasal accent and twang peculiar to the inhabitants of America —

"Stranger, I guess this Cairo is a tarnation rummy place?"

Seeing no reason to dispute this by no means rash assertion, I readily conceded the point; and, by way of carrying on the conversation, ventured to remark that —

"It certainly is a very curious and interesting old place, and the inhabitants no less so."

He: "That's so, sirree; they *are* queer beggars, and so *are* their wimen."

This also was an indisputable fact, and I acknowledged that they were a strange race, strongly wedded to old customs, and as strongly opposed to innovations.

He: "Stranger, yew don't roost here, I guess?"

I: "No; I am just travelling for a few months, and shall leave Cairo in two or three days' time."

He: "In what line may you be travelling, stranger?"

Now, of course I knew what he meant, but thought his remarks were so original, not to say impertinent, that I must not omit this opportunity of extracting some amusement, and provide material for my diary. I therefore replied —

"Oh! I came by the P. and O. line to Alexandria, by rail here, and now my lines have fallen in pleasant places."

"Guess yew don't quite fathom me. What's yer business, and where are you going tew?" said he.

I then gave him the names of a number of places in Egypt and the Soudan, enumerating them as rapidly as I could, so that I am quite sure my nasal friend was very little the wiser for the information.

He enshrouded himself in a huge cloud of smoke, vigorously expectorated once more, and regarding me fixedly for a moment, exclaimed —

"By Jupiter! stranger, that's a large order. Opening up a trade or colon*ize*, I guess."

I suppose, because I told him I was travelling with six other gentlemen, he thought we were going to start a colony somewhere, and then annex all the adjacent country, which, by the way, would certainly be a very good thing for the Egyptians and the Soudanese, and very probably for ourselves also. However, I gave him to understand that we were simply travelling for pleasure, exploration, and sport. Notwithstanding this, my Yankee acquaintance was determined to turn me inside out if he could; he, therefore, was so complimentary as to say —

"Well, now, I guess you are a gentleman?"

To this I answered —

"Thanks; I trust your surmise is a correct one;" and I might have said, but I did not, "Sorry I cannot return the compliment."

I have often heard of the pertinacity of an American reporter, but it appears to me that the bump of inquisitiveness is not by any means confined to them, but pervades the whole community. There was no shilly-shallying, no delicate, nicely-worded hints and adroitly-put questions; but my interrogator was determined to find out all about me if he could, and so he asked me how long I had been in Cairo, how old I was, if I was married or single, how many children I had, if I lived on my money, and lots of the most impertinent questions, and finally finished up by saying, "Guess you are a Britisher?"

Having, as he thought, pumped me pretty considerably, he was good enough to take me into his confidence, and tell me all about himself, and his belongings, and "*hew* his father had left him a pile," adding, "Guess I spend some, and move about a bit." I could not help saying —

"I think you are wise to pursue that course; travel will improve you a good deal, and, like the marble statuary in the Baulac Museum, it will put on a little polish."

He eulogised the States and the inhabitants thereof, and was apparently under the impression that America was the only place worth speaking of, winding up with the quite unnecessary announcement —

"I'm 'Merican."

"Oh, yes," I replied; "I knew at once you were an American."

"Yes; is that so?" said he. "Hew did ye know that, stranger?"

"Well," said I, "by your accent, the estimate you form of your country, and, pardon me for saying so, but no one but an American would have asked me such questions as you have, or manifested such a desire to find out all about me and my affairs."

He did not appear to be at all annoyed at this remark, but merely said—

"By thunder! stranger, you are a queer coon. Will you come and liquor?"

I declined with thanks, and left young America to ponder over the inscrutable ways and manners of the "darned Britisher." He was evidently the offspring of a parent who, perchance, had "struck ile," and had never before forsaken his ancestral home in search of travel and adventure; and, if such was the case, we must excuse the young man. As soon as I left him I sought my bedroom, chronicled the above conversation in my diary, and retired to bed, where I slept soundly.

The following day I and three others formed a party for a visit to the far-famed pyramids of Gizeh. We chartered a carriage, taking our lunch with us; and from the time we left Shepheard's Hotel until we returned that hateful word, "Backsheesh," resounded in our ears; indeed, I should say that there is no word in the Egyptian language so frequently on the tip of an Arab tongue as that. I should suppose that the pyramids of Gizeh are about ten miles from Cairo. There is a pretty good road, which was constructed by the former Khedive, Ismail, specially to accommodate the Prince of Wales when he visited the place some years ago. During our drive we could almost have imagined that a line of sentries had been posted all along the road specially to utter that horrid word, "Backsheesh," so continuously were our tympanums offended with it. Arrived at the base of the Great Pyramid, we are immediately surrounded by a considerable number of Arabs, who are all anxious to assist us in the ascent, of course, for a small consideration; but one of our party having been there once before, knew how to set about matters in a business-like way, so he demanded at once the presence of the Pyramid Sheik, who very soon came. We told him we did not want all this crowd of Arabs, but two each would be sufficient. Accordingly he allotted us these, but as he suggested that a third would be desirable to push us up from behind, we had him. Those who have ascended the Great Pyramid are not likely to forget the dusky demons who accompany them.

I commence the ascent with my body-guard, who appear now to look upon me as a piece of brittle china, and are most anxious to prevent me using my limbs in my own way—they will not let me take a step without their assistance. Directly I had started I found my body-guard considerably augmented, and notwithstanding repeated warnings that I did not want them, and that they would not get any backsheesh, they stuck to me all the way up and back. For the time being I belong solely to these energetic, incessantly-chattering Arabs, whose most strenuous efforts were now put forth to damaging my ball and socket joints.

I have to ascend 203 steps—the lower steps are about four feet high, and few of them less than three feet anywhere. The two Arabs in front get on to the step I have to land on; each seizes an arm, one gets behind, and the hoisting process begins. The latter gives the cue, and with a loud "Ha-hu," up I go from one step to the other. This game goes on with great rapidity, until I had got about half-way up, where I think it advisable to rest awhile. So down I sat, but soon found that instead of three Arabs I was at once surrounded by about a dozen, all talking most vehemently to me at the same time. It was in vain to protest—all had curiosities, scarabei, little images, and ancient coins, some of them curious, no doubt dating back to the time of Adam. For a small consideration they were all anxious to place these in my possession, and all were shouting into my ear, "Autica effendi, autica." At last, for peace sake, I bought a small image of a defunct Pharaoh from one, and from another three or four copper coins, all, of course, the only genuine. In vain I protested against having any more. I had no peace until I had bought something from each one; in fact, I had no quiet until I turned all my pockets inside out, showing conclusively that I had spent every piaster with them. After resting awhile, we continued the ascent, and after a succession of ha-hus, tugs, and hoistings, I at last found myself on the summit of the Great Pyramid, and well rewarded for the trouble I had taken.

Here, in this bright, clear atmosphere, I saw stretching out for miles on the west the Libyan Desert, and reaching out before and around us in vast extent the classic and historic hills, rivers, and plains of Ham and Mizraim, Heliopolis, Memphis, Mount Mokattam, Sakhara, the beautiful city of Cairo, with its numberless mosques and slender minarets, skirted by the outstretched Nile, bearing on its placid bosom hundreds of dahabeahs, and on its banks tall waving palm-trees. Nearer is the village of Gizeh, and closer still the remaining pyramids of Gizeh, the granite temple, and the sphinx, the whole forming a picture that cannot be effaced in a life-time.

It is said with some truth, "Time tries all," but I have also heard it said that "the pyramids try time," and, upon my word, it almost seems so, when we think of their great antiquity. Here they have stood for thousands of years in majestic grandeur, looking down on many Pharaohs and many dynasties, and witnessing the rise, greatness, and decline of a once mighty nation. Abraham, Isaac, Jacob, Joseph, and Moses have gazed on these huge piles of masonry, which raised their lofty heads long, long before Abraham in a day of famine sought bread at the hands of Pharaoh.

When I had spent some time in gazing again and again on this beautiful scene, and thoroughly succeeded in obtaining a mental photograph of it, I commenced the descent, and found I could get down much more comfortably without assistance than with; but this the pertinacious Arabs would not hear of, they said, on account of the danger to me. But my own private opinion was that they wanted to earn good backsheesh by persistent attention. I resigned myself to my fate, and at last reached the foot of the pyramid by a series of jumps and bumps very trying to my spinal column, and which joggled my internal economy most unpleasantly.

After a short rest, we explored the interior, a rather difficult achievement in some parts. We had brought a good substantial luncheon with us from the hotel, which we thankfully disposed of at a house, or palace, near by. This was specially built, I believe, either for the Prince of Wales or the Empress Eugenie, I really forget which. After lunch we visited the sphinx, two or three tombs, and the other two pyramids, settled up with the sheik, and drove off to our hotel; and not until I reached the steps of the hotel did I hear the last of that hateful word "Backsheesh." When I retired to rest I dreamt of a pocketful of large copper coins and scarabei, an armful of defunct Pharaohs, an army of lithe, sinewy, swarthy, impecunious Arabs, amongst whom I had scattered a ship-load of piasters, and "still they were not happy."

Before I have done entirely with the pyramids, I think I ought to say something about them, as those at Gizeh are the most remarkable. This group consists of nine, and comprises three of the most remarkable monuments in existence—those of Cheops, Cephren, and that of Mycerinus, the last-named much smaller than the other two. Herodotus, who was born about 500 B.C., tells us that in building the great pyramid of Cheops it took 100,000 men working incessantly for 30 years to complete it; 10 years of this 30 was spent in making a causeway 3,000 feet long, to facilitate the transportation of the stone from the Turah quarries. Herodotus describes the method of building by steps, and raising the stones from layer to layer by machines, and finally of facing the external portion from the top down. Its present height is 460 feet, the original height was 480 feet.

The extent of solid masonry has been estimated at 82,111,000 cubic feet. It at present covers 12 acres. The only entrance is on the north face, 49 feet above the base, though the masonry has been so much broken away that the *débris* reaches nearly up to it. A passage, 3 feet 11 inches high and 3 feet 5½ inches wide, conducts from the entrance down a slope at an angle of 26° 41', a distance of 320 feet 10 inches to the original sepulchral chamber, commonly known as the subterraneous apartment; it is carried, reduced in dimensions, beyond this a distance of 52 feet 9 inches into the rock, though for what purpose remains a matter of conjecture. The sepulchral chamber is 46 feet long by 27 feet wide, and 11½ feet high. From the entrance passage another branches off and leads to several other passages and chambers. One of the latter, known as the *Queen's Chamber*, is situated about the middle of the pyramid, 67 feet above the base; it has a groined roof, and measures 17 feet broad by 18 feet 9 inches long and 20 feet 3 inches high. The other, called the *King's Chamber*, is reached by an offshoot from the Queen's Passage, 150 feet long. Its dimensions are 34 feet 3 inches long by 17 feet 1 inch wide, and 19 feet 1 inch high. The chamber is lined with red granite highly polished, single stones reaching from the floor to the ceiling, and the ceiling itself is formed of nine large slabs of polished granite extending from wall to wall. The only contents of the apartment is a sarcophagus of red granite, which, judging by its dimensions, must have been introduced when the building was proceeding. It is supposed to have contained a wooden coffin with the mummy of the king, and that these long since disappeared when the pyramids were first opened and plundered. We do not see these pyramids as they originally were. The outer casing of polished stone has been removed and utilized in constructing the mosque of Sultan Hassan. These pyramids were built between 5,000 and 6,000 years ago. Great was the antiquity of Thebes before European history begins to dawn. It was declining before the foundations of Rome were laid, but the building of the great pyramids of Gizeh preceded the earliest history of Thebes by 1,000 years. Whilst speaking of Thebes, I'll just mention that there are to be seen to-day the tomb of the great Sethos, Joseph's Pharaoh, of his greater son, Remeses II., and of Menophres or Meneptha, in whose reign the Exodus took place. In the tomb of Sethos, coloured sculptures cover 320 feet of the excavation. There is to be seen the draughtsman's handiwork in red colour, showing the designs that were to be executed by the sculptor, and the corrections in black ink of the superintendent of such works, and although these sketches were made 3,000 years ago, they are still quite clear and fresh-looking. On the east side of the pyramid, half buried in sand, is the wonderful colossal Sphinx, his head 25 feet high and back 100 feet long, all one stone.

CHAPTER VI.

HELIOPOLIS—THE SHOUBRA ROAD—BEDROSKYN—MITRAHENNY—MEMPHIS—SAKHARA—APIS MAUSOLEUM—WORSHIP OF THE BULL APIS—TOMB OF KING PHTA—MEET THE KHEDIVE—ENGAGE SERVANTS FOR THE SOUDAN.

My next visit was to Heliopolis on donkey-back. I was told that it would be a nice ride, but nothing to see except an obelisk when I got there. Notwithstanding this, I felt very desirous of visiting this ancient seat of learning, where Moses had lived and "become learned in all the wisdom of the Egyptians." Accordingly Ibrahim and I started off. Leaving the citadel and tombs of the Caliphs on my right, I had a pleasant ride of about two hours or so from Cairo through avenues of acacias and tamarisk trees, a large plain covered with a luxuriant growth of sugar-cane, citrons, lemons, oranges, ricinus, cactuses, olive trees and palms.

Before reaching the mounds of Heliopolis is a well of fine water on the border of a grove of citrons and palms, and in the midst of these is a venerable old sycamore enclosed by palisades and regarded with veneration by the Copts, as the place where Joseph, Mary and the infant Saviour rested on their flight into Egypt. Although a very aged tree, it cannot be, of course, as old as the legend affirms. It is, however, a very pretty spot, sheltered from the busy hum of life, embowered in citron thickets, which resound with the music of birds, and with tall, waving palm trees, on the trembling branches of which large vultures rock to and fro. I approach the site of Heliopolis on a dead level, and find that it stood formerly on an artificial elevation, overlooking lakes which were fed by canals communicating with the Nile. With what history does this place teem! Here, or in the vicinity, Jeremiah wrote his Lamentations. Thales, Solon, Pythagoras and Plato studied here. From the learned priests of Heliopolis, Plato —who studied here for several years—is believed to have derived the doctrine of the immortality of the soul and of a future state of rewards and punishments. This neighbourhood was probably the scene of the Exodus of the Israelites, and here was the most celebrated university in the world for philosophy and science. It was here that Potipherah, the priest or Prince of On, resided. Here Joseph married his daughter Asenath, who became the mother of Ephraim and Manasseh. Now what do I see? This once famous city of the sun, the Heliopolis of Herodotus and Strabo, the On of Joseph, the Bethshemesh of Jeremiah, the university of the world at that time, with its collection of colleges and temples, avenues of sphinxes and extensive dwellings of the learned priests, dazzling palaces, obelisks and splendid edifices has been almost blotted out, and as I stood there absorbed in thought, and feebly endeavouring to picture to myself this place as it once stood, teeming with life, wealth and power, those beautiful words of Shakespeare, our immortal bard, came floating through my mind as very descriptive of what I now saw—

> The cloud-capt towers,
> The gorgeous palaces,
> The solemn temples,
> The great globe itself,
> Yea, all which it inherit,
> Shall dissolve,
> And like the baseless fabric of a vision,
> Leave not a wreck behind.

All was now desolation, if I except the massive foundations of the Temple of the Sun, which are still visible in a few places. The one solitary object that serves to mark this once celebrated city is an obelisk of solid granite, 62 feet high, the last monument of a temple that once vied in magnificence with those of Karnak or Baalbeck, and which has been pointing to the sky from the time of the old monarchy for more than 4,000 years. It bears the name of Osirtesen I. (Joseph's contemporary), the first great name in Theban history, builder of the older and smaller part of the great temple of Karnak and King of Upper and Lower Egypt, and probably where I then stood looking at, but unable to decipher the hieroglyphics on this obelisk, Joseph and Moses (who had both been admitted to the priest cast) had stood before me. *Sic transit gloria mundi.*

I had now seen all there was to see, and was pleased that I had made this visit, so I mounted my donkey and got back to Cairo. It happened to be Friday, the Mahomedan Sunday. On this day all the rank and fashion can be seen between four and six driving up and down the Shoubra Road. This is lined by a splendid avenue of trees, which meet overhead, thus forming a delightful shade. It was now about 4 p.m.; I performed a hasty toilet and set off for a carriage drive down this road. I found it thronged with visitors and a goodly sprinkling of officers, amongst whom I saw the now famous Arabi Pacha. Mounted sentries also were posted at intervals each side of the road as the Khedive usually takes a drive there every Friday about 4 or 5 p.m. I had not been there long ere he came sweeping down with his escort.

Next day I devoted to exploring the ancient (probably the most ancient city in the world), Memphis, the Noph of the Bible, and its necropolis, Sakhara. According to Herodotus its foundation was ascribed to Menes, the first King of Egypt. If this was so it would be about 6,000 years old, and it is said that the art of building was known centuries before his time.

It is quite a good day's work to perform this journey in the blazing sun. I get an early breakfast and leave at 7.30 on my donkey, accompanied by Ibrahim on another donkey, in possession of my luncheon. The distance to the railway station is about two miles. Here I procure tickets for ourselves and the two donkeys, proceed to Bedrashyn, a distance of about ten miles, then remount and pass through the village of Mitrahenny, then a very fine palm-grove, on to the site of ancient Memphis, once a large, rich, and splendid city, remarkable for its temples and palaces. As late as 524 B.C., at the time of the conquest of Cambyses it was the chief commercial centre of the country, and was connected by canals with the Lakes Mœris and Mareotis. Some distance from the village of

Mitrahenny I saw near the pathway a colossal statue of Rameses the Great in excellent preservation. It is composed of a single block of red granite, polished. It was originally 50 feet in length, but has been mutilated, and now does not measure more than 48 feet. It lies on its side in a pit by the wayside, which, during the inundation of the Nile, is filled with water. On its subsidence the alluvial deposit is scraped off sufficiently to show the statue to travellers. Vast mounds of broken pottery and statuary are to be seen about here and Sakhara, probably burying the ancient city. Sakhara is about two miles or so from Memphis, and the greater part of the ride lies through sandy desert. It lies, in fact, on the edge of the Lybian Desert. It is remarkable for its ancient monuments, among which are 30 pyramids. The great step pyramid is said to be even older than the pyramids of Gizeh. Besides these 30 there are the ruins of a great many others, and numberless grottoes, sarcophagi, the Ibis catacombs, and Apis Mausoleum, which was discovered by Mariette Bey. He observed the head of a sphinx protruding from the sand, and remembering that Strabo described the Serapeum of Memphis as approached by an avenue of sphinxes, he at once commenced his explorations in search of the temple in which Apis was worshipped when alive and the tomb in which it was buried when dead. The sand-drift, after immense exertions, was cleared away, and the avenue was laid bare from a superincumbent mass, which was in some places 70 feet deep. Conceive, if you can, the splendour of this imposing approach; no less than 141 sphinxes were discovered *in situ*, besides the pedestals of others. The temple to which they led has disappeared, but the tomb remains.

I go down hill, nearly up to my knees in sand, with my guide. A great door is unlocked and thrown open, we then light our candles and explore. We proceed a considerable distance through a passage or tunnel, and then find ourselves in a large vault or tunnel some 200 or 300 yards in length. Chambers lead out of it on either side as large as an ordinary sitting-room, and about 12 feet high, in each of which is a ponderous granite sarcophagus, polished. Placed on the sarcophagus like a lid was a granite slab of great size and weight, the whole weighing about 20 tons. Near the subterranean cemetery of the bulls are the groves or pits of the sacred Ibis also formerly worshipped. These are enclosed in earthenware vases; the bones and broken urns now lie scattered all around. These huge blocks of granite were actually transported from the quarries near Syene to Memphis, a distance of nearly 600 miles! I carefully examined one sarcophagus containing the embalmed dead deity. It was carved all over with sacred hieroglyphics, sharp and clear in their outlines, and the polish on the marble bright as it was 3,000 years ago. I saw between 30 and 40 of these sarcophagi here.

The worship of the bull Apis was celebrated with great pomp and splendour, and he was regarded as the representative of Osiris.

His interment would cost as much as that of any king or conqueror. It was necessary that he should be black with a triangle of white on the forehead, a white spot in the form of a crescent on the right side, and a sort of knot like a beetle under his tongue. When a bull of this description was found he was fed four months in a building facing the east. At the new moon he was led to a splendid ship with great solemnity and conveyed to Heliopolis, where he was fed 40 days more by priests and women, who performed before him various indecent ceremonies. After this no one was suffered to approach him. From Heliopolis the priests carried him to Memphis, where he had a temple, two chapels to dwell in, and a large court for exercise. He had a prophetic power which he imparted to the children about him. The omen was good or bad according as he went into one stable or the other. His birthday was celebrated every year when the Nile began to rise; the festival continued seven days. A golden patera was thrown into the Nile, and it was said that the crocodile was tame as long as the feast continued. He was only suffered to live 25 years, and at his death he was embalmed and buried in these sarcophagi amidst universal mourning till the priest had found a successor.

When I emerged once more from this mausoleum and struggled up through the sand I paid a visit to the tomb of King Phty or Phta, said to be 5,400 years old. His sarcophagus is similar to those I had just visited, and is contained in a nice lofty room, the walls of which, as are the walls of the chapel outside, plentifully and excellently sculptured, and quite fresh in appearance, though so ancient. I do not remember all I saw represented on the walls and tombs, but amongst other things there were lions, giraffes, ostriches, sacred Ibis, owls, crocodiles, elephants, buffaloes, a boat floating on the water with a man in it, and in the water fish of different kinds, Egyptians fishing, harpooning the hippopotamus, agricultural pursuits, ploughing and sowing, treading out the corn just as they do now, the butcher sharpening his knife, the butcher killing the animal whilst another holds him down, hunting, battle scenes, &c., &c. Some figures on the wall had been painted red; the paint is still good and not at all frayed. In another excavation, after leaving this tomb, I saw a mummy; but I must not expend too much time over this place, although I feel quite disposed to keep on talking of it. We cannot leave the plain of Memphis without recurring to the most memorable event in all its eventful history. It was probably here that Moses and Aaron stood before Pharaoh and demanded that he should let the people go. This was the spot where "Pharaoh rose up in the night, he and all his servants, and all the Egyptians; and there was a great cry in Egypt, for there was not a house in which there was not one dead."

Ruminating on the mutability of human affairs, I mounted my donkey, had a long ride through beautiful palm groves, and finally emerged from the village of Gizeh on to the main road from the pyramids and over a handsome bridge across the Nile to my hotel. When half-way across the Nile, I observed the Khedive and his escort coming along, so I got off my donkey to watch him pass. I took off my hat to him, and he acknowledged my salutation with a gracious bow. As I returned homewards, in imagination I saw these glorious cities of old Egypt peopled. I tried to picture to myself—feebly, I dare say—the splendour and wealth of those people, the magnificence of the designs carried out, the result of which was that neither before nor since has the sun shone on anything like such superb, massive, and imposing temples, palaces, and tombs in the world. Thebes, with its hundred gates, was perhaps the most splendid city in the world for many centuries. Then there were Luxor, Karnak, Philæ, Elephantine, Baalbeck, Dendera, Aba-Simbal, Abydos, Esneh, Edfau, Silsilis, and other places, all decorated with palaces, temples, pyramids, tombs, and sphinxes, &c., on the same magnificent scale; but all have shared the same fate, and their stupendous ruins are all that remain to strike the stranger with awe and wonder.

About two days after our arrival in Cairo, our party was augmented by the arrival of Mr. W. D. James, Mr. A. James, and Mr. Percy Aylmer, Mahoom, a black boy; who had been rescued from the Soudan some years beforehand; Jules, George, and Anselmia, the three latter European servants. Here we engaged Suleiman as a sort of general manager for the caravan; he had travelled through the Soudan with Sir Samuel Baker; Ali, a very good cook, and Cheriffe, who made a very good butler, and had been accustomed to travel as a kind of steward on the Nile boats.

CHAPTER VII.

THE LAND OF GOSHEN—ANCIENT CANALS—SUEZ—HOWLING DERVISHES—ECLIPSE OF THE MOON AND STRANGE BEHAVIOUR OF NATIVES—LEAVE SUEZ—WHERE THE ISRAELITES CROSSED THE RED SEA—PASS MOUNT SINAI—CORAL REEFS ABUNDANT.

OUR next move was on to Suez by rail, a day's journey through another very interesting portion of Egypt, the land of Goshen, the home of the Israelites for 430 years. A good deal of country near the line of railway is now under good cultivation, supplied by the Sweet Water Canal. The earliest attempt that we are acquainted with to construct a canal was by Rameses the Great. It was between 50 and 60 miles in length, and left the Nile at Bubastis, reaching into the neighbourhood of Lake Timsah. Upon it Rameses built his two treasure cities, Pithom and Raamses near Ismailia, mentioned in the 1st chapter of Exodus, and there is little doubt that the Israelites, who were then in bondage, laboured at these cities, and the canal 3,000 years ago. It is probable also that the canal dated far back beyond this time, for the Egyptians had been great in canal making 1,000 years or more before then: One of the greatest marks of Rameses was the covering the whole of Egypt with a network of waterways in connection with the river. They served a double purpose—they greatly extended the supply of water and the area of cultivation, and were invaluable for defensive purposes. Many centuries after this Pharaoh Necho took this canal in hand 500 or 600 years B.C. He undertook to adapt it for navigation and prolong it to the head of the Arabian Gulf. He is the only Egyptian monarch whose name appears connected with maritime enterprise, and he was so zealous as to perfect the formation of a ship canal connecting the Nile with the Red Sea. He carried the great work as far as the Bitter Lakes, and then abandoned it, warned by an oracle to desist, after expending the lives of 120,000 fellahs. Herodotus actually *saw* the docks, which as a part of the plan, he had constructed on the Red Sea. One conqueror succeeded another, and the works got neglected and the canal choked up. The Romans again carried on extensive repairs and alterations, but on the downfall of the Roman Empire anarchy and confusion prevailed, and all public works were allowed to fall into dilapidation. The canals were choked up, and remained unnavigable till the Arab conquest of Egypt. Under the vigorous administration of Amrou they were reopened, and corn and other provisions were conveyed along them for the use of Mecca, Medina, and other Arabian towns. A very great deal could be said about their ancient canals, but I have only time to glance *en passant* at a little of the ancient history of the places I passed by. In the evening we arrived at Suez, 76 miles east of Cairo. There is very little to interest or amuse at Suez, but here we were obliged to remain for nearly a week by reason of stoppages in the canal, which are frequent. The day after our arrival we took donkey rides down the Mole, which is 850 yards long, to see after our provisions, tents, &c., which Mr. James and his friends had got together for our campaigning in the Soudan. We found them, and there sure enough was a stambouk (a native boat something like a fishing smack) not only full but piled up with everything that we could possibly require, and the collecting of which must have necessitated a great deal of forethought. Two days after our arrival, Mr. J. B. Colvin, of Monkham's Hall, Waltham Abbey, arrived by steamer from Australia, to join us, thus completing the party. During our stay here there happened to be an eclipse of the moon. This appeared to have a very disturbing influence on the native element, as I should think that every tomtom in Suez was called into requisition and incessantly beaten all over the town during the eclipse to drive away the evil spirits. If it did not succeed I have no hesitation in saying that all the good spirits (ourselves) would very soon have vanished if we could. We had ample time to explore the town both by day and night, and amuse ourselves as well as we could by donkey rides down the Mole, boating, fishing and bathing, but whilst bathing we were careful not to go far from shore for a header or remain in long, as sharks are so plentiful in the Red Sea. One evening, two or three of us were wandering about at night and heard strange noises issuing from a small building. We were sufficiently inquisitive to go up a narrow passage to ascertain the cause. There we found about a dozen very dirty howling dervishes in the odour of sanctity (a decidedly strong odour we thought) performing their senseless and absurd mode of worship with great energy. They were in a dirty room, having a damp, uneven, earthen floor, the dimensions of which were about 7 feet high, 7 feet wide, and perhaps 10 feet long. Very little light or air could find its way in. The weather was very hot, and the sudoriferous glands of these unsavoury gentry were in an abnormal state of activity. Need I say that we remained here a very short time? We were all thoroughly tired of Suez, and anxious to get on to Souâkin, but unfortunately, amongst all the steamers blocked in the Suez Canal, we could not hear of a single one bound for Souâkin. The *Agra*, a British India steamer, was bound for Jeddah, on the opposite coast, so Mr. James telegraphed to London, asking the Company to let us be taken to Souâkin. They acceded to the request. Accordingly, on the 8th December, we got on board, unloaded the stambouk, and started off for Souâkin, *the* port of Nubia, and indeed of Central Africa, since made historical by our slaughter of thousands of Arabs in that neighbourhood. The places of interest pointed out to us on the Red Sea coast were Moses' Well, Mount Sinai, and the spot where the Israelites crossed. Here the arm of the sea is 12 miles wide, and just here Pi-hahiroth before Baal-zephon is the one and only opening in the mountains. Here one million and a half of the Israelites—men, women, and children—passed through in the night, whilst the army of Egypt pursued them. After a most agreeable but very warm voyage (90° F. in the

LANDING PLACE AT SUÂKIN.

shade) of 3½ days we reached Souâkin. During our last day at sea Captain Smith was very careful in his navigation, as the Red Sea, particularly in that last day's voyage, abounds in coral-reefs.

CHAPTER VIII.

ARRIVAL AT SOUÂKIN — THE SOUDAN — BEDOUIN ARAB PRISONERS IN THE SQUARE, NOT "ON THE SQUARE" — IVORY—ENGAGE CAMELS—SHEIK MOUSSA—SOUÂKIN—SLAVES—TRAGIC END OF A DOCTOR—HADENDOWAH ARABS—AN ILL-FATED MISSIONARY ENTERPRISE.

WE were now just about to land in the Soudan, and as that word is, as I am writing, in everyone's mouth, it would be as well to say something about it before I go any further.

The Soudan, or Beled-es-Sudan, Land of the Blacks, has since the Middle Ages been the common name of the vast extent of country in Central Africa, which stretches southward from the Desert of Sahara to the Equator. The name was originally applied by the Arabs, but with great latitude of signification, different authors giving it to the different parts of the territory with which the varying routes across the desert made them acquainted. Later geographers divide it into High and Low Soudan. Many include Senegambia in it. High Soudan stretches from the sources of the Niger, Senegal and Gambia, to the Upper Nile, or, at all events, to the south of Lake Chad, and embraces the mountains of Kong and of Upper Senegambia, the kingdoms of Ashantee, Dahomey, Mandingo, Houssah, and Feelah. All this country is richly watered and wooded, distinguished by a luxuriant tropical vegetation and by deposits of gold. Low Soudan stretches on the north of High Soudan, eastward to Kordofan, and northward to the desert. This district is partly level, partly undulating, and partly broken by chains of lofty hills rising within its own limits. Its situation between the desert on the north and the mountains which border it on the south, with a climate destructive to foreigners, and a lawless and predatory population, make it one of the most inaccessible regions in the world. In the south, where it is watered by the Niger, Lake Tchad, and their tributaries, it assumes a fertile and cultivated appearance. The inhabitants contain numerous nations of different races, chiefly of the Negro, Fulde, or Fellatah stems, together with many Arab colonists.

This is what Sir Samuel Baker says about the

Soudan in the *Contemporary Review:* " Before the White Nile annexation the Soudan was accepted as a vague and unsatisfactory definition as representing everything south of the first cataract at Assouan, without any actual limitation; but the extension of Egyptian territory to the Equator has increased the value of the term, and the word Soudan now embraces the whole of that vast region which comprises the Deserts of Libya, the ancient Merve, Dongola, Kordofan, Darfur, Senaar, and the entire Nile Basin, bordered on the east by Abyssinia, and elsewhere by doubtful frontiers. The Red Sea alone confines the Egyptian limit to an unquestionable line. Wherever the rainfall is regular the country is immensely fertile; therefore the Soudan may be divided into two portions—the great deserts which are beyond the rainy zone, and consequently arid, and the southern provinces within that zone, which are capable of great agricultural development. Including the levels of the mighty Nile, a distance is traversed of about 3,300 miles from the Victoria N'yanza to the Mediterranean; the whole of this region throughout its passage is now included in the name ' Soudan.' "

We had on board Captain Gascoigne and Dr. Melidew, of the Royal Horse Guards. They were also bent on a shooting expedition in the Soudan, but did not accompany us farther than Souâkin. There were several other passengers on board bound for India.

We landed at Souâkin on the quay, in a large open square. One side is occupied by what is absurdly called the palace, a large building in which the Governor transacts his official duties, the opposite side by the custom-house, the other by a guard-house, whilst the opposite side was not occupied by any building, but was open to and contiguous to the Red Sea; it was, in fact, the quay.

Here I saw nine tons of elephants' tusks ready for shipment. The average weight of each pair of tusks would be somewhere about 36lbs. I computed that about 560 elephants would have been slaughtered to make up nine tons of ivory; and if elephants are killed at that rate, people may well exclaim about the scarcity of ivory. What next attracted my attention was about 60 Bedouin Arabs in heavy chains, wandering about in this large open square. These poor fellows had to pay their gaolers 100 dollars a month. The Maria Theresa dollar which is in use in the Soudan, and preferred to any other coin, is worth 4s. of our money. They had to find their own food, or rather their tribe did so. I was told that at one time they were a strong tribe, and had come over from Arabia. They had at one time 8,000 camels, but they had dwindled down to 2,000, as whenever they failed to pay the taxes some of their camels were seized. I cannot speak with any certainty of their offence, but somehow or other they had incurred the anger of the then Governor of the Soudan, Ali Riza Pacha, about a year beforehand. He clapped them into irons, and there they seemed likely to remain, unless some more kindly-disposed Governor superseded him. This fortunately happened not long before our return to Souâkin in the following April, when Ali Dheen Pacha was appointed, who soon liberated them.

The inhabitants of Souâkin are principally Arabs, a few Greek and Italian merchants, and two Englishmen. The Government usually have a garrison of about 300 Nubian troops stationed in an undefended barrack on the mainland, about a mile from the town.

Blind to their own interest, the Egyptian Government obstructs traffic by the heavy duties which it levies. Cattle and sheep, which can be obtained from the tribes in the neighbourhood, are sent by hundreds annually to Suez by sea. Were it not for the heavy duties imposed, I should say that a large trade ought to be done with Suez, which is but three and a half days from Souâkin. There is a telegraph line to Kassala. They have large numbers of camels for sale or hire, but no horses, mules, or donkeys. The water is collected during the wet season in a large reservoir about a mile from the town; there are also two or three wells at the same place.

We soon introduced ourselves to Mr. Brewster, an Englishman, and head of the custom-house; and he in turn sent for Achmet Effendi, the Civil Governor of Souâkin, to whom he introduced us. Of course, there followed the inevitable salaaming, coffee and cigarettes, so customary in the East. Our business was very soon explained; we wanted about 80 camels provided without delay to transport ourselves and our baggage across the desert to Kassala. The camel sheik, Moussa, was sent for, and soon appeared—a really picturesque, handsome-featured man, almost black, possessed of gleaming, regular teeth, wearing a snow-white turban and loose white robe, precisely like the ancient Roman toga. *En passant*, I cannot help thinking that the slang word "togs" is derived from the word toga.

The Sheik Moussa promised to provide us with the camels within three days; and, strange to say, he did so, a singular instance of a man keeping his word to one in the East. I know that my experience amongst the officials in Turkey was very different—there everything was put off until to-morrow. A day would be fixed for me to call at the Seraskierat, or War Office, and when I went I was usually met with the reply, "Yarrin sabbah, effendi" (to-morrow, sir), or "Ywash, ywash" (by and bye), not once or twice, but I daresay five or six times. Another inconvenient phrase which is always on their lips if one wants any money from them, and which is spoken trippingly on the tongue, is "Para yok" (no paras), in English, "I haven't a farthing."

It soon became known that there was a "Hakeem Ingelese," as they called me, in our party, and I very soon had many patients, amongst whom was a child of one of the Bedouin Arabs.

In the afternoon I improved my acquaintance with Mr. Brewster, who had officially resided here four years, and, of course, knew most of the people and the customs of the place. There are a great many good and curiously-built houses with flat roofs, built of blocks of white coral, and a great many tent-like structures constructed with reeds, stalks of palm leaves, and matting, which is very cheap and abundant, made by the natives out of palm leaves. Mr. Brewster was good enough to escort me over Souâkin, and give me all the information he could about the place and people. As we strolled on he pointed out the home of a slave-dealer, who then had several slaves—children and young girls. These could easily be transferred as ivory, dhurra, or something of the kind, as old Achmet Effendi connived at slave-dealing, and would shut his eyes to the transaction provided his palm was crossed with a couple of dollars per head. The little children realize from 30 to 40 dollars a head, and young girls 70, 80, or 100 dollars.

"Why," said I, "in England it is supposed that the slave trade has been abolished in Egypt long ago. When in Cairo I saw the slave-market, but was told no slaves have been sold there for the past three or four year."

"Ah," said he, "you will find, when you get further into Africa, that it is still carried on, and more openly than it is here. When they have been captured they are driven across the desert just like cattle to some quiet place on the Red Sea coast, where there is a stambouk waiting; there shipped and taken across to Jeddah in a day or so, and sold by public auction." The only other Englishman resident at Souâkin was Mr. Bewlay; he had at once lived in Jeddah for a time, and he assured me that he had often seen slaves sold there. *Apropos* of my profession, Mr. Brewster related a very interesting, and, to me, a very instruc-tive anecdote, which served to enlighten me considerably as to the peculiar line of thought which sometimes permeates the native brain, and to the still more peculiar line of action which it leads to. He told me that about three years or so before our arrival a German doctor, who had settled there, whilst attending a native, had occasion to perform some trivial operation which was not attended with the success which he desired or anticipated, as unfortunately for the native, and subsequently for the doctor, the former was so inconsiderate as to expire a day or two afterwards. The doctor could truly say after this, "A doctor's lot is not a happy one," inasmuch as the friends of the defunct Arab paid him a visit, and in a marked but highly objectionable manner, showed what they thought of the doctor's services in a way that did not commend itself to me, and which, for want of a better illustration, we will call "a new way of paying old debts." The worthy leech was requested, in so pressing a manner that refusal was out of the question, to accompany these friends of the deceased, and *nolens volens*, they escorted him to a large open space just outside the town, where dhurra and other things were sold, and there they remunerated him, not in dhurra, not in sheep, not in goats, not even in money, but in a most cutting manner, for they fell upon him with their knives and literally chopped him to pieces. Reader, "would you be surprised to hear," that on learning this I was extremely careful not to perform any rash operations, and that my ministrations to the lame, the halt, the sick, and the blind, should be successful. At all events, it is a source of great gratification to me that they were not so unsuccessful as to necessitate the sudden and unlooked-for departure of any of my patients to their happy hunting-grounds.

The Hadendowah Arabs are the most numerous tribe in the neighbourhood of Souâkin, and are, for the most part, good-looking men; they are very dark, approaching to blackness, have good, well-formed features, large dark eyes, arched black eyebrows, and face, on which as a rule there is little or no hair, and nearly every Arab, here and elsewhere, that I met with, is possessed of the most beautifully white, regular, and sound teeth possible. There is little doubt but that this is due to the simple manner in which they live; their chief food is dhurra (sorghum vulgare). This contains $11\frac{1}{2}$ per cent. of gluten, our wheat only ten per cent. This is the wheat of Egypt, and is the food of camels, horses, and men. Camels, however, get very little of it, as a rule, unless on a forced march, or are owned by a man who can afford it. It grows to the height of nine or ten feet, and is very prolific. I never counted the seeds in a head of this sorghum, but Sir Samuel Baker did, and he says that in one single head he found 4,840 grains. The Arabs, speaking generally, are not big-boned men, but are lithe, active, and sinewy. Their hair is bushy, frizzly, long, and black, which they wear very curiously; they often take as much trouble with it as any West-end dandy would do. A parting is made around the crown from one temple to the other; the hair on the top is combed up and kept short—perhaps an inch long—the rest is combed down, and stands out in a bush all round the head to a distance of three or four inches; a thin piece of stick, like a skewer slightly bent towards the sharp point, is stuck through the hair at the top, and is often used to stir up the population, which is no doubt very numerous. I have often seen their hair white with fat, which they plaster on most abundantly when they can get it, and as few wear any covering over their shoulders when they are exposed to the heat of the blazing sun, this drips down on to them. They wear a bundle of charms secured just above the elbow, a tope, or loin-cloth round the waist, which reaches down to their knees, and very many a ring in one nostril. Nearly all of them carry a shield and a long spear weighted at one end. The Hadendowhas are much given to lying and laziness.

During the time that we remained here we were

fully occupied in preparing for our journey across the desert from Souâkin to Kassala, a distance of about 280 miles; we cut up old boxes, made new ones, and sorted out what provisions, &c., we should require. I arranged my medicine-chest and surgical instruments so that I could get at what I might want easily. We got a little shooting, sand-grouse, flamingoes, pelicans, and herons; wandered about the town and frightened all the children in the place, who thought we were slave-dealers come to steal them. The principal slave supply is obtained from the White Nile and Darfour; Khartoum, I believe, is the principal slave mart.

At nights we stretched ourselves out on the divan that ran round the room in the palace, and slept head to feet all round. This room adjoined and looked out on the square in which the Bedouin prisoners were confined; frequently in the early morning they woke us up with their clanking chains, or by indulging in their peculiar mode of devotion. The day before we started on our journey, Mr. Brewster said —

"Well, Doctor, I hope you will all return alive and well, and not be so unfortunate as a party that Dr. Felkin accompanied a year or two ago."

"I am sure I quite indulge in the hope of returning to England in a sound state," I replied. "But tell me about the misfortunes of the party you speak of."

"That is done in a very few words," said he. "Six missionaries went from Souâkin and six from Zanzibar, meeting eventually in the wilds of Africa, sent out by the English Church Mission Society, to reclaim lost sheep. They were not happy in the selection of a suitable spot for evangelising, as only three of them and Dr. Felkın returned to Souâkin, looking considerably the worse for wear; the others had succumbed to fever, dysentery, and spears. Indeed, I am not quite sure that some of them were not eaten."

CHAPTER IX.

THE START ACROSS THE DESERT—MY CAMEL SERVES ME A SCURVY TRICK—THE CAMEL, ITS HABITS AND TRAINING.

THREE days after our arrival at Souâkin there were some very heavy showers of rain. Mr. Brewster informed me that it was eighteen months since it last rained there.

On the fourth day after our arrival about 80 hired camels were brought into the large open square to be laden with the tents and baggage of every description. I wish I could adequately describe the scene that ensued—the camels groan and bellow without any provocation, as if they were the most ill-used animals in existence; the Arabs shout and wrangle with each other as they adjust the loads on the haweias (a kind of pack-saddle), clutch one another by the hair of the head, after the manner of women when quarrelling, and shake the offending head about most vigorously. Our head-man, Suleiman, walks round and distributes his favours very impartially—a tug of the hair for one, a box on the ears for another, and a flick of the coorbatch (a whip made of hippopotamus hide) for another. This scene lasted for about three hours, and when at last they did start, they formed a very long hamlah, or caravan. The head of one camel is tied to the tail of the one in front, a long piece of rope intervening to allow for the long stride of the camel. We posted our letters—the last for some time to come—for England, to say that we were just starting on our Arab life across the Nubian desert. The caravan having started, each of us sees to his riding camel being got ready. We are some time in starting, getting our makloufas (camel saddles) properly and securely adjusted, and our little belongings, such as rifles, revolvers, saddle-bags, travelling satchels, &c., fixed on them. Each one has a zanzimeer hung on to a strap by the side of the camel. The word zanzimeer requires explanation; it is a large leathern bottle, capable of holding three or four quarts of water. As, in our journey across the desert, we should perhaps be sometimes two or three days before we came to any well, we had to provide a water-camel, whose business was to carry two large barrels full of water for domestic purposes. Each of these had a padlock on them, so that the Arabs could not get at them just whenever they felt inclined—a very necessary precaution, as they are so very careless, would take the spigot out of the barrel, quench their thirst, and as likely as not insecurely replace the plug, and let the water waste, which would be a very serious calamity. The mode of mounting and sitting on a camel is peculiar; my legs don't hang down each side of him in stirrups, but hang down in front of the saddle each side of his neck or crossed over the neck. No stirrups are used: The camel, of course, is on the ground, with his legs tucked under him; I approach his side and give a sudden vault or spring on to the makloufa. This must be done with great dexterity and quickness, unless the attendant has one foot placed on his fore-leg, as the camel gets up *instantly* as soon as I leave the ground, so of course, unless I am quick and dexterous, the result is disasterous; in other words, the camel gets on to his legs, and I go off mine on to my back. I watched the process of mounting very carefully, as it was my first experience of camel riding. I attempted and succeeded in doing the same as my pattern, and when my camel got up (which he did pretty quickly, and not without considerable danger and inconvenience to me), I felt that I occupied a very high and somewhat precarious position. However, I

I

soon got accustomed to the peculiar motion of a camel. A hygeen, dromedary, or riding camel, can go on a shuffling kind of trot (which is infinitely preferable to a fast trot or walk) at the rate of about five miles an hour, and I am sure that anyone who rides 25 or 28 miles a day, under the burning rays of an African sun, will think he has done quite enough, although on some occasions we have made forced marches and travelled 30 or 33 miles in one day. There were no hygeens at Souâkin; we therefore rode our caravan camels. A hamlah, or caravan camel, is capable of carrying considerably over 3 cwt. for very long distances, travels at the rate of $2\frac{1}{2}$ miles per hour, and will go steadily on for 12, 14, or 16 hours without stopping to eat or drink. He only requires water every fourth day, and can go without (on a pinch) 5 or 6 days, but when he does drink it is as well to let out his girths a few inches, or he will burst them. The twigs and leaves of the mimosa and kittar bushes, the scanty herbage of the desert, is all he requires, except whilst making forced marches, when he requires a certain amount of dhurra, because he has no time for grazing. This useful animal may well be called the ship of the desert, for if it were not for him, the enormous extent of burning sand which separates the fertile portion of the Soudan from Lower Egypt would be like an ocean devoid of vessels, and the deserts would be a barrier absolutely impassable by man. During the season when fresh pasture is abundant camels can go for weeks without water, provided they are not loaded or required to make extraordinary exertions; the juices of the plants which form their food are then sufficient to quench their thirst. The flesh of the young animal is one of the greatest luxuries; of the skins tents are made; the various sorts of hair or wool shed by the camel are wrought into different fabrics; and its dried dung constitutes excellent fuel, the only kind, indeed, to be obtained throughout vast extents of country. In order to qualify camels for great exertions and the endurance of fatigue, the Arabs begin to educate them at an early age. They are first taught to bear burdens by having their limbs secured under their belly, and then a weight proportioned to their strength is put on; this is not changed for a heavier load till the animal is thought to have gained sufficient power to sustain it. Food and drink are not allowed at will, but given in small quantity, at long intervals. They are then gradually accustomed to long journeys and an accelerated pace until their qualities of fleetness and strength are fully brought into action. They are taught to kneel, for the purpose of receiving or removing their load. When too heavily laden they refuse to rise, and by loud cries complain of the injustice. Those which are used for speed alone are capable of travelling from 60 to 90 miles a day: Instead of employing blows or ill-treatment to increase their speed, the camel-drivers sing cheerful songs, and thus urge the animals to their best efforts. When a caravan of camels arrives at a resting or halting-place, they kneel, and the cords sustaining the loads being untied, the bales slip down on each side. They generally sleep on their bellies: In an abundant pasture they generally browse as much in an hour as serves them for ruminating all night, and for their support during the next day. But it is uncommon to find such pasturage, and they are contented with the coarsest fare, and even prefer it to more delicate plants. Breeding and milk-giving camels are exempted from service, and fed as well as possible, the value of their milk being greater than that of their labour. The milk is very thick, abundant, and rich, but of rather a strong taste. Mingled with water it forms a very nutritive article of diet. The young camel usually sucks for twelve months, but such as are intended for speed are allowed to suck and exempted from restraint for two or three years. The camel attains the full exercise of its functions within four or five years, and the duration of its life is from forty to fifty years. The hump or humps on the back of a camel are mere accumulations of cellular substance and fat, covered by skin and a longer hair than that on the general surface. During long journeys, in which the animals suffer severely from want of food, and become greatly emaciated, these protuberances become gradually absorbed, and no trace of them left, except that the skin is loose and flabby where they were situated. In preparing for a journey, it is necessary to guard the humps from pressure or friction by appropriate saddles, as the slightest ulceration of these parts is followed by the worst consequences: insects deposit their larvæ in the sores, and sometimes extensive and destructive mortification ensues. I have often seen crows pecking away at sores on a camel's side, and was surprised to see how little notice it takes of them. After all, I must say of the camel, that he not only groans and roars when he is too heavily laden, but at all times without the least occasion, and although it may appear mild, docile, and patient, it is frequently perverse and stupid. The males especially are at certain times dangerous. It is surefooted, too, as I have often experienced in travelling over mountains so precipitous that no animal but a camel could have carried such heavy loads as I have seen it do without accident. All breeds of camels could not do so, but those belonging to the Hadendowah Arabs, between the Red Sea and Taka, are very sure-footed. The camels most highly thought of in the Soudan are the Bishareen; they are very strong and enduring, but not so large as many others. There is quite as much difference in the breeds of camels as of horses, and as much differance in riding a hygeen and baggage camel as there would be in riding a nice springy cob and a cart horse. Amongst the Arabs a good "hygeen," or riding dromedary, is worth from 50 to 150 dollars; the average value of a baggage camel is about 15 dollars, but I believe our average ran up to 30 or 35 dollars.

CHAPTER X.

OUR FIRST CAMP—TORRENTS OF RAIN—JULES BARDET—CAMEL-DRIVERS BEHAVE BADLY—SULEIMAN IN TROUBLE—CAMEL-DRIVERS GET UPSET—THE DESERT—TWO OF US LOSE OUR WAY—JULES SUFFERS FROM DYSENTERY—SAND-STORM—A PILGRIM DIES ON THE ROAD, ANOTHER IN THE CAMP—JULES' ILLNESS—CAMP SPLIT UP—LOSE OUR WAY—ENCAMP SEVERAL DAYS IN THE DESERT—ARAB HUTS—THE MIRAGE—A LION.

AFTER this digression and short dissertation on the camel, I will return to the subject of our journey. We now formed a tolerably numerous company, ourselves seven, three European servants, Suleiman, Mahoom, Cheriff, and Ali, the cook, with an assistant, four or five native servants, and nearly thirty camel-drivers. George, one of our servants, and I had some trouble in getting our makloufas properly adjusted on our camels; consequently, we were behind the others in starting. I also made a call on Mr. Bewlay, who pressed me to remain to luncheon. As I knew that this was to be a short march of about three hours, I did so. I then bade adieu to Mr. Bewlay (one of the nicest and most gentlemanly fellows to be met with), and commenced my journey, thinking I should soon overtake my comrades, but in this I was greatly mistaken. I had reached the middle of the town, amongst the bazaars, when the eccentric conduct of my camel was quite alarming, exciting grave apprehensions respecting the safety of my limbs, I being quite a novice in the art of camel-riding. Down he flopped without the least preliminary warning, whilst I held on to the makloufa as if I had been in a hurricane. I plied my coorbatch on his tough hide; the only effect it produced was to make him open his mouth (to such a width that it could easily have accommodated a human head) and groan away with most stentorian voice. At last an Arab succeeded in getting him on his legs, and away he went at such a jolting pace that I experienced the greatest difficulty in keeping my seat. Down he flopped again in the same unceremonious manner as before just in front of a projecting part of the Police Station.

"Well," I mentally ejaculated, "this is, indeed,

too much. I will not be placed in such jeopardy as this any longer."

I lost no time in dismounting; Sheik Moussa was sent for, and at once promised to find me a tractable beast. George remained with me. We had no sooner unburdened the camel, and got under the projecting roof of the Police Station, than down came the rain in torrents; then I felt thankful that my camel had proved so awkward and disobedient. Two hours and a half elapsed ere a respectable camel was brought. By that time the rain had ceased, and George and I resumed our journey in comfort.

When we arrived at camp at 6 p.m., we found the tents pitched and everyone changing their clothes, except Jules; they had all been drenched to the skin. This was a favourable opportunity for me to deliver a lecture on sanitary precautions. I therefore did so, warning all Europeans to remember that we were not now in England, but in the tropics, where the days were excessively hot and the nights not only cool, but often very cold at this time of the year; always to change wet clothing as soon as we got to camp; never to expose themselves to the burning rays of a tropical sun without helmets; and last, but not by any means least, to be extremely careful as to the quality of water they drank, and always to see that the zanzimeers were well washed out before they were replenished. Well, I know that in England, whilst practising my profession, I have met with extremely clever people who not only know their own business, but that of everyone else, and are most ready with their unasked-for advice. They are quite encyclopedias of knowledge, or, at least, they would have one think so. They apparently listen, with folded arms and the head a little bit on one side, in the most attentive manner, literally drinking in all the doctor is telling them when he forbids this and orders that, and yet will use their own judgment or sense—presuming, of course, that they have any—and the moment his back is turned they exclaim—

"Pooh! what an old fidget that doctor is. I know that when poor Mrs. Smith was ill her doctor didn't do ought like that, but let her have a glass of stout for dinner, and ordered her a glass of hot whisky and water at bed-time, poor thing, and that was what kep her up."

When the doctor very impressively says, "Now, Mrs. Thompson, your friend is very ill—I wish you to be careful to give her so-and-so and avoid so-and-so," Mrs. Thompson says, "Yes, doctor—I quite understand;" and Mrs. T., being a very garrulous, and also a very knowing personage, will begin a long rigmarole about her first husband's case some 20 years before, and how beautifully she nursed him through an illness of "seven week," as she calls it, and brought him round, she, of course, not having had her clothes off for four weeks, nor a wink of sleep for ten nights, till she was a perfect "shada," but still able to articulate, poor thing. Unless the poor doctor now bolts off, she will then confidentially commence a history of three or four other cases in which she was, of course, eminently successful. These very clever people, so wise in their own conceit, are really very dangerous people, and I always look after them well. Of course, Mrs. Thompson may think the medicine "strong enough for a horse," as she expresses herself, and will administer it if *she* thinks it suits the case, and exercise her very discriminating faculties in the way of diet, and matters of that kind; but at the end of a week Mrs. Thompson—who has, of course, seen many similar cases—expresses to her neighbours and confidants (who look upon her utterances as oracular) her dissatisfaction with that ere doctor, and is determined on his next visit to favour him with what she is pleased to call a bit of her mind. She does as promised —

"Well now, doctor, what do you think *is* the matter with poor Mrs. Smith ? She don't seem to get on at all. I remember when poor Mrs. Rodgers, my second husband's first wife's cousin, was laid up with —"

But, reader, you may imagine the rest; I can very well. I have used the preceding imaginary conversation " to point a moral and adorn my tale."

In our camp I had a very headstrong Mr. "Cleverity," if I may say so, to deal with. Jules, before we started, was working away, sorting the baggage, &c., in his shirt sleeves after passing through the rain, getting thirsty, and drinking bad claret and beer, such as he could obtain in the place. Indeed, his absorbing powers were remarkable— he resembled a huge dry sponge, which, when dipped into a basinful of water, absorbs it *all*. I ascertained, from one who knew him well, that this absorbing tendency was not altogether induced by the heat of the climate, but that it was his normal condition which he always suffered from in England, where he lived a life of comparative ease and indulgence. I only knew Jules absorb water when he could not get anything stronger. I had warned him at Souâkin not to get wet, as the evenings were so cold, and now, on arriving at camp, here he was again wet to the skin, helping to pitch tents and put things ship-shape ; but, with a thirst unquenchable, he was continually drinking water which was the colour of pea-soup, but not *quite* so thick.

"Now, Jules," said I, "remember what I told you at Souâkin. You are going the right way to get dysentery."

He replied —

"Oh, I am all right, doctor. I am not an old woman, or a piece of barley-sugar. I shall take no harm."

The sequel will show how disastrous was his disregard of my repeated warnings, and very much grieved I was for two reasons : one was the loss of a really good-hearted fellow, who had proved a faithful and affectionate servant to his master, who thought very much of him, for many years; the other was, that although I used every effort to save him, and many a time was unable to sleep on account of the anxiety the case caused me, so much so that I frequently visited his tent in the night, yet all was of no avail. Added to this, I was excessively and incessantly annoyed by the fussy interference of two amateur doctors in camp, who, as educated men, ought to have known better than to worry me seven or eight times a day with useless suggestions of a shadowy character as to the treatment of a complaint of which they knew absolutely nothing. They were great examples of an old adage, " A *little* knowledge is a dangerous thing."

In the evening of our first day's camping out, just after dinner (we dined at 7 p.m.), down came the rain again, causing us all to scamper off to our respective tents; spades were out, and trenches dug round, and there we remained until morning. At 6 a.m. we were up, and saw no more rain for several months; indeed, not until I reached Venice in the following May.

It was about 10 a.m. next day ere our caravan started. The sun blazed out with a scorching heat, causing us to feel as if we were in a Turkish bath from the evaporation which took place, and our solid leather portmanteaus, which were thoroughly saturated the day before, to curl up like match-boxes. Before we started on our second day's march across the desert our camel men were told they were to go on until 6 p.m., and Suleiman was commissioned to see this order carried out. We often went on in front of them in the morning, on the look out for a shot at a desert gazelle; but it was singularly noticeable that about 1.30 p.m. we were all somewhere in the neighbourhood of Cheriff, our butler, who was in the charge of the canteen on a camel. Unless we made a forced march, we usually breakfasted about 7 a.m., luncheon at 1.30, dined at 7, and retired to rest at 9 or 9.30 p.m. After luncheon we frequently lay down on our rugs, smoking cigarettes and reading some book, long after the caravan had passed us. This day we did so, but judge of our astonishment when, at four o'clock, we came upon some of our camels browsing; others had not been unburdened, and nearly all the camel-drivers were in a circle, with uplifted spears.

We soon ascertained the cause of this; there was poor Suleiman, our head boss, the centre of attraction for these Hadendowab Arabs, with their uplifted spears, who were angrily jabbering away. To the question, "What's the meaning of this, Suleiman? they were to have gone on until six o'clock," he replied, "Yes, I know, gentlemen, that I tell them they no stop till I say, and I catch hold of one mans to stop him take the load off the camel, and now they say they spear me if I don't leave them alone."

He pointed out the ringleaders of what looked like mutiny against authority, and as soon as he had done so, in true old English fashion, a few well-directed blows put about five Arabs in the prone position; all pulled out revolvers, and made them pile their spears, which were at once secured, tied in a bundle, and given in charge to the English servants. They were then made to re-load all the camels, and, at great inconvenience to ourselves, we re-start at 6.30, and march until nearly ten, just to let them see that they could not do as they liked, and that we were masters and not they. This assertion of authority had a most beneficial effect on the native mind. It was past eleven that night ere we dined, and I retired to rest at half-past twelve, with a feeling of general bruising and dislocated vertebræ easily accounted for, as I was unaccustomed to the peculiar motion of a camel, which has a knack of shaking up one's liver in a most effectual manner. Referring to my diary, I find that on our third day's march, Dec. 17th, the temperature was 82° F. in the shade at 1.30 p.m. I generally took the temperature when we halted for luncheon, which would usually be about one or half-past. We could do with the dry heat very well as we were mounted, but now, in consequence of the late heavy rains, we felt it very relaxing, and just like a Russian vapour-bath. The Red Sea was still visible to the east of us; to the west, a large tract of desert, backed up by impassable rocky mountains. We now saw desert gazelles for the first time, and one of the party brought one down, thus providing dinner for the evening. We marched from 9 a.m. until 6 p.m., came to water then, and pitched our tents near to it. We generally had very good water, but here it had a brackish taste; still, with the aid of four bottles of champagne, we managed to slake our thirst tolerably well. So far the mimosa and kittar bushes were abundant, particularly dur-

HADENDOWAH ARAB CAMEL-MEN.

ing the first two days, but on the fourth day we saw very few indeed, and marched through absolute desert, saw nothing but the burning sands, and huge rocks of volcanic origin. We filled our barrels, zanzimeers and girbas with water before we started, and again marched from ten till six; temp. 81° in the shade. A girba is the skin of a gazelle dressed. It is dressed in the following way by the Arabs:— They get the chopped red bark of the mimosa tree, and put in the skin with water, it is allowed to remain there for three or four days and then it is converted into leather. This day we encamped at a place called Settareb. On the fifth day we again made the usual march, and shot two gazelles. We started off at nine—and left the caravan to follow. About 11 a.m. one of our servants caught us up with the information that some of the camels had been lost. Messrs. A. and W. James returned to see about them, and found that it was a dodge of the camel-drivers, who thought they would try to sneak back to Souâkin. The camels were easily found; the two camel-drivers were tied together, marched into camp, duly admonished and punished. At 5 p.m. we come to water, turn out all the brackish water, fill our barrels, &c., and march until 6 p.m.; temp. 82° in shade. Dine at 7.30, bed at 10 p.m., but before going to bed we had all the camel-drivers up, some of whom appeared inclined to be mutinous. We gave them a sound lecturing, and let them distinctly understand that we would not stand this kind of thing any more, and that the next offence would be punished with the coorbatch. Our camping ground is called Wadi Osier. The next day, our sixth in the desert, Mr. F. L. James and I had a somewhat unpleasant experience. After luncheon, as usual, we all rested awhile, allowing the caravan to go on. Mr. F. L. J. and I, who were absorbed with our books, remained long after our comrades had proceeded on their journey. When at last we did start, we were surprised to find how late it was getting. Knowing that there is little or no twilight in these parts, we hurried on, hoping to catch the caravan ere darkness overtook us, but could not do so. Darkness comes on—a most profound darkness, too—and we lose the track; we dismount and light matches to see if we can find it again. We don't, however, succeed in doing so. Nothing now remains but to remount our camels and trust to them and Providence. On we go, at the rate of four miles an hour. The silence of the tomb and the darkness of Erebus surround us; not a glimmer of light could be seen in any direction, not the sound of a wild animal, of a bird, or even the rustling of a leaf, or the sigh of the softest zephyr. When we had

gone on thus for about an hour, neither seeing a
light, nor hearing a sound, we began to get uneasy,
not knowing if we were going in the right direction,
but knowing full well that it might prove to be a
serious matter if we strayed off into the limitless
waste of the desert. Every now and again I fired a
shot from my revolver, but I might as well have
used a pop-gun. Now the stars begin to make their
appearance; by them we see that we are, as we think,
pursuing some track. We now dismount, and finding
that revolvers are useless, Mr. James gets his rifle
and lets off one barrel. We wait, and anxiously look
for a corresponding flash; hear we could not, as by
this time a slight breeze had sprung up, and was
blowing from us towards our caravan. Another
barrel is now fired, but no reply. We were now
rapidly coming to the conclusion that we should have
to tie our camels to a mimosa bush, and sleep out
without food, and what was still worse, without
water, as both our zanzimeers were nearly empty.
Still we perseveringly jogged on, and after a time
discharged another barrel. In a few minutes' time
we see a slight flash, which appears to be so far off
that we cannot make out whether it is in the heavens
or on the earth. Not a sound reaches our ears. Our
cartridges are also nearly exhausted, and we have all
but made up our minds to sleep out, but try the rifle

once more. This time both barrels are discharged one after the other. We look out anxiously; not a sound reaches us, but we see a corresponding double flash a long way off, and are convinced that this comes from our camp. We see certain stars over the spot, and for these we steer. When we had jogged on for another hour and a-half, we see a glimmering light like the flicker of a lantern (it really was a huge bonfire)—another half-hour, and we can plainly see lanterns moving about, and to our great relief and that of our friends, we gain the camp at 9 p.m., thoroughly hungry, thirsty, and tired. The temperature this day was 86° in the shade; my ears and nose were quite scorched, and smarting from the heat of the sun.

On arriving in camp I found Jules very ill indeed. On the fourth day he came to me in the evening complaining of a bilious attack. I gave him something for it. In some respects he was better by the evening of the fifth, and on the morning of the 6th bilious vomiting had ceased, but in the evening, judging from the symptoms, I was afraid that formidable complaint, dysentery, was setting in. However, I kept this to myself, at present, not wishing to alarm the camp, and hoping that treatment might prove beneficial. We dined at 10.30, and retired to bed at 12 p.m. When I say we retired to bed I literally mean that, not to a shake-down sort of thing with a rug over me and a portmanteau for a pillow, but a comfortable bed with a comfortable pillow, in a comfortable tent, and cocoa-matting on the ground. There really was an air of comfort about all our surroundings. We had comfortable shut-up and open-out chairs, a comfortable folding-up table, each a nice portable india-rubber bath, and, whenever we encamped by water we each had a bath before breakfast and another before dinner. As for eatables and drinkables, the most fastidious would not turn up their noses at those. We had sufficient champagne and claret to last us during the whole campaign; a freezing machine, so that we could have these iced in the hottest weather. We had gozogenes and any amount of seltzer-water, and when we fell short of that we used Eno's fruit-salt in the gozogenes. We had Peek Frean and Co's. biscuits, Cross and Blackwell's excellent Chutnee pickles and pickalili, tomato sauce, asparagus, green peas, plum puddings, French jams, minced collops, kidneys, tinned soups from Fortnum and Mason's, Piccadilly, and everything else one could think of to insure comfort in eating, drinking, and sleeping. Some ascetics would say we were of the earth, earthy, but I maintain that if you mean to keep a *mens sana in corpore sano* one may just as well—and a great deal better—build up the waste tissue from time to time and travel with every comfort, if one can afford it, as do the reverse. I have tried both; whilst campaigning in Turkey, when I have been on the march with the army, I have indulged in the luxury of a small onion and a limited piece of somewhat indifferent bread for breakfast, washed down with a drop of water, the same again for luncheon, and the same again for dinner, " and still I was not happy," for I could comfortably have disposed of breakfast, luncheon, and dinner at one sitting without the slightest inconvenience. The ground was my bed, the canopy of heaven was my tent, the twinkling stars my lantern, and a stone or water-jug with a coat rolled round it was my pillow. I shall endeavour to avoid the slightest exaggeration in this book, and will go so far as to say that the former mode of travelling is by far the most comfortable, and, in my humble opinion, the most conducive to health.

Again I find myself branching off, and cannot give any guarantee but what I may still do so. All I ask is that my readers will overlook this little failing of mine.

7th day.—We found water here, and of course replenished everything with this valuable fluid. The mimosas were scanty and very stunted here. During the night and all this day a great wind has been blowing, producing a most blinding sand-storm, fortunately at our backs, or we should not have been able to proceed. No one can form any idea of the intense discomfort of a sand-storm, unless he has been in one. I may close up my tent and be roasted inside. I may lock up my portmanteau, which fits pretty closely, and have it in my tent, the lock covered with leather, yet when I go to bed I find the sheets brown with sand, the most secret recesses of my portmanteau and the lock filled with sand, and my writing-case also, which is inside. I open my mouth to speak, and I can masticate sand, if so disposed. I eat—all my food is full of sand. I drink, not water, but water and sand. In fact, sand is everywhere; eyes, nose, mouth, ears, hair, brains, and everything else has a mixture of sand about it. I chance to leave a book, a pair of boots, or anything else outside my tent, they soon become invisible, and are covered inches deep in sand. Here we found great difficulty in pitching our tents, as there was nothing but sand to drive the pegs into, and then we came to rocks. Three or four days ago a lame woman and a man joined our caravan, and two days ago two men, all bound for Kassala, all pilgrims from Mecca. They were allowed to accompany us, and we fed them. To-day we miss the woman, and on inquiry find that she was knocked up *en route* yesterday, and so her companion left her to die, and probably when we discovered this she had been picked clean by jackals and vultures. Such is the value put upon human life out here.

8th day.—The sand-storm still rages with unabated violence. We decide not to go on, but encamp here to-day. We are, however, obliged to move our tents to a place that is a little more sheltered, as at present it is absolutely miserable. Jules still very ill. Temperature 86° in the shade. In the day time the fierce heat of the sun rendered the interior of the tents like ovens. Outside the sand reflected the heat. Although producing great personal discomfort, our sufferings were nothing to what poor Jules endured, who is now unmistakably suffering from dysentery badly. Under any circumstances this is a grave complaint to have, but under present circumstances, doubly so; that which he requires is impossible to obtain, namely, absolute rest and a suitable diet. The poor fellow complains to-day of incessant thirst, and everything he gets to eat or drink is impregnated with sand, which it is impossible to avoid.

About 12 meridie, Mr. Phillipps, who was passing across the camp, saw the two pilgrims whom we had allowed to join the caravan, two brothers. One was supporting the head of the other in the blazing sun. The poor fellow's eyes, nose, ears, and hair, &c. were full of sand. He said his brother was ill. I was at once called to him, and found him *in articulo mortis*. Very little could be done for him, and in twenty minutes' time he died. His brother borrowed a spade, dug a shallow grave near the camp and buried him, putting a mound of little white stones on the grave. In my journey across the desert I frequently came across these graves, sometimes two or three together, sometimes 20, 50, or 100. Occasionally skeletons of camels were met with. In the present instance, the poor fellow who died looked very emaciated and weak, probably exhausted by constant marching and a deficient supply of food. But he had accomplished the pilgrimage to Mecca, and I suppose he died a happy man.

9th day.—Poor Jules is so ill to-day that I cannot consent to have him removed. The camp is accordingly split up, Mr. Phillipps and I, with a few camels and attendants, remaining behind. The sand-storm is abating, but the heat is very great and trying to Jules. A gazelle was shot to-day. I cannot say that gazelle is a particularly toothsome morsel under our circumstances. We are obliged to cook it on the same day that it has been killed: The flesh of a desert gazelle is hard, and has very little flavour. Our comrades left us about 10 a.m., and directly they had gone down came the vultures for pickings.

10th day.—Jules still very ill, but in some respects a trifle better. We decide on advancing to-day, if possible, and encamp a little longer when we get to water. Accordingly we strike our tents and help the camel men to load, send them on, then see to our own. We do not get off until 4.30 p.m. Half-an-hour afterwards we come to a dry river course, on each side of which are dhoum palms and other trees. We saw a couple of jackals sneaking off here, but did not get a shot at them. We trusted to one of our Arabs to show us the way. When we had gone on for about an hour, he suddenly stopped in the middle of a great sandy plain, said he was not sure of the way, and as it was getting dark, thought we had better stop until daylight. On hearing this Mr. Phillipps retraced his steps, and was absent about two hours. I now became anxious about him, and every now and then fired off my revolver. Fortunately I happened to have a box of matches with me, and kindled a fire, then Mahoom and I tore up all the stuff that would ignite. Half-an-hour afterwards Mr. Phillipps found us, but he had been unsuccessful in his search for the road. However, we kept up the fire, hoping some of our camel men would see the signals of distress, which fortunately they did after a time; at last one of them found us. In the meantime Jules was lying on the ground exhausted, with a rug thrown over him. Our man led us to where the other camels were. Now we had another bother : one of the camels had thrown his load off; the old fellow who was in charge was lying on the ground, said he had got a pain in his stomach, and we must stop there, as he could not possibly go on. We roused him up, gave him a good shaking, and made him come on. But he soon stopped again, and laid down to sleep, most coolly saying he could not go any further. The fact is that just before we started he had eaten a large quantity of raw meat, had, in fact, thoroughly gorged himself. However, there we left him, and went on another two or three miles. Halted at 10 p.m. and kindled a fire, had a cup of cocoa, a bit of bread, rolled ourselves up in rugs, and lay on the ground. Jules suffered much from this, as the nights were so cold.

11th day.—Up early, feeling stiff, cold, and hungry. Marched until 10 a.m. (four hours), intending to rest during the excessive heat of the day, as my poor invalid was almost too weak to set up. About 3 p.m. Mr. F. L. James appears on the scene, and tells us that the camp is only about four miles off, at a place called Waudy. We get there about 6.30 p.m., and find the camp pitched near a well surrounded by dhoum palms. Temperature to-day, 88° in the shade. This being Christmas Day, we had some excellent plum puddings, made by Crosse and Blackwell, iced champagne, and other luxuries for dinner.

12th day.—Jules was very ill indeed to-day, thoroughly prostrated by his complaint, which had increased in intensity—it was quite out of the question for him to attempt to move. We held a council, and decided that as there were a few huts and goats, and a well, that it would be advisable to let Jules rest here awhile, for now we could get a little milk for him twice a day. Accordingly on the 13th day the camp was split up. Messrs. A. and W. James, Colvin, and Aylmer went on to Kassala, whilst Jules, Messrs. Phillipps, F. L. James, and I remained behind. Here we rested for five days, and what with treatment, diet, and rest Jules improved daily.

On the 16th day we rigged up an augarip (a kind of litter), with an awning of matting and palm leaves to keep off the sun, and on the 17th day this was slung across a camel. Jules got into it, and off we started at 7.30 a.m., marching until 7.30 p.m. Much too long a journey for Jules, who was again thoroughly knocked up and exhausted. I suggested now that such marches were too long, and that our best plan was for me to start off early with Jules, say 6 a.m., and march until 10, then rest until 4 and go on until 7 or 8 p.m. This was agreed to.

18th day. January 1st, 1883.—I visited Jules at 6 a.m.; found him no worse. We started at 8, halt at 12, rest until 2, and go on until we catch up the caravan, at 8.30 p.m. Jules complained bitterly of these long journeys, which were so exhausting to an invalid. Medicine was now out of the question, as the rolling motion of the camel made him very sick. At the mid-day halt we found some empty huts in the desert. These we explored, and found rather interesting. In several of them I found a hole in the floor, the use of which is rather singular. The good wife of the house uses this. She gets certain fragrant barks and frankincense, burns them in the hole, then stands over them, having her dress drawn round her, to fumigate herself and make herself acceptable to her husband. In England, of course, this is not at all necessary. We passed through a fine palm-grove to-day by a khor, and shot three gazelles.

19th day.—March again about 12 hours. Jules worse. Again I pointed out the bad effect of these long marches on the invalid.

20th day.—Ten hours' march to-day; halt near a deep well and a large palm-grove. Here I shot a fine golden-crested eagle. Jules frightfully done up, and rapidly going the wrong way.

21st day.—On the march at 9 a.m. We marched the greater part of this day across an awful desert, where no living thing except ourselves could be seen. No shelter was attainable for the mid-day lunch. Temperature 92° in what shade we could manufacture. During several hours of the day I saw that optical illusion which so often mocks the thirsty traveller, called the mirage—mirage, called by the Arabs, Bahr esh Sheitan, "The Devil's Sea." By a strange refraction of the atmosphere, plains of arid sands seem to be rippling lakes of water as far as the eye can reach, lapping the base of stupendous mountains of rocks, and bathing the roots of the stunted mimosa bushes. This day marched nearly 14 hours. Jules takes scarcely anything, is rapidly sinking, and again complains of these long marches.

22nd day.—Another 12 hours' march. See mirage again for hours. Encamp at Fillick. Here there is a military station and a telegraph office.

23rd day.—Mirage again. Shot two gazelles, four bustards, and five guinea-fowl. Appear to be getting into a better country. Jules much weaker, pulse scarcely perceptible. Ten hours' march to-day.

24th day.—Eleven hours' march to-day, and, I am thankful to say, the last day's march across the desert. Temperature 93° in the shade. Since 11 a.m. we have travelled through much better country, and after our late experience it was quite refreshing to see a luxuriant vegetation once more, such as dhoum palms, colocynth, tamarisks, nebbucks, heglecks—not stunted mimosa bushes now, but different kinds of mimosa trees and various trees and shrubs. The place I am speaking of was quite like a gentleman's park. Here also were ariels, gazelles, bustards, parroquets, eagles, vultures, and jackals. About seven, and pitch-dark, we, for the first time, heard the roar of a lion not far off. Our sensations were of a creepy character, and would, perhaps, have been more so had we known what we did when we got to Kassala—that he had lately dined, at separate times, on four human beings.

CHAPTER XI.

ARRIVED AT KASSALA—DESCRIPTION OF KASSALA—WE BUY CAMELS AND HORSES—THE MUDIR GIVES A DINNER—JULES' DEATH AND BURIAL—HYÆNAS—ARAB PATIENTS—MAHOOM'S HISTORY—DEMETRIUS MOSCONAS ON SLAVERY—MENAGERIE AT KASSALA.

WE arrived at Kassala at 8 p.m., and found the camp pitched about a quarter of a mile, or less, from it, close to a garden full of fine trees of various kinds; in fact, between this garden and a very wide river bed. This river is here called the Gash, but nearer to Abyssinia it is called the Mareb. Jules' exhaustion and pulseless condition was most alarming. I succeeded in obtaining some eggs and milk; these I mixed with brandy, and had this mixture administered to him every half-hour.

Whilst we were dining, at 9 p.m., we heard the peculiar cry of hyænas, which literally swarm round the camp at night and make an awful row. I daresay there would be 150 or 200 come round every night after dark, and when we retired to our tents, and the lights were put out, they would not only come close to, but actually into the camp; I can assure the reader that I am not, as it is called, drawing the long bow when I say that I have seen one poke his head in at my tent door more than once. We remained here many days, and sometimes the hyænas would be so troublesome and noisy that it was a by no means uncommon thing for one of us to get up in the night, go to the edge of the camp in our night-shirt and discharge the contents of one or two barrels into the noisy crowd. This had a quieting effect, and we often found one or two dead hyænas in the morning, the rest having scampered off.

We found Kassala a very warm place, for in the middle of January the thermometer registered 90° in the shade. It is situated about 1,900 feet above the level of the sea, is surrounded by a wall made of mud bricks baked in the sun, and plastered over with mud and the refuse of cows. The wall is loop-holed for musketry, and surrounded by a deep fosse. The exports of the Soudan are ivory, hides, gum arabic, senna, bees' wax, and honey—the latter obtained chiefly from the Abyssinian border.

The Kassala Mountain, which is just outside Kassala, is an enormous, almost perpendicular, mass of granite, several thousand feet in height, rising straight out of the plain, and can be seen for many miles in all directions. The population was in 1882, something like 25,000, without reckoning the garrison, which consisted of about 1,000 Nubian troops.

There are large numbers of cows, goats, sheep, and camels in the neighbourhood, and a great deal of camel-breeding is carried on here.

When I left England, the thought occurred to me that it would be a good idea to take out some knives, razors, beads, and so forth, both as presents and for barter. I, therefore, provided myself with some common knives, about a dozen of a better class, and half-dozen hunting-knives from Mr. T. B. Hague, of Sheffield; a couple of dozen of Mappin and Webb's, and Heiffer's shilling razors, which were much prized by the Arabs. These I found very useful at Kassala, as I bartered some of them for a dozen beautiful long ostrich feathers, and a handful of shorter ones. The natives were well pleased, and so was I.

January 8th.—We were now comfortably encamped, but, alas! too late for Jules, who was fearfully emaciated and prostrate. I visited his tent twice in the night, at one and four o'clock, but could do very little more for him, and I fear he will soon go. All the camels that we hired at Souâkin will have to return there with their drivers. One reason our friends preceded us to Kassala was to let it be known that we wanted to buy or hire camels. The result was not exactly what we anticipated, for they kept them back awhile. When at last they were brought for inspection, the most extravagant prices were demanded, whilst many of them were absolute screws. We also required a few little horses for hunting purposes; the dealers were as knowing as horse-dealers in England, and that is saying a great deal.

January 9th.—Jules is evidently sinking fast. I visited his tent five times in the night, but could do little for him beyond giving him drink twice. Mr. W. James and Mr. Aylmer had taken lessons in photography before leaving England, and were each provided with a good apparatus. With these they took many interesting views in different parts of the country. This day the Mudir (Governor) of Kassala sent his two little boys and ponies to be photographed. Whilst we were at breakfast to-day an Arab brought two playful little leopards, which he had stolen from their nest. I could have bought them for a couple of dollars each, and probably should have done so had I been on my way home. The Mudir paid us a visit at noon, inviting us all to dine with him; but Mr. Phillipps and I could not go on account of Jules's illness, which now will be of short duration. I understood afterwards from those who did go that the dinner consisted of 15 or 18 courses. About 5 p.m. I visited Jules, and found him asleep, but evidently sinking. Mahoom, who was my servant during the whole campaign — and a very good boy he was, too — attended well to him, and frequently sat up at nights with him. At 10 p.m. poor Jules breathed his last. The particulars of his illness, together with other curious and interesting medical notes, can be found in an article of mine in the *British Medical Journal*, September 23rd and 30th, 1882. As soon as he was dead I washed and laid him out. M. Demetrius Mosconas, a Greek living in Kassala, was good enough to at once see about some kind of coffin, covered with black cloth, shaped thus — ▭ This was to be sent early in the morning.

January 10th.—At 10 a.m. the coffin was brought. Jules was put in it. On the corpse were laid sprays of green shrubs all round. At 11.30 he was carried to his last resting-place by natives, all of us following; the Union Jack being placed on the coffin.

The weather was fearfully hot, and the roads very dusty. He was buried in a garden where three other Christians had been buried. Mr. F. L. James read the burial service, and we remained by the grave until it was filled up, which was very quickly done in the following manner: The earth had been thrown up each side of the grave, eight Arabs stood each side with their backs to the grave, and as soon as the word was given they, with their hands, pushed the earth between their legs, filling the grave within about ten minutes. A cross was afterwards made of ebony by Mr. Phillipps, and placed at the head of the grave. This concluded our last duty to poor Jules.

When we returned to camp, four horses and four camels were bought; after lunch Messrs. Colvin and A. James, with Suleiman and a few servants, started off for the Atbara in quest of camels, as these people were holding theirs back in the hopes of making a good thing by so doing. Korasi, on the Atbara, is considered one of the cheapest and best places to buy camels.

January 11th.—Soon after my arrival at Kassala it became known that there was a "Hakeem Ingelese," as they called me, and I very soon found that my patients daily increased in number. Every morning after breakfast there was I, wearing my pith helmet, in the broiling sun, with Mahoom as interpreter, for two hours or more attending to a large number of Arabs—men, women, and children—who squatted round my tent on their haunches in a semicircle. I frequently saw 60, 70, or 80 patients a day. I did not charge them anything; probably, had I done so I should have materially thinned out the applicants for medical and surgical relief. It is a strange thing, but human nature is (in some respects) pretty much the same in Central Africa as it is in England.

Ali Mahoom's history, poor boy, was not, in early life, a very bright one, as he was stolen by the slave-dealers. He said —

"I remember very well, sir, when dey took me. My mother was out when a lot of mens come down and took all de little childrens dey see. Dey took me with dem to Khartoum, and dere my mother found me. Dey let her stop with me for a long time. She begged dem to let her have her little boy back, but dey say, 'No, unless you steal two little children; den you shall have him back.' Den I was sold to somebody else; after dat Gordon Pasha find me, and he take me and give me to Mr. Felkin, and he has been good to me ever since." He gave me the name of the country he came from, but I forget it, adding, "It is the next country but one to the Niam-Niams."

I had heard they were cannibals, so I said to Mahoom —

" What do they eat, Mahoom ? "

" Dey eat de flesh of beobles," he replied.

" But," I said, " why don't they eat antelopes and other animals ? "

" Dey say de flesh of beobles is much nicer," he replied.

He, of course, was disgusted with them. I found also that if a relation dies they bury that relation in close relation to them, that is, at the entrance to the hut; and if a baby, they send it to the relatives they have most respect for, and these relatives, to show their respect for their friends, eat the baby— cooked, I presume, but that I am not sure of.

About noon M. Demetrius Mosconas (who spoke English fairly well, and is, in a certain sense, a brother) asked me to go and see his son, who was very ill. I did so, and found him suffering from acute rheumatism. Mosconas, it seems, was engaged by the Government in sinking wells in some outlying districts, and his son, who partly superintended this work, must have contracted this disease by sleeping out, as, although the days were very hot, the nights were often excessively cold, and I have often known the thermometer sink from 90° at 1.30 p.m. to 45° or lower by 11 p.m.

I had a talk with Mosconas about slavery, and

learnt very conclusively that it exists pretty openly in this part of the Soudan. He informed me that the woman (his servant) who had just brought us two small cups of coffee was a slave, one of a dozen owned by an Arab woman, and she realized a living by letting them out on hire. He paid three dollars per month for the hire of this slave. He also told me that Georgie Bey, an Arab Army doctor, who left Kassala for Khartoum the day before our arrival, sold two of his slaves before he went. This Georgie Bey was since killed with Hicks Pasha's army near Souâkin.

Another bit of information which Mosconas gave me was that some Arabs and Greeks breed from slave-women, who are kept for profit just as cattle are in England. The children born under these circumstances are sold by their fathers.

Having had a long chat with Mosconas, I next paid a visit to Herr Schumann's collection of wild animals. I found a large building and yard occupied by them. Schumann himself was away some distance from Kassala, amongst the Beni-Amir tribe, where he had a zareeba. He collected animals there, and sent them on to his manager at Kassala. Just before the rainy season commenced, about May, he would go on himself, with quite an army of attendants, across the Nubian Desert to Souâkin with his collection; then take them to London, Liverpool, Hamburg, Vienna, and America, where they would be sold. Here he had four giraffes, four gazelles, three fine antelopes, as tame as lambs, a nice, amiable little baby elephant, five young lions, chained to rickety old posts, which rattled up, as they darted at a passer-by, in a very alarming manner, nine infant leopards, two or three young hyænas, eight ostriches, some wild hogs, baboons, tiger-cats, and other animals.

CHAPTER XII.

CAMELS FROM THE ATBARA—THE MUDIR—GORDON PASHA'S CHARACTER IN THE SOUDAN—FERTILITY OF THE SOUDAN.

JANUARY 15th.—Messrs. Colvin and A. James, with their attendants, returned this afternoon from the Atbara, having purchased thirty-four camels. This rather astonished the natives here, who had no idea that we could do without theirs, and quite thought we should be obliged eventually to buy their camels, and of course give them a good price. Whilst our friends were gone to the Atbara, we bought sixteen camels, eight ponies, a number of sheep, and some milk-giving goats, so that we could have milk with our porridge every morning for breakfast. It was decided to-day that we must hire a few more camels for our march from here to the Beni-Amirs, and leave Kassala on the 17th.

January 16th.—Mosconas dined with us to-night;

he says that a year ago King John's nephew, of Abyssinia, whilst fighting with some of the Arab tribes, was killed, and that a Shukeryiah Arab took out his heart and ate it on the spot. He said that these Hadendowahs, Beni-Amirs, Shukeriyahs, Hamrans, and others, are always fighting, either with the Abyssinians or amongst themselves, and that in consequence of the frequent raids made by the Egyptian governors on the Arabs for taxes, the latter frequently hide their money in the ground, putting oil on it to prevent discolouration. He also informed me that the present Mudir of Kassala was a very sharp fellow, and extremely successful in squeezing money out of the poor Arabs, but that Gordon Pasha, when he was Governor of the Soudan, was very kind and lenient, frequently remitting taxes when he thought they were unduly pressed.

Now my own opinion of Gordon Pasha is that he was a just, honest, and honourable man, whose sole aim was, not to extort all he could from these poor Arabs, and so make himself popular at head-quarters, but to do that which was simply right between man and man, just to those who employed him, and to those whom he ruled. I believe I should not be far wrong in saying that all Egyptian governors who preceded and succeeded him were *extortionists*. What a charm his name had in the Soudan, amongst different tribes in different parts! I have noticed that when Gordon's name was mentioned the Arab's countenance would become radiant with pleasure, as if calling up recollections of a good friend in bygone days, and with a significant, "Ah! Gordon Pasha," they would begin to expatiate on his good qualities in such a way that I could not help thinking that he had more influence amongst them than any man living. The fact is, that these poor down-trodden Arabs had, unknowingly, adopted one of our own texts, "Prove all things, hold fast that which is good." Gordon Pasha was kind to them, and when he passed his word he would keep it, whether it clashed with the interests of the Khedive or not. He was the only man as a governor whom they trusted as children would their father, and who never forfeited their confidence. All his actions were summed up in the words justice, truth, and duty.

> A wit's a feather,
> A chief's a rod,
> An honest man's the noblest work of God.

As I am writing this (March 30th, 1884), I cannot help thinking that, had Gordon Pasha been sent out to the Soudan nine months ago, before the wave of rebellion had increased to raging billows, sweeping over the land, we should have been spared the painful events which have taken place there quite lately, and by this time the Mahdi would have been little heard of. Then Gordon Pasha would have come on them like the noon-day sun, and all the tribes would have flocked round him as a deliverer, whilst the Mahdi would have been powerless, and relegated to the obscurity from which he had sprung. What a country Egypt and the Soudan might become under British rule! In Lower Egypt we should form a net-work of canals in communication with the Nile, as in the days of Pharaoh; then thousands upon thousands of acres, which to-day look sterile deserts, would be made to yield enormous quantities of sugar-cane, cotton, flax, dhurra, &c., and at least two crops in the year could be obtained. Politics I have nothing to do with. I am simply giving an expression to an opinion which I formed when in the Soudan and Egypt. This opinion I expressed in January, 1882, when in the Soudan, and subsequently very many times since in England. It is a source of great satisfaction to me that so eminent an authority as Sir Samuel Baker, F.R.G.S., entertains the same ideas. As things now are, extensive cultivation in the Soudan would be almost useless, the only means of exporting their products being by the very slow method of camels to the nearest seaport; taxes would increase, and the only people who would derive any benefit would be the Egyptians, not the

Arabs. If we ruled there we would appoint an English governor, who would let the Arabs live on their own industry, if they had any, and, if not, bring the fallaheen there, and take only a reasonable share of taxation. We should put down a railway from Souâkin to Kassala, from there to Massawah and elsewhere. We should sink wells, and erect engines which would pump up sufficient water to irrigate thousands of acres of the most fertile land. These lands require no manuring, nothing but clearing, scratching the rich alluvial deposit, and putting in the seeds. The crops when gathered could then be transported by rail to Souâkin, which would soon become a flourishing port, could, in fact, be transferred direct from central Africa to any English port within three weeks or so. Senna, coffee, tobacco, cotton, sugar, flax, dhurra, wheat, oats, oranges, lemons, and I don't know what, could be grown there without the least trouble, besides which, hides, honey, beeswax, and other things would be abundant. I was so struck, soon after we left Kassala, with the immensely fertile appearance of the soil, and the vast extent of country capable of cultivation, and of producing two crops a year at least, that I mentioned this to Mr. Colvin, as we rode side by side on our camels, afterwards making a note of the same in my diary.

Every night of our stay at Kassala the monotonous beating of the tom-tom would commence about 8 p.m. and continue incessantly till about twelve, accompanied by the most extraordinary shrill trilling note of a female every now and then. It seems there had been a death in the family, and on all occasions of great joy and sorrow this unpleasant musical entertainment is at once provided. Mosconas tells me that, after a death, the mourners go on in this kind of way every night for about a month, and a very irritating performance it is to our untutored English auditory nerves. We found the white ants very troublesome here. They are very destructive little insects, and, I believe, will destroy everything but iron and stone. If a strong, solid, leather portmanteau be left on the ground for two or three nights, they will destroy it, but if two stones, sufficient to raise it an inch or two from the ground, be placed underneath, they will not touch it, and if we encamp on sand we are safe from them. They destroyed all the matting laid down in our tents during the few days that we were here, although it was taken up and beaten every day. Scorpions as well as white ants were frequently found underneath the matting. This is very cheap, indeed; we therefore secured a fresh lot.

CHAPTER XIII.

LEAVE KASSALA—CHARACTER OF THE COUNTRY—MEET BENI-AMIR ARABS ON THE RIVER BED—THE BAOBOB TREE.

ALL being ready, we started off from Kassala at 3 p.m. on the 17th January, intending to reach Heikota within three days. We encamped at 8 p.m., and next day were off at 9 a.m., marching until 6 p.m.—temp. 90° in shade. Fine trees became more numerous; the country looked much greener, and water was usually obtainable every day simply by digging a few feet in the sandy river-bed. This day we passed through a large field of dhurra. To guard this from elephants, birds, and buffaloes several platforms were erected in different parts of the field about 10 or 12 feet high, and on these boys and men spent the whole day unsheltered from the scorching rays of the sun—which was like a ball of fire—cracking whips and uttering hideous noises. We came across distinct and recent tracks of a lion, two full-grown and one young elephant. I also saw a few monkeys, a musk cat, several young tiger-cats and hundreds of guinea-fowl. We shot on the march one eagle, two ariels, and two gazelles; the latter are not so hard and dry as those in the desert.

On the 19th we made the usual march, encamping at Ashberra. The general character of the country has now become much more varied and interesting. This day we travelled through tall grass, about 10 feet high, for a long time—perhaps an hour. When we got out of this we found ourselves encountering the prickly thorns of the mimosa and kittar bushes. We had now done with caravan routes entirely, and my camel-riding capabilities were fully tested as I go up and down hill; now over rocky hills, down steep banks and across dry river-courses, then through a forest of dhoum palms, dodging as I go the great projecting strong branches, which appear strong enough almost to decapitate or sweep me off my camel. Then, by way of variety, we pass through a mile or two of the horrid cruel thorns of the mimosa and kittar trees, which every now and then bury themselves in my flesh, and tear my clothes and helmet as I duck my head to avoid having my face lacerated. The camel, of course, walks on in the most unconcerned manner, just as if he was on open ground, taking no notice whatever of these obstructions, but brushing past them as if they were twigs or straws. Everything, even the smallest of the mimosa tree, is armed with long, strong, very sharp thorns. Each thorn is as sharp as a needle and about an inch long; indeed, the native women use them as a cobbler does his awl, and I have often seen a woman using the thorn to pierce a girba and shreds of the palm leaf to sew it up with. The thorns of the kittar bushes are quite semicircular in shape, very near to each other, not long but very strong, and each successive thorn crooks in a different direction to its predecessor—one crooks up and the other down. When they catch hold of any-one they stick to him as close as a brother. If my clothes get entangled, I must stay and pick myself out, or if I elect to go on without doing so, I must submit to having my clothes, and perchance my flesh, effectually torn across. We saw *en route* a great many baboons, vultures of course always, eagles, thousands of doves, guinea-fowl, and recent tracks of elephants, lions, and leopards. Mr. Phillipps and I, whilst stalking some gazelles in a large palm-grove, lost the caravan for hours, and just as we emerged from it on to the wide river-bed of the Mareb we came upon a large number of the Beni-Amir tribe in that semi-nude condition, which is so fashionable amongst them, watering their goats and cattle. We dismounted and joined the sable throng, made them understand that we should like some goat's milk, which they gave us, after which we showed them our pocket and hunting knives, revolvers, and watches. We were at once surrounded by an admiring throng of our new acquaintances, who seemed greatly pleased with what they saw, but when I applied my watch to the ear of one his surprise and delight was immense, for he had never in his life seen a watch before. The ticking tickled him greatly, so much so that he pushed all his friends forward one after the other to participate in his joy. However, as the long bushy hair of these fellows was streaming with fat, I observed caution.

January 20th.—We were off at 9.30, and had not far to go ere we reached Heikota, where the Beni-Amir tribe then lived. This was the shortest march we ever made, for we arrived there at 11 a.m., amongst the most luxuriant vegetation, encamping just by a huge baobob tree (*Adamsonia digitata*), 51 feet in girth. Large as this may seem, it is not by any means as large as they grow—they are frequently 60 to 85 feet in girth. The trunk is not above 12 feet high ere the branches are put forth. The flowers are in proportion to the size of the tree, and followed by a fruit about 10 inches long. This looks like a greenish pod or capsule, having a bloom on it such as we see on a plum; on breaking the capsule we find a large number of granular-like substances very much resembling pieces of white starch packed closely together, which have an agreeable sub-acid flavour. When this white substance, which is very thin, is dissolved, and it does so readily in the mouth, we came to a dark, brownish little stone, very much like a tamarind stone in appearance, but smaller. When dry, the pulp, by which the seeds are surrounded, is powdered and brought to Europe from the Levant, under the name of *terra sigillata lemnia*—the seeds are called *goui*.

CHAPTER XIV.

ENCAMP AT HEIKOTA—SHEIK AHMED—HERR SCHUMANN AND HIS ZAREEBA—WE MAKE A ZAREEBA—THE MAHDI—EXCITEMENT IN THE VILLAGE—HORRIBLE TRAGEDY—SHEIK AHMED DINES WITH US—THE MAGIC LANTERN—LIONS VISIT US.

ERE we could pitch our tents we had to cut down a number of young palm trees, and clear away a quantity of tall grass, &c. Whilst doing so Sheik Ahmed, of the powerful Beni-Amir tribe, who paid us a visit, gave us a good deal more of manual labour by advising us to make a zareeba (a fence of prickly trees), assigning as a reason, and a very substantial one, the fact that lions came down every night, and often made such a noise as to disturb his slumbers, but that we had nothing to fear from his tribe. He said further that boa-constrictors and scorpions were very common, leopards also. We found traces of the latter whilst clearing.

Sheik Ahmed, or Achmet, is said to be one of the most powerful Sheiks in the Soudan; he certainly was far and away the best sample of a Sheik that I have seen anywhere. His head was kept shaved; on it he wore a tight-fitting white skull-cap. He was almost black, and of a determined aspect, but his features were good, and his teeth white, sound and regular; his eyes were keen, black and glittering as a hawk's; he was dressed in spotless white and scrupulously clean; quick in action, thought, speech, and appearance. One might almost say really that he was an educated man, for he could both write and read, and certainly looked a remarkable, shrewd, and intelligent man. During the piping times of peace he could be a merry fellow of infinite jest; and he and I cracked many a joke together by the aid of an interpreter. He could also be a fierce warrior when necessary, and bore marks, some deep ones, too, of many a skirmish he had been engaged in. "Beware of entrance to a quarrel, but being in at it, bear thyself, that thine opponent may beware of thee." The latter half of this proverb, I think, would be quite applicable to our friend, Sheik Ahmed, as all his wounds were in front; the first part, I fear, he would be rather regardless of, probably, indeed, more of the temper of an Irishman handling a shillelagh at Donnybrook fair, exclaimng—" Will ye jist thread on the tail of me coat, now?" And I assure you, reader, that had you known Sheik Ahmed you would hesitate ere you trod on his caudal appendage, if you discovered it. I have heard that he is one of the most powerful vassals under the Khedive, and that should occasion require he could put in the field about 10,000 horsemen and tribesmen.

These people, over whom the Sheik seemed to possess great control and authority, are quite pastoral in their pursuits, and own such enormous flocks and herds as would astonish any ordinary mortal. These are every night driven in from grazing to a large zareeba on the river-bed. I was irresistibly reminded here of the patriarchs of old. Here was this Sheikh with four wives and I don't know how many children, the leader or petty sovereign of a large and powerful tribe, over whom he possessed absolute power, and, as I said before, owning these flocks and herds. On the river-bed of the Mareb the tribe, or a part of it rather, lived, their dwellings simply consisting of a few stakes driven into the sand, over and around which is a covering of tall grass and matting made from the palm leaves. They live in this neighbourhood as long as there is anything for their flocks and herds to eat; when there is not, like locusts, they move off a few miles to pastures new. Then, when the wet season commences, they clear off to the mountains or desert, else the tetse fly would destroy the animals. They seem a contented lot, and may truly say, as a deceased M.P. once said, "My riches consist, not in the vastness of my possessions, but in the fewness of my wants."

They live simply, on milk, honey, and dhurra principally, and to that fact may be attributed the beautifully white sound teeth they possess. I think I ought to say that the Sheik was good enough to ask me to stay with the tribe for three or four years, and as an inducement was good enough to say that if I would he would give me four wives, thus placing me on a par with himself. However, I neither embraced this tempting offer nor the sable females, and here I think the utterances of the deceased M.P. would be peculiarly applicable. When the Sheik, who was very friendly, left us, he accepted our invitation to dinner at 7 p.m. Quite close to our camp was another zareeba; in this dwelt Herr Schumann and his wild animals. He had, when we were there, three young elephants; two females, and one rogue (the latter, being a rather fierce little fellow, was chained by the leg), a few young lions, wild cats, leopards, and 15 young ostriches about the size of Dorking fowls.

Apropos of the Mahdi, I find the following in to-day's paper:

"April 2nd, '84—An Austrian dealer in wild animals, writing from Kassala to friends in Vienna, gives some information about the Mahdi, whom he knows personally, and with whom he has frequently transacted business, the Mahdi himself having for years past dealt in wild beasts for the different European Zoological Gardens. He is described by the writer as a very cunning impostor, and as an instance, it is related that a short time ago he suddenly appeared with a number of warts on his right cheek, these having been artificially produced by the aid of a German called Schandorper, formerly a clown, and afterwards a hairdresser, now in the service of the Mahdi. The reason was that the legends about the expected Mahdi speak of him as having such marks. Like the beasts he formerly dealt in, the Mahdi sleeps in the daytime and transacts business during the night." I have no doubt whatever that our old acquaintance, who was the only animal collector I ever met with, is the author of the preceding, and I think a very credible man.

In the evening, just before dinner, we heard near our camp a great number of women and children, accompanied by the inevitable beating of the tom-toms, and that wild, peculiar trilling note of a woman to which I have before alluded. Being desirous to find out as much as I could of the habits and customs of these people, I got Mr. Colvin to accompany me to ascertain the cause. We went and found a great number of women shouting and chanting, whilst a number of their braves were executing a war dance with spear and shield, others in the meantime sharpening their spears. Of course we were at a loss to account for the extreme activity and evident warlike preliminaries, and returned to camp not feeling certain whether these sharpened spears would not on the morrow make unpleasant incisions in our intercastal spaces—at least Mr. Colvin, who was a very facetious and witty fellow, humorously suggested this. On returning to camp we passed Herr Schumann's zareeba, and told him what we had witnessed, asking him the meaning of it all. He narrated the following tale of blood: The day before our arrival at Heikota, when we were in the immediate neighbourhood, probably about the time we were encamping, a number of the Basé people from the village of Sarcella had come upon the children of the Beni-Amirs driving the flocks and herds in for the night. They then perpetrated a deed which makes one shudder to think of, for they were not satisfied with simply slaughtering these unoffending children, but doing so in a most horrible manner; in short, they ripped them open with their knives, and drove off about 2,000 head of cattle. In consequence of this the Sheik had given the word to his men to prepare for action, and they were now doing so, intending to make an attack on the village of Sarcella in the morning.

In the evening we had a champagne dinner; the Sheik studiously avoided the champagne, and had the shocking bad taste to prefer raspberry vinegar and water. Herr Schumann also joined us, but, like a Christian, partook of champagne.

We pretended not to know anything of this slaughtering business, so asked the Sheik what was the reason of all the commotion amongst the tribe. He related the same story, adding that he should get his men together in the morning and attack these Basé (that means kill all they could lay their hands on) and get his cattle back again. How ably he carried out his destructive intentions I will tell the reader later on. The customs are somewhat peculiar in this part of the world. Supposing I and my party, who are not Beni-Amirs, enter the Basé country from the Beni-Amir tribe, and they should be at enmity with them at that time, they would regard us as enemies. Knowing this, we told the Sheik we were very sorry this had occurred just now, as we intended to explore that country, and his fighting might make it a very difficult, if not impossible matter to do so. However, with the true instincts of a gentleman sheik, he accommodated himself to all parties, very readily acquiesced in our views, and was good enough to postpone his bloodthirsty intentions for a few days.

After dinner we chatted round the camp fire for awhile, smoking the "calumet of peace," to use a Cooperian phrase, and retired to our different tents to rest 9.30 p.m. The Sheik, ere he left us, accepted an invitation to breakfast next day at 7 a.m. If we are late birds in England, we are early ones in the Soudan.

January 21st.—True to his appointment the Sheik breakfasted with us this morning. He was not only punctual, but he literally *did* breakfast; there was no finiking and fiddling about with his food, for he disposed of it in a most straightforward manner. Imagine an opening in the pavement for the reception of coals, and you have a pretty good idea of the rapid disappearance of food down the œsophagus of our friend. We commenced with porridge and milk; a dish evidently highly appreciated by the Sheik; then we had minced collops, kippered herrings, gazelle, stewed kidneys, wild honey, French jam and coffee, to all of which Sheik

Ahmed did ample justice. After breakfast many warriors drop into camp, and, in their fashion, squat round in a circle on their haunches. One of the spears was covered with leather as a sign that they were at peace with us. A great and long pow-wow ensued as to our future journey; we should want to buy or hire camels for going through the Basé country, as those we had hired at Kassala would have to return from Heikota.

Last night we were rather disturbed by the noise of lions, and this morning, within about a dozen yards of my tent, I found their footprints, fortunately outside the zareeba. I dare say I spent about an hour or so at my tent this morning attending to a large number of natives, and afterwards visited others in their own tents on the river-bed. In some instances I was obliged to crawl in on my hands and knees. When I had finished my morning's work I took up my shot gun and strolled off in quest of some beautifully plumaged birds which were abundant here and brought home an eagle, paroquet, laughing-bird, falcon, and shreik, which I skinned after luncheon.

We again invited Sheik Ahmed and Herr Schumann to join us at the festive board at 7 p.m.; we also told the former to let his people know that at about 8.30 p.m. there would be what they call a *funtasia.* Just before 7 p.m. the Sheik arrived and behaved himself in quite a gentlemanly manner. He was dressed in spotless white, and was so particular as to borrow a pen-knife from me to clean his nails with (a great instance of the civilizing effect of Englishmen). Although we drank iced champagne and claret, he stuck to raspberry vinegar and water, which he consumed with great relish. He was rather clumsy with a knife and fork; indeed, almost the only breach of manners that he perpetrated was to finish up the repast (just before coffee was brought) by plunging the teaspoon into the preserve, scooping out as much as it would conveniently hold, conveying it to his mouth and replacing the spoon in the preserve; this mode of eating has its inconveniences.

Another peculiarity of his was a singular habit that one requires to get thoroughly accustomed to to really appreciate; he generally indulged in it largely at meal times when conversing, and having his face directed to the object of attack. I scarcely know how to describe it, and perhaps ought not to do so in polite society, but that I wish to tell my readers exactly what kind of a man this was. It was a method (not unfamiliar even to English ears) of producing a peculiar vibration or concussion of the atmosphere by a noise proceeding from the mouth;

some polite people would call it an eructation, but that is not sufficiently explanatory. It is familiarly and vulgarly known as "belching," and so frequently did it occur at meal times that it became known amongst ourselves as "the genial belch of the Sheik." I suggested that probably it was a complimentary proceeding on his part, but I must say if it was so we could readily have forgiven this *too* frequent formality. After dinner a great many of his people assembled (no women, and very few children) to witness the mysteries and wonders of the magic lantern, or *fantasia*. Would that I had the pencil of an artist to delineate the picture which the *Graphic* or any other illustrated paper would have been glad to have reproduced. Here we were encamped in equatorial Africa; we had five tents pitched amongst waving dhoum palms, tamarisk, and tamarind, nebbuck, baobob, hegleek, ebony, and other trees, and the usual luxuriant growth of tall grass and young palms. About three hundred of these dusky-skinned, almost black, agile-looking fellows, wearing simply the tope or loin-cloth, the foremost squatting on their haunches, the rest standing behind, the Europeans in white clothing, and the picturesquely-dressed Sheik in his white turban and robes. It was a weird, wild scene, when viewed by the flickering light of the lanterns as they moved about the camp, but when the moon shone out, shedding a soft, bright light on the scene, it certainly was a most charming and interesting picture. Amidst it all could be seen three hundred glittering spear-heads, making the picture complete. How easily, had they been so disposed, could these wild sons of the Soudan have made an end of us, but I am happy to say this ceremony was not included in the evening's programme. We placed a wet sheet across the entrance to one of the bell-tents, and as the Queen (whom they called the Sultana) the Prince and Princess of Wales, the elephant, lion, rhinoceros, hippopotamus, giraffe, ostrich, crocodile (snapping his jaws together), and other animals with which they were familiar, appeared on the canvas, the delight of these grown-up children was manifested by loud expressions of approval. When the Sheik, his retinue and people took their departure, we further astonished them by letting off rockets and illuminating their way with red and blue fire. If I went out there again I should certainly take out a galvanic battery, which I am sure would astonish and amuse immensely. We here engaged fresh camel-men, huntsmen, horse-boys, and servants, at rather high wages, on account of the rumoured ferocious character of the Basé, the Sheik taking a pretty good share of the wages himself. All camels were bought, not hired; when we wanted to hire we were cheerfully assured by the owners that we should very likely all be killed by the Basé or Kunama people, and they would lose their camels. The Sheik was presented with a capital bell-tent, a rifle, and a good musical-box, which played six airs, others, with razors, butchers' knives in sheaths, topes, beads, knives, scissors, small portable looking-glasses, &c., all of which were productive of great wonder and joy. Sheik Ahmed, in return, sent us a present of ten sheep and ten milk-giving goats, so that now we had sixteen goats, which furnished us with plenty of milk every morning to our porridge. As we intended resuming our journey on the morrow, we were all busy writing letters to England, which Herr Schumann engaged to forward to Kassala.

CHAPTER XV.

PATIENTS AT HEIKOTA—LEAVE HEIKOTA—GAME IN THE BASÉ COUNTRY—SEE OUR FIRST LION—A LION INTERVIEWS THE AUTHOR—TETÉL, NELLUT, AND OTHER GAME KILLED ON THE MARCH.

ON the 22nd January we were up in good time, as there was a good deal to be seen to ere we continued our march. We intended to return to Heikota after exploring the Basé country, which we thought would occupy about four or five weeks. It would not, therefore, be necessary to take all our baggage with us; accordingly, a considerable quantity was left behind in Herr Schumann's zareeba until our return —assuming that we should do so. I was, as usual, busily occupied after breakfast in attending to my patients, who not only came from close by, but from long distances on camels. It had got noised abroad from Kassala that there was a "Hakeem Ingelese" travelling with these gentlemen, and whenever we encamped anywhere for a day or two many patients came to visit me. They appeared inordinately fond of my pills, and would swallow them with as much avidity as boys in our country swallow lollipops. To judge from what was expected of me, they must have thought that I was endowed with almost supernatural powers. One boy was brought to me whose hip had been dislocated a year or so before; another person who had been positively blind from ophthalmia two years, hoped I could let in a stream of welcome light: Alas! poor fellow, I could not make the blind see, or the lame walk, under such circumstances. However, I was often able to effect cures in some and relief in other cases, and when we returned to Heikota many grateful patients came to thank me; one would give me some dhurra, another a skin of milk, an Arab knife, a spear, a sheep, and so on. Gratitude even is pleasing to a doctor, although sometimes a scarce commodity. We did not succeed in making a start until 4 p.m.; halted at six. The Sheik, who came part way with us, on returning to his tribe, said he would join us in the morning, and see us well on the way ere he interviewed the Basé at Sarcella, whom he had an account to settle with. During our various conversations with him he informed us that we should find abundance of shooting of every kind in the country—elephants, lions, leopards, porcupines, wild cats, hyænas, buffaloes, jackals, giraffes, ostriches, rhinoceros, antelopes of different kinds, gazelles, oterops, ariels, maarifs, mehedehét, tetél, nellut, dick-dick, baboons and monkeys; all kinds of birds; falcons, Egyptian hawks, rollo-birds, paroquets, eagles, vultures, doves, quail, partridges, sand-grouse, guinea-fowl, and I don't know what besides—all of which was quite true; there was really enough of shooting of every description to satisfy the most ardent sportsman. He also advised us, when we got into the Basé country, not to have our guns, rifles, and revolvers in cases, but ready at a moment's notice, night and day, and this advice we strictly followed during the whole of our journey.

'On the 23rd we marched nine hours, encamping at a place called Toodlook. Our sleep was rather disturbed in the night by the noise of lions and hyænas, which came very near the camp. We marched to-day through varied scenery and pretty country—now along the Mareb, then for two hours across country, through jungle, again coming on to the Mareb, across it, and over a plain studded with trees and shrubs, finally encamping by the side of the Mareb. Whilst our tents were being pitched, Messrs. A. and W. James and I reconnoitred, soon coming near to a place where there was some water. Suddenly we discovered, about two hundred yards from us, a fine lion lying down on a little elevated land, no doubt on the look-out for some unsuspecting antelope coming to drink. Mr. A. James ran back to camp for his rifle, crept up, without arousing the suspicion of the noble beast, and fired, but not being near enough, missed him. The lion simply got up and calmly turned off into the jungle, where it was deemed unadvisable to follow him. On our way back to camp we saw one place where there had evidently been a desperate struggle between a lion and his prey; the former evidently had the best of it, as we saw a long trail, he having dragged his supper into some long grass and young palms.

On the 25th we were up and off in good time, leaving Suleiman and the English servants to follow in charge of the caravan. Last night a rather curious adventure occurred to me, which might have had a curious termination. When we arrived at a camping-ground I usually selected the spot for my tent, quite regardless of where the others were going to be pitched. On this occasion I had done so, and ordered it to be pitched under some trees close to young palms and tall grass, some distance from the others. Suleiman remonstrated with me for doing so, saying that the Basé or lions might come down in the night. However I would have it so. Every day whilst we dined a large camp-fire was lighted, as the nights were very chilly, although the heat was so great in the daytime. Around this we smoked and chatted over politics, English friends and the events of the day, and plans for the future, skinned birds or animals, wrote letters, or posted up diaries. At half-past nine or ten o'clock we gradually melted away one by one to bed. On this night I was the last, having stayed to have an extra pipe. At last I lighted my lantern, was walking off to, and had nearly reached, my tent, when I was startled by a low growl issuing from a thick growth of young palms, about a dozen yards from my tent; there was no mistaking the nature of the growl, and I rapidly executed a retrograde movement, poked my head into the nearest tent, calling out to the semi-sleeping occupants thereof, "I say, did you hear that salutation just as I was going to my tent?" Answer by Mr. F. L. James and Mr. Phillipps, "No; what was it, doctor? We were just going to sleep." "Why, it is a lion close to my tent, and there is no mistaking it." They laughed immensely, and seemed to think it a good joke, but jumped up and came with me towards my tent, I think slightly incredulous. Their incredulity was, at all events, quickly dispelled, as the lion, by another louder expression of opinion, gave us distinctly to understand that he was not only in unpleasant proximity to, but had his eye on us. Again an *extremely* rapid retrograde movement by the trio ensued, and a joking remark from Lort Phillipps, "Doctor, you will be dragged off to-night, as sure as fate," and a consoling remark from Mr. F. James that the lion was perhaps hungry. We seized some burning brands from the fire, and piled on a large number of dried palm leaves in front of my tent. I then retired to rest in peace, and when I arose in the morning my friends were, I hope, pleased to find I was not in pieces. We heard both lions and panthers in the night pretty near to us, but so long as they did not visit the camp we did not care. In the morning at breakfast the Sheik was highly amused by an account of my night's experience, and extremely jocular over it. This day we killed two tetél on the march, and caught fifty-seven sand-grouse in a net, but only kept sufficient for dinner and luncheon. One of our courses at dinner was an omelette of ostrich eggs.

CHAPTER XVI.

WE ARRIVE AT THE BASÉ OR KUNAMA COUNTRY—THE VILLAGE OF SARCELLA—MURDER OF MR. POWELL AND PARTY—MY CAMEL AND I UNCEREMONIOUSLY PART COMPANY—THE FIRST BASÉ WE SEE—ENCAMP AT KOOLOOKOO—OUR FIRST INTERVIEW WITH BASÉ—THEY MAKE "AMAN" WITH US—THEIR APPEARANCE—DESCRIPTION OF KOOLOOKOO AND THE BASÉ PEOPLE—THEIR HABITS AND CUSTOMS.

FROM January 26th to 28th nothing of importance took place. A day seldom passed without nellut, tetél, and gazelle falling to someone's rifle. We were all busy during leisure hours in writing letters for England, as we should not be able to do so or receive any again until our return from the Basé country to Herr Schumann's zareeba, where Mr. James had arranged all letters and papers from Kassala were to be brought. We often saw baboons gambolling about, also tracks of elephants, lions, and panthers. The Shiek says we are now in the neighbourhood of giraffes, ostriches, and buffalos. This day he leaves us to fight or come to terms with the Basé, and graciously condescends to act as our postman as far as Heikota, promising to see that our letters are forwarded from there to Kassala. He tells us that his men are at Sarcella, where they have about 1,000 of the offending Basé shut up in a cave; they were now waiting for him ere they took any further action. What transpired we did not learn until we returned to Heikota. That I will describe when we return there.

January 29th.—We are now in Basé territory. We have for days past done with caravan routes or paths, and travel over rocky mountains, large plains, jungle, river-beds, and through a forest of tamarind, tamarisk, palm, baobob, nebbuck, hegleek, and mimosa trees. On the branches of the latter we frequently saw lumps of gum arabic, as large as walnuts, which had exuded through the bark.

At 4 p.m. we saw a Basé village on fire, and rightly surmised, as we found out afterwards, that the Beni-Amirs had been the authors of this. Just after breakfast, before the camels were brought, we shot eight partridges and ten quail, which were handed over to the cook. Some were prepared for dinner, and some for luncheon next day. We also shot on the march a buck tetél; the prime bit was, of course, reserved for our dinner, and was more like roast beef than the flesh of any other animal I tasted; the rest was given to our attendants. We encamped by the side of the river-bed, where we found water on digging to the depth of 7 or 8 feet. Ere we could encamp we had to set to with axes and clear away a number of young palms and mimosa bushes, make a zareeba, and before retiring for the night look to our rifles and revolvers and see that we had plenty of cartridges ready in case of emergency, as we flattered ourselves that we were like the Bristol, Sheffield, or any other boys in England who slept with one eye open. At all events we had heard sufficient of this country to know that it would be unwise for us to be caught napping, especially as we noticed some of the natives spying about soon after we had pitched our tents. About midday we sighted the village of Sarcella, the inhabitants of which Sheik Ahmed had gone to interview, and whom Suleiman designated as "a very bad peoples." There is very little doubt that Suleiman was right, if all we heard about them was true, for in 1869 or '70—I am not sure which—Mr. Powell, wife, little boy, and all the Europeans were spitted on their long spears. They now lie buried in

Bassaleg churchyard, near Newport, having been brought home by his brother, Mr. Powell, M.P., who fearfully avenged his brother's death. Whilst I was in the Soudan I saw by a newspaper which we got, that this gentleman lost his life in a balloon.

January 30th.—Made a short march to-day, namely, from 10.30 a.m. until 4.30 p.m., encamping at a place called Wo-amma, playfully christened and ever afterwards known as "Whoa Emma." The country was to-day very mountainous and difficult for the caravan, to say nothing of ourselves. I distinctly recollect that on this very day, whilst travelling along a plane, one of the horse-boys came trotting quickly along, causing my camel not only to shy, but to bolt when I was quite unprepared for any such *contretemps*. A spectator would, doubtless, have been much amused. I was not. For the space of about 20 yards I bounded like an india-rubber ball on the makloufa; then came suddenly to grief from my lofty elevation, the distance from the camel's hump to his feet being considerable. I fell with a regular bang on to my hip, which felt very painful for some days afterwards, and had the mortification to see my belongings gradually parting company with the camel—my rug, then my satchel, a basket, zanzimeer, &c. The camel was caught after some trouble, whilst I and they were gradually picked up, I with rage in my heart, for this camel, being a bolter, had served me several scurvy tricks before; for instance, if we came to any little declivity, the beast would persist in making a trot of it, greatly exciting my apprehensions. Again, when we came to a narrow pathway I would duck my head where there were overhanging boughs of prickly shrubs; he, thinking I was going to thrash him, would at once bolt, and when he had rushed through I should find my head and hands were like a pincushion. I could then knock my helmet out of the trees and at my leisure pick out the horrid thorns with which my head and hands abounded. Once I was nearly swept off the wretched beast as he bolted in this way. A strong chain of cactus was across our way, catching me in the middle. I saw the danger in time, and clutched hold of the makloufa with all my might, on I might have been found suspended amongst the trees. It broke, fortunately, and I escaped, but I never shall forget how angry that camel frequently made me, what self-restraint I was obliged to exercise, for if I chastised him he would bellow and bolt again, to my great danger and annoyance. I had in England extracted many human teeth in my time, but this day I extracted an elephant's tooth, and brought it home as a curiosity. However, I think I ought to say the elephant was not alive, and that on the march we passed the skeletons of two others, which, I have no doubt, furnished some excellent repasts for the natives. These were not all we passed calling for notice, for some of our men came upon two of the Basé people; the first sample of these curiosities we had seen. One was in a baobob tree gathering the pods and throwing them down to the other, who was collecting them in a basket. These so-called ferocious savages appeared terribly alarmed when our men came upon them. The one on *terra firma*, with the true instinct that "self-preservation is the first law of nature," bolted like a shot, but our men captured him. The other was afraid to come down until one of the English servants discharged the contents of one barrel of his rifle, and let him know by the aid of Beyrumfi, our interpreter, that the contents of the other would be lodged in his frail tenement of clay unless he was more sociable. This persuasive kind of argument appeared very effective, for down he came, and I am sure both he and his companion, who, doubtless, were accustomed to be hunted like wild beasts, were agreeably surprised when they each received a pocket-knife and a bit of bread and meat. Remembering the injunctions of Sheik

Ahmed, and with Powell on the brain, we took precautions against surprises—set to work and made a zareeba round the camp, lighted camp fires, and looked well to rifles and revolvers. The latter we kept under our pillows; the former at the heads of our beds, ready at a moment's notice. Sentries were posted, and occasionally relieved, whilst one of us (whoever chanced to awake) went round to see that they were doing their duty. The man who was not, felt unhappy next morning, as he received an intimation from the coorbatch before breakfast that there had been a certain direlection of duty on his part.

January 31st.—We marched eight hours to-day, encamping at Fodie on the dry river-bed, close to some wells. This was a very fatiguing march for the caravan, on account of our luggage, which was much obstructed by trees. We travelled through quite a forest of these. Where there were no trees the grass had been burnt for miles round. Many quail and sand-grouse were shot to-day.

February 1st.—After a short march of four hours only, we encamped on the broad, sandy river-bed of the Mareb, very near to the village of Koolookoo, which we could see high up amongst the rocks of a mountain on the opposite side. Each side of the Mareb was plentifully lined with overhanging trees of all kinds, and amongst the twigs of some could be seen many hundreds of the beautifully constructed nests of the weaver-bird. Not very far from the Mareb, at the base of the mountain, in which these Basé at Koolookoo lived, were the remains of a mud house in which Mr. Powell had once lived. This was, I believe, as far, or nearly so, as he had penetrated.

The Kunama, or Basé country, is quite a *terra incognita*, and, as far as we could ascertain, we are the first and only Europeans who have explored that country at all. This being so, I shall expend a good deal of time in saying all I can about this country and people. We shall have to thank Messrs. W. D. James and Percy Aylmer for a map of that country, and also for some photographs of the people and scenery, which will be found in Mr. F. L. James's book. This book I have not yet read, and shall not do so until my own is in the publisher's hands, for fear I may unwittingly adopt any of his theories or expressions, but rather prefer to be perfectly independent of it, and give *my own* ideas and description in my own way, be they good, bad, or indifferent. No two men agree on any subject, and it is *very* probable that Mr. F. L. James and I may materially differ on *many*. So that I shall not be termed a copyist, I shall neither reproduce the map or photographs, but trust to sketches taken to the best of my poor ability, but which, I hope, will convey a pretty good idea of the kind of place and people that we sojourned amongst for a while. Very well, then, after this exordium—probably the longest I shall make—I will continue my narrative, as the dog would say of his caudal appendage.

This was the first Basé village we had come to, and ere we could go any further it was necessary that we should interview the Shiek of this village, and explain the object of our visit. We made an ostentatious display of our rifles and guns, twenty-four in number, and placed them against the bank ready for immediate use if necessary, whilst each of us sported a six-chambered revolver in our waist-belts. When we had—as we thought—taken sufficient precautions against surprises or treachery, we were curious to see these much-dreaded savages, whom report said were capable of any sanguinary deed (could, in fact, murder with a smiling face), and although their neighbours lived on their borders, they appeared to know little more about them than we did ourselves. Whilst we lunched within easy reach of our rifles, we sent forth one Beyrumfi, " our guide, philosopher, and friend" (and the only man who knew anything of the language) to the village. When we had finished our luncheon, we got our field-glasses, and on the very summit of the rocky mountain we saw all the women and children, and a few of the men, looking down on us. Half an hour afterwards, winding round by a circuitous pathway, on sloping ground, and occasionally hidden by trees, we could now see Beyrumfi, accompanied by seven or eight of the Basé, each carrying his spear and shield. When they appeared on the edge of the river-bed in single file, headed by Beyrumfi, the Sheik's son (a fine, strapping, well-made fellow, who took his father's place during his absence) dropped his shield, and, without stopping, drove his spear quivering into the sand; his example was followed by all the others. They all marched briskly across the river-bed, whilst we, in our English fashion, stood up and shook hands all round, which, under such circumstances, was much more agreeable than kissing all round. Sheik junior, if I may call him so, was about 5ft. 10in. in height, as straight as a dart, and not by any means over-dressed, for he wore nothing but a bit of soft leather, very much the shape and size of a man's bathing drawers. He got the twig of a tree and broke it with us as a sign of friendship. All then squatted round on their haunches, with their knees under their chins (their customary mode of resting themselves), and Beyrumfi explained the object of our visit. This was satisfactory. The Sheik then borrowed a two-edged sword from Beyrumfi, placed it on the ground with the point directed towards us, put his *naked* foot on it, and delivered a short harangue, the purport of which was that we were in his country now, and as long as we remained neither he nor his people would harm, but do all they could to assist us, and that we were now his brothers. However, he could really only speak for his village. This is what is called making "Aman"—that is, swearing peace and friendship, and that we will trust one another; but we didn't. On hospitable thoughts intent, we ordered a large bowl of cooked meat; our new acquaintances soon squatted round, and judging from the rapid disappearance of the food, I should imagine that a larger bowl would have done very well. We gave each of these fellows small presents, amongst other things an empty claret bottle each, which was much prized, but to the Sheik's son we gave a few extra things, such as a tope or loin-cloth, a razor, a knife in sheath, needles, pins and thread, a velvet necklet, and a waistcoat striped yellow and black. He at once invested himself with the order of the tope and yellow and black waistcoat, to the great admiration of his friends, who continually made a clucking noise with the mouth, just as we do to urge on a horse; from their point of view it meant how wonderful, how nice, and what a swell you are. The claret-coloured lead-capping of bottles, which had been thrown on the ground, they gathered up, using them to decorate their hair with, or as an addition to their necklaces. Our rifles and guns were still leaning against the bank, just to show how well armed we were. Now, finding the natives were so friendly, and that they had left their spears on the other side of the river-bed, we ordered our rifles to be taken into our tents; still, however, retaining our revolvers. Of course a long pow-wow ensued. Whilst this was going on the women and children were not idle in the village, for they stood out on various places of vantage, looking down on their braves. We lent the Basé field-glasses to look at them, and it was most amusing to hear their expressions of surprise, with any amount of the clucking accompaniment, as they saw how near the glass brought their friends to view. After a while they returned to their village, upon which several of their friends, finding not only that we appeared reasonable beings, but that we had given several presents, paid us a visit, no doubt hoping that we would serve them in the same way. Of course the wonderful Ingelese exhibited to all these visitors their rifles and revolvers, accompanied by an elaborate explanation of their killing powers. Beyrumfi explained all this amidst a shower of cluckings. We had been told by Sheik Ahmed that the Basé were no better than beasts, that they lived in holes in the ground and in caves; we resolved to see for ourselves, and so told the Sheik that we would pay him a visit on the morrow, which we did. They don't absolutely live in holes in the ground like rabbits, but where the rocks lean against one another, or project out, forming an awning, they utilize these accidents to convert such a place into a dwelling; they also have many well-made huts. In these particulars they differ from wild beasts, but I think in most other particulars they very much resemble them. As for their being the ferocious savages represented to us, I must say that they appeared more afraid of us than we were of them. I formed an idea that they had a cowed, hunted look, and well they may have, as the Egyptians squeeze all they can out of them on one side, and the Abyssinians on the other, and the reason they live in such places amongst rocks difficult of access is that if attacked, they can roll these rocks down on their assailants. The attire of both men and women is extremely simple and scanty. The women wear a short skirt reaching from the waist to the knees, most of them a large ring in one nostril. Many of them are not bad looking; their black hair is not profuse, but inclined to be frizzly; this is plaited down, whilst bits of metal, brass rings or beads, are frequently interlaced. All have lovely teeth. In stature they are rather short and when young possess rather graceful, well-formed figures. Either beads, metal, or some other ornament surrounds the neck, the arm, just above the elbow, the wrists and ankles. Very many, both men and women (the Arabs as well), have the scars of burns about the size of a shilling. I do not know whether it is so in all cases, but in very many, if they are in pain in any part of the body, they apply a hot iron button (technically known as the actual cautery). A very common custom is to decorate the chest, abdomen, and back (sometimes one of these, sometimes all of them) with a series of little cuts, into which a dye called kohl is rubbed in. Kohl is also much used by the Basé to stain their eyelids all round, which produces a bluish-black stain. Whilst speaking of this dye, I may say that it is supposed this was the very thing which Jezebel used to improve her personal appearance. The difference between the Basé men and women in the matter of dress and ornaments is that the men, instead of a short tope or skirt, wear a bit of thin leather round their loins (like a rather scant pair of bathing drawers), and a scratcher in their hair. I saw some moderately big boys attired in the most inexpensive suit conceivable; namely, an anklet and bracelet of metal, and a bit of a porcupine's quill in the left nostril.

Speaking generally, the men are well-formed, agile-looking fellows. These Basé people are quite hemmed in in their small country, on the one hand by the Abyssinians and on the other sides by different tribes of Arabs, with whom they appear to have little or no communication or dealings, and if they venture out of their own country they are hunted down by the Arabs just like wild animals. The Arabs of the Soudan are darker than the Abyssinians, but the Basé are much darker than the Arabs and speak a different language. The Basé are quite a different race to their neighbours, and more nearly approach the negro type. They are blacker than the Arabs, but not the coal-black of the negro; their hair is shorter, more crisp and woolly, than the Arabs, but not the absolute wool of the negro. The Arabs have good regular features, lips and noses like our own; the Basé are the contrary, and more resemble the negro in this respect and their high cheek-bones, but they are not nearly so pronounced as the negro. Their foreheads, as a rule, are rather narrow and receding. I was obliged perforce to depend on Sheik Ahmed, and more particularly on Beyrumfi, for all the information I could glean respecting these people. They say they have no religion. Sheik

Ahmed, speaking very contemptuously of them, says "that they have a rain-maker who promises rain, when it is pretty sure to come; but if he makes several promises and the rain does not come, he goes"—to that bourne from whence no traveller shall return. In the little matter of marriage, their laws and ceremonies are extremely simple, for they marry their sisters, their daughters, their cousins, and their aunts, possibly their mothers and grandmothers. Courtship is brief and primitive. A Basé man fancies a Basé girl (presumably not his own daughter); he tells the nearest male relatives so, father or brother—good; he then presents him with a few yards of calico or some skins, the same also to his bride, and she becomes his.

Now with regard to their diet. I cannot help thinking that this admits of considerable improvement. As they are not possessed of large flocks and herds like their neighbours, the Beni-Amirs, they have not much milk or meat, neither have they so much dhurra as an article of diet. They obtain meat occasionally when they can ensnare an animal; the *kind* of meat is rather a secondary consideration for they will eat the meat of lion, panther, elephant, monkeys, lizards, or giraffes with as much gusto as that of antelope or buffalo. They are not so particular, either, as they ought to be, for they consume all except the skin and bones. They also eat the roots of young palm trees, the outer covering of the dhoum palm nut, nebbuck, and hegleek nuts, the fruit of the baobob, wild honey, and a certain, or rather an uncertain, quantity of milk and dhurra. They do not indulge in baked baby, and I am quite sure that their carnal longings are never satiated with cold or roast missionary, as there are no missionaries there, but it has occurred to me that this place is virgin soil for missionary enterprise, as there does not appear to be any religion that requires eradicating from their minds.

In the evening of the 2nd February a dirty-looking old fellow (a sheik from Aidaro), paid us a visit, bringing with him a gourd of wild honey as a peace offering, made "aman" with us, and of course received his presents.

I was much struck when visiting the village with their beautifully made baskets; so closely woven are they as to enable them to carry milk or water in them without a drop oozing through.

CHAPTER XVII.

WE LEAVE KOOLOOKOO, ACCOMPANIED BY A NUMBER OF THE BASÉ—THE MAGIC LANTERN—SEE BUFFALO AND GIRAFFE FOR THE FIRST TIME—TWO BUFFALOS KILLED—A BASÉ FEAST—CURIOUS BASÉ DANCE—THEY DRY THEIR MEAT ON LINES IN THE SUN—A WOUNDED BUFFALO—HOODOO, CHIEF SHEIK OF THE BASÉ, VISITS US—A COLUMN OF SAND—A LEPER—THE BASÉ SQUABBLE OVER THE MEAT—WE ARRIVE AT ABYSSINIA.

On the 3rd February we made a further advance, starting at 11 a.m., and encamping at 4 p.m., again on the river-bed, at Aibara. This day we marched for the space of five hours through a forest; the heat was very great, and the ground over which we travelled was full of large, deep cracks, often two or three inches wide, caused by the contraction of the earth, which had been subjected to a continuous baking by the hot sun since the rainy season. Oftentimes could be seen the great footprint of an elephant, now quite a moulded one, having been there since the rainy season. On leaving Koolookoo we were accompanied by about 80 or 100 of the inhabitants, having nothing with them but spear and shield. We knew what this meant—that we should have to provide them with food—a rather large undertaking considering that our own party, including camel-men, horse-boys, and servants, numbered about 40 or 50. Accordingly a delicate hint was conveyed to our new body-guard, that our own people would first of all have to be provided with food; then if there was plenty of meat to spare they would be quite welcome to it. To this arrangement they amiably acceded. On *terra firma* we could have made a good stand with our rifles and revolvers in case of attack, but had these Basé thought proper, at a preconcerted signal, to make an onslaught on our long straggling caravan, I am afraid we should have fared very badly, notwithstanding our being well armed. However, I think their principal reason for coming with us was to have a continual feast of meat, an article of diet they were capable of stowing away as capaciously as a lion would do, and with as little ceremony. In the evening three sheiks paid us a visit, each going through the ceremony of "aman." After dinner the magic lantern was exhibited, and this excited their astonishment even more than it did that of the Beni-Amirs. I do not intend to go into a description much of hunting-scenes, as they would occupy too much space, and I do not think that the frequent repetition of such scenes would be interesting to the generality of my readers; besides which I have no doubt Mr. F. L. James has done this in his book. Suffice it to say that as there was abundance of game of every description, scarcely a day passed without plenty being brought into camp.

February 4th.—Off at 10.30 a.m., halt at 5 p.m.; pitch tents at Maissasser, on the bank of the Mareb, and quite close to jungle. About 12 o'clock, as our camels were slowly winding along the bed of the Mareb, a grand bull buffalo, an enormous beast, dashed right across in front of us, raising quite a cloud of dust. This was the first buffalo we had seen; at half-past 4 p.m. we saw three more, and just afterwards a giraffe. There was a good deal of chuckling now at the prospect of sport in store, and we resolved to encamp here for the next two or three days. To-day we saw miles of country on fire. The country looks much greener in this neighbourhood; trees and jungle abundant, and water much nearer to the surface.

February 5th.—Last night, about 11 o'clock, just as I had gone to sleep, I was considerably startled by several rifle shots, one after the other. In an instant I was out of bed, rifle in hand, rushed out of my tent in my slippers and night shirt, not knowing what to think; the first idea naturally was that we were being attacked. Messrs. F. L. James and Phillipps, who slept in another tent, were also out, clad in the same airy costume as myself, and, like me, each with a rifle in his hand. All this was the work of a minute — we had scarcely time to say, "Whatever is the meaning of it all?" when close behind my tent, amongst the thick stems of the tall grass, there was a sound as of a rushing mighty wind. This was enough; the whole affair was explained at once; we knew directly that this was nothing less than a herd of buffalos, and I am very thankful that they just avoided my tent, which could as easily have been upset by them as a box of matches. It seems that just after we had gone to bed, the others, Messrs. Colvin, P. Aylmer, W. D. and A. James, "from information received," took their rifles (it was a bright moonlight night) and stole out cautiously to the edge of the jungle. There they saw a herd of buffalos drinking, and into it they discharged their rifles with pretty good effect, for about 11 o'clock this morning one of the herd was found dead in the jungle pretty near to camp. A camel was sent to the spot to bring home the quarters for food, and the head, of course, as a trophy. A great number of the Basé were pretty quickly on the spot; then there ensued such a scene as I had never before witnessed, and which almost baffles description. I will, however, endeavour to describe it, as some of my readers might like to be furnished with particulars. Invalids, persons of delicate organization and others, might, however, like to omit this little account of a Basé feast, which I assure them will not have an appetising effect. I may here say that there is not the least occasion for me to draw on my imagination and indulge in what some people facetiously call "crackers," which I have not and shall not do, as there is no necessity for doing so, there being abundance of material of a strictly veracious character which I cull from my diary, written carefully down at the time. Incredible as some accounts may appear, I must ask my readers to accept these facts without the usual formula *cum grano salis*. Very well, then, I will write down, and you, reader, can read, mark, and inwardly digest (if you please) *without* the usual proverbial pinch of salt, a description of a scene that I was an eye-witness of, and if I should somewhat interfere with your enjoyment, when called from labour to refreshment, don't blame me, but blame the Basé. All I can say is, that this is not what incredulous people call "a traveller's tale," but a "true story." Do not say, "It strikes me that he doth protest too much."

I recollect to have seen somewhere or other a pamphlet entitled "The Stomach and Its Trials." That useful organ in the human body of Basé does not appear to be subject to usual inconveniences, but accommodates itself to circumstances, not unlike an india-rubber bag. The only trials I saw them suffer was trying how much they could stow away without causing a rupture of that viscera.

Well, to continue. As soon as the animal was opened they fell upon the intestines like hungry wolves. Oh! such a scramble for tit-bits. There were our dusky friends very soon ankle-deep in the viscera, and about 20 pairs of hands clutching at them. Two would perhaps get hold of the same piece, and pull away like a couple of dogs, until a knife produced a solution of continuity. Another group could be seen hacking away at pieces of the liver, and cramming the warm, quivering morsels into their mouths. One could be seen stuffing a lump of fat into his mouth with one hand, the other at the same time would be industriously employed in rubbing this adipose tissue into his hair. Another appeared to have a predilection for kidneys; and so this disgusting feast went on, until the whole interior of the animal was consumed, without such absurd preliminaries as cooking.

One would naturally suppose that I should be busy at my medicine-chest next day, but not one of them even so much as troubled me for a pill afterwards. They might truly say, "We are fearfully and wonderfully made;" and after this exhibition of digestive powers, I should be obliged to coincide with them. When they had gorged themselves like boa-constrictors, I should not exaggerate if I said that they presented a most filthy and disgusting spectacle. Their proportions were quite aldermanic, and their mouths, faces, and arms up to the elbows were smeared with fat and gore. Had this buffalo lived a month or two longer she would have become a mother.

We do not consider very young veal wholesome, but whether the Basé thought this *very* young buffalo would be a delicacy they must not touch I know not; at all events it was brought into camp. We gave it the Basé, who appeared quite pleased. In less than ten minutes afterwards we saw three of them engaged in tearing it limb from limb, and eating it without going through the formality of cooking. The quarters of buffalo, senior, were divided between our men and Basé; the hide was cut up into sections and given to the sheiks and others to make into shields.

Messrs. Colvin and Aylmer shot to-day two mehedehét. This is a very beautiful antelope, possessing a very rough coat, a fine pair of horns, slightly curved and annulated; is about 13 hands high, and in colour much resembles the red deer. Messrs. F. L. and W. James stalked an ostrich for two hours, but did not succeed in bringing him down.

We were encamped on a little plateau by the side of the Mareb, close to a great jungle. On the opposite side of this wide river-bed were very many trees of different kinds, and on both sides rocky mountains. Just by our camp, on the sandy river-bed, the Basé were encamped. Notwithstanding their mid-day feast on the uncooked internals of the buffalo, they were ready and willing for another set to in the evening—this time of cooked meat. Whether this second gorge had a stimulating and intoxicating effect on them I don't know, but just as we were off to our various tents for the night, at 9.30 p.m., we heard strange noises issuing from the Basé camp. Messrs. A. James, Colvin, and I were curious to ascertain the cause, so down we went amongst them, and this is what we saw, and what I have some difficulty in describing:—

All the Basé were engaged in a peculiar dance,

four or six abreast, and so close to each other as to be almost touching; those behind always treading in the footsteps of those in front, whilst each one held his spear aloft at arm's-length. What they were saying I don't exactly know, but it was a dance of joy celebrating their feast of meat. A few words as a solo would be sung, then all would join in chorus. This went on for about half an hour; then they broke up and went through a wild war-dance—now flying forwards and darting out their spears at an imaginary enemy whilst protecting themselves with their shields, then nimbly retreating, crouching and springing like wild cats. It was a novel and singular spectacle to see nearly a hundred of these black savages, with their glittering spears, agile as monkeys, leaping in and out between about 30 flickering fires on the river-bed. Like the Pharisee of old, I could not help (mentally) exclaiming, "Thank God I am not as these men are."

I then retired to rest, and slept peacefully and soundly until the following morning.

February 6th.—Soon after breakfast we saw, stretched from tree to tree near the camp, what appeared like clothes-lines with stockings suspended on them to dry. The Basé had made ropes out of the palm-leaves, and on these the meat which they could not then dispose of hung in strips and festoons to dry. When dried, they would stuff them into gazelle skins, or bags of some kind, for future use. To-day about 40 of them returned to Koolookoo, well-charged with meat, both in their own skins and that of gazelles; the rest remained with us.

This morning another buffalo, which was wounded on the night of the 4th, was found, but not dead. He, however, received his *coup de grace* from Mr. Colvin's rifle, but not until he had made a furious charge, though so badly wounded, fortunately without any ill-results. A wounded buffalo is about as dangerous and fierce an animal as can be met with, and will charge most savagely if he is only within five minutes of death, provided his limbs will support him. We had plenty of meat brought into camp, for in addition to this buffalo, two nellut, a mora, and two buffalos were shot. Temperature at 1.30, solar thermometer 150°, wet bulb 66°, dry bulb in shade 90°.

This has been rather an exciting day, as Mr. W. James saw and stalked three giraffes, but was not successful in getting near enough for a shot. Sali, the tracker, saw three ostriches and a rhinoceros, the latter pretty close to him, and I two full-grown elephants a distance off, but none of them were bagged. No doubt had these elephants been followed up for a day or so they could have been got at, but they were not. Messrs. A. James and

Colvin followed them up next day for many miles, but not far enough.

February 7th.—Messrs. Colvin and A. James, who went in quest of the two elephants, returned about 4 p.m., without having seen them. In the evening Hoodoo, chief sheik of the Basé, paid us a visit, bringing with him a pot of wild honey as a present. He went through the formality of making "aman" with us, after which he squatted on his haunches in the usual native fashion.

During a long pow-wow which ensued, I was busy making mental notes of Hoodoo, not by any means complimentary to that august personage. He was a dirty-looking old fellow, as scantily dressed as his colleagues, nearly black, with an ill-favoured, sinister cast of countenance, and not by any means a man whom I should place unbounded confidence in. He received several presents, amongst others a bernouse and a rather gorgeous-looking abia (a cloak-looking kind of thing), with gold braid ornamentation around the neck. He seemed mightily pleased with these. He then joined his comrades' camp, and we went to our dinner.

This was rather a nice camping-ground, but quite unsheltered from the sun by trees. However, we provided a shelter by cutting down some young trees, fixing them in the ground and making a covering of matting, tall grass, and palm leaves, which were obtainable close by. So great was the heat now that the ink dried in my pen ere I could write three lines on a page of foolscap. However, I was fortunately provided with Mappin and Webb's stylographic pen, which is really invaluable in such hot climates. Always about 12 or 1 o'clock a slight breeze would spring up, producing occasionally a very curious phenomenon. A very high column of dust (perhaps half a mile in height) would come whirling and waltzing along right through the middle of the camp, and so long as it was not hidden by trees or mountains I could see it spinning on and on, looking in the distance like a column of smoke. A good deal of sport was obtained in this neighbourhood, chiefly buffalos and antelopes of different kinds.

February 8th.—We struck our tents and were in marching order by 11 a.m. After an easy journey through some pretty good country, where vegetation was abundant, we encamped at 3 p.m. on a nice bit of land by the Mareb amongst many tall trees and shrubs, which afforded a good shade. Here we purposed remaining for a week at least, as big game of all kinds was plentiful, and here for the first time we found rhinoceros' tracks. This place is called Maiambasar, and is situated on the border of Abyssinia. Water is near the surface here. During the journey I have noticed that as we have got nearer to Abyssinia we have found the water nearer the surface. We heard panthers, hyænas, and lions last night near camp, but lions are not so plentiful as they were a few days ago.

February 9th.—Abdullah, a black boy, who looks after my camel, has been walking very lame during the last few days, having considerable swelling at the knee. I find he has a large abscess, produced by a guinea-worm. He comes from Algeden, which is about five days from here between Kassala and Souheet. He says guinea-worm is very common there and on the White Nile.

Strange to say, all returned to camp in the evening without having obtained game of any kind, although out all day. Mr. Alymer, whilst in search of game, suddenly came upon a rather curious scene. There, on the mountain side, scarcely sheltered from the burning rays of the sun, was an old man suffering from leprosy, miles away, apparently, from any human being or habitation. Food and water had been placed near him, to which he could help himself. Mr. Aylmer informed me that the surrounding atmosphere was charged with the stench arising from the decomposed food which was scattered around the place. I should say that most probably that old man furnished a meal for one of the wild beasts ere long.

February 10th.—Two buffalos and two nellut

killed this day. One, a bull buffalo, was an enormous beast, and probably the hero of many a fight, for one of his horns had been knocked short off, one eye knocked out, whilst his forehead was covered with scars—evidently a disreputable, cantankerous old buffalo. His carcase was given to the Basé, who were well pleased with the donation. The Koolookoo Basé who came with us through the country would, I daresay, have divided the meat amicably between them, as their Sheik was with them, but their number had been materially increased by other Basé.

In the evening, during the division of the spoil, just outside our camp, a great difference of opinion prevailed as to *meum* and *tuum*. Knives, clubs, spears, and staves were freely brandished amid a chorus of yells and shouts, ending in a scramble for the joints and pieces of meat. Some of them secured a reasonable share, and trotted with it; others, again, not so fortunate, would intercept a fugitive caressing, perhaps, the thigh of the deceased buffalo. Then a desperate struggle would ensue between them, five or six pulling away in different directions. Fortunately all was settled without bloodshed, peace reigned in the camp, and we all retired to our respective tents at a respectable hour.

CHAPTER XVIII.

THE DEMBELAS ATTACK US, MAHOMET WOUNDED, NARROW ESCAPE OF TWO OF OUR PARTY—ACTIVITY IN CAMP, WE MAKE A ZAREEBA AND FIRE THE COUNTRY—HOLD A COUNCIL OF WAR—OUR SILENT AND DANGEROUS RIDE—HOODOO'S SAGACITY—ARRIVAL IN CAMP OF MAHOMET, WOUNDED—WE RETREAT — MAHOMET'S DEATH AND BURIAL.

FEBRUARY 11TH, 1882, was the most memorable day of the whole campaign. Thinking it was not safe to leave the camp without protectors, Messrs. W. D. and A. James and I remained in camp, whilst Messrs. F. L. James and Colvin went out in one direction and Phillipps and Alymer in another, in search of big game. Each party went out mounted on ponies, which had been bought for the purpose at Kassala and Heikota. Each party took an agreegeer, or huntsman, a horse-boy, camel-boy, and camel with them, the latter for the purpose of carrying home the game. They started soon after 8 a.m., Messrs. Phillipps and Aylmer went in the direction of some mountains on the Abyssinian border, whilst Messrs. James and Colvin took the opposite side of the Mareb. We amused ourselves in camp in reading, writing letters, or posting up diaries. Keeping my diary carefully and correctly posted up day by day was a duty which I most religiously attended to before ever I retired to rest, however fatigued I may have been by the day's march. Incidents and impressions written down at the time are more likely to be correct than if left to memory. From my diary I quote the following particulars:—

"About 1.30 p.m., just as we were about to sit down to luncheon, Messrs. Aylmer and Phillipps came into camp looking considerably chop-fallen and exhausted, and having only one horse between them. Of course we did not expect either party home until 5 or 6 p.m., so I said to Aylmer—

"'Hallo! how is it you are back so soon, and looking so precious serious?'

"'I can tell you, doctor, this is no laughing matter,' said he, 'for we have been attacked by the Abyssinians or Dembelas, and very likely they will soon be down on our camp.'

"This certainly did look a serious business,

especially as we had no zareeba round the camp; so I said —

"'Well, the best thing we can do is to have our luncheon at once; then we shall be more fit for work.'"

The wisdom of this suggestion was apparent, and at once acted upon. Whilst it was being brought I strapped on my revolver, brought out my diary and entered the above conversation. Mahomet Sali and others were at once sent out as scouts in search of Messrs. James and Colvin, with a promise of five dollars each to those who brought them into camp. We then sat down to luncheon, and the following account was given of this affair, and was duly entered in my diary immediately afterwards, as we did not know when we might be attacked, and I was desirous of leaving my diary posted up complete to latest date.

Aylmer's story:—"We had got about eight or nine miles from camp on the sandy river-bed, quite in a hollow, precipitous rocks and trees on each side of us, when suddenly about 30 strangers, who turned out to be Dembelas, appeared. We thought they were Abyssinians, because they were so much lighter in colour than Arabs, and, of course, quite different in every respect from the Basé. Some of them seized our hands and commenced kissing them profusely, exclaiming 'Aman, aman,' at the same time beckoning us to lay down our rifles. Now, although we thought they were friendly, we did not think it wise to be so confiding as this, until Mahomet, the agreegeer (who, we supposed, knew more of the customs of these people than we did), lay down his, beckoning us to do the same, saying it would be better to do so. One fellow, wearing a felt hat, was more demonstrative even than the others. Well, we followed Mahomet's example; no sooner had we done so (we had four rifles with us and about 50 cartridges) than they were immediately seized, and a struggle ensued for their possession. The man wearing the felt hat seized a valuable elephant rifle, vaulted on to the back of Mr. Phillipps's horse and galloped off. Attached to the saddle of that horse was his revolver, a number of cartridges, and a field-glass. The horse-boy vanished like smoke, whilst his horse was taken possession of by another of the enemy. They attempted to spear the camel-boy, missed him and speared the camel. Phillipps received a blow from the butt-end of a rifle which would have prostrated him had not his helmet protected his head. He, however, turned round, closed with his assailant, and succeeded in wrenching the rifle from him. I pulled the trigger of my revolver, but on account of sand, which obstructed it, I could not discharge it.

"In the hubbub which ensued Mahomet could nowhere be seen, and about 8 or 10 Basé (who had accompanied us, with the intention of having a feast and cutting up the animal into quarters) vanished at once. We were now alone, and by this time there were about 100 yelling demons brandishing their spears, whooping and leaping about. Under such circumstances we thought discretion the better part of valour, so we fled with one horse between us, and have made the best of our way to camp, riding and walking by turns."

This really was very alarming news, and we quite expected that we should soon be fully occupied in defending ourselves from an attack.

We now resolved to fire the country all round and construct a strong zareeba. Before I fell to with the axe I once more sought out my diary and chronicled the above. All then fell to with a will, cutting down all the prickly trees in the neighbourhood, dragging them round the camp and so forming a very strong zareeba. This was no joke when the solar thermometer registered about 150°, and the heat was 100° in the shade.

Whilst we were thus employed the horse-boy made his appearance, streaming with blood, his flesh being torn by the cruel thorns as he rushed blindly on. We now set fire to all the tall grass and bushes in the neighbourhood. The terrific speed with which it spread was surprising, miles of country were soon in flames. The crackling of the grass and trees resembled more than anything else the most fierce hailstorm I ever saw.

Now the camel-boy turned up and this was his account of the affair:—Just as he leaped off the camel he saw Mahomet on the ground, whilst one of the Dembelas darted his spear at him several times; then left him writhing. He went to his assistance, and helped him along some distance, whilst poor Mahomet supported his intestines (which had gushed out) in his tope. At last the poor fellow sank down under a tree, saying—

"I can go no further; I shall soon die. Save yourself; make haste to camp and tell the gentlemen to make a strong zareeba at once as they will certainly be attacked, probably to-night."

By this time Messrs. F. James and Colvin, who had been found by the scouts, arrived. We at once held a council of war, and determined not only to go in search of Mahomet, but to attack the Dembelas if we could find them, leaving two of our company in camp to command the men in case of attack. All the neighbouring Basé, we found, had bolted—Elongi, the Sheik from Koolookoo, and his men, alone remained, and promised to stand by us and fight for us if necessary.

Our armoury consisted of about 22 shot-guns and rifles, and about a dozen six-chambered revolvers. All the camel-men and native servants were armed with spear and shield. Having provided ourselves each with rifle, revolver, and cartridges, our two European servants; Suleiman, Ali, and Cheriff also; we called up our native servants. To the most trusty of these, including Beyrumfi, our guide, Mahomet Sali, Sali, the tracker, and Ali Bacheet, the head camel-man, we entrusted the remainder of our firearms, but unfortunately most of them had to be instructed in the use of them.

I provided myself with a few bandages, lint, and my pocket case of surgical instruments, and feeling that we were embarking on a very perilous enterprise, left instructions respecting my immortal diary, which would convey full information up to the time of our departure from camp.

Just as we were getting into the saddle who should turn up but the Chief Sheik, Hoodoo, who left our last camping place the morning after his arrival. He *appeared* surprised at all this commotion. Whether he was really so or not I do not know, but I am sure, from the very first, I did not feel that I should repose in him the trustful confidence of an innocent child.

Our little army consisted now of Messrs. F. L. and A. James, Phillipps, Aylmer, myself, six of our men with firearms, the Koolookoo Sheik, and 15 of his men with spear and shield. We started off, on what *might* prove to be our last journey, about 4 p.m. And I think we shall all remember that silent ride of eight miles up the sandy river-bed of the Mareb to Abyssinia, shaded often by trees which thickly adorned the banks. We well knew, as we approached Abyssinia, that each bush may conceal an enemy, who might at any moment spring out on us unawares, and knowing this, each one clutched his rifle with a firm grip, ready for instant use, and determined to sell his life dearly if the worst came to the worst. I felt that our present position was something like that of Fitz-James, when he held the interesting conversation with Rhoderick Dhu which Sir Walter Scott so graphically describes —

> Instant, through copse and heath, arose
> Bonnets, and spears, and bended bows;
> On right, on left, above, below,
> Sprang up at once the lurking foe;
> From shingles grey their lances start,
> The bracken-bush sends forth the dart,
> The rushes and the willow-wand
> Are bristling into axe and brand,
> And every tuft of broom gives life
> To plaided warrior armed for strife.

> That whistle garrisoned the glen
> At once with full five hundred men,
> As if the yawning hill to heaven
> A subterranean host had given.

No one spoke above a whisper as we stole silently and quickly on, until at last we arrived at the scene of the scuffle.

> It was a wild and strange retreat,
> As e'er was trod by outlaw's feet.
> The dell, upon the mountain's crest,
> Yawned like a gash on warrior's breast.

Here, and in the neighbourhood, we searched about for Mahomet or his assailants. We spent two hours thus unsuccessfully, until darkness warned us it was time to return to camp.

> The shades of eve come quickly down,
> The woods are wrapped in deeper brown,
> The owl awakens from her dell,
> The fox is heard upon the fell;
> Enough remains of glimmering light
> To guide the wanderer's steps aright,
> Yet not enough from far to show
> His figure to the watchful foe.

As we were returning, our attention was attracted to a large baobob tree full of vultures. Sali and Mahomet Sali thought we might find Mahomet's bones, picked clean by these foul birds, near the tree. We, therefore, searched that neighbourhood, but found him not.

Darkness had come on ere we had retraced our way any distance, and we returned as silently as we had advanced, keeping well on the alert until we neared the camp.

> In dread, and danger, all alone,
> Famished and chilled, through ways unknown,
> Tangled and steep, we journeyed on;
> Till, as a rock's huge point we turned,
> Our camp fire close before us burned.

It was about 10 p.m. by the time we got to camp. Dinner was soon on the table. This we at once discussed, also our plans for the next day. The line of action determined on was this—sentries were to be posted about the camp, and a few outside to guard against surprise. These, again, would be looked after by Suleiman. We should load up in the morning, and return to our former camp, first of all having another hunt for Mahomet. We could not divest our minds of the idea that we ought to attack these Dembelas if we could find them, and thought that perhaps our dirty old friend Hoodoo would assist us with some of the Basé. Accordingly, whilst seated round the camp fire after dinner, he was sounded on the matter, and promised £100 if he would lend a 100 of his people next morning. Hoodoo mentally said, " Hoo dont." As a cautious look stole over his black face he raised his eyes from the camp fire for a moment, stealing a furtive glance at us; then, as he slowly shook his head, replied —

"I and my people will be here after you are gone, and if I was to do so the Abyssinians would come down on us, burn our villages, kill our men, and take our women and children as slaves."

I assure you, reader, that when that old man shook his head he did not shake all the sense out of it. There was a good deal of logic in his remarks, and it is highly probable that had the old man accepted the offer made, he and many of his braves would soon have been translated (to use an orthodox phrase), and the merry dollars would have danced off into possession of the Dembelas; therefore the old man " deserved well of his country." Indeed, his diplomatic action would almost entitle him to the appellation of a grand old man, though he did not look it.

February 12th.—The stillness of the night fortunately was not broken by the clash of arms, and I awoke, refreshed by a sound sleep, at 6 a.m. Whilst we were at breakfast Mr. F. James proposed that we again ask Sheik Hoodoo to let us have 200 of his men to assist us in making a raid on the enemy, and if he would not, that we should send the caravan back to the last camping place, and take about 20 of our own, as we were not at all satisfied to leave poor Mahomet (who might still be living) to his fate. Hoodoo was accordingly approached with the same result as before, he adding —

"I am at peace with them, and I cannot make your quarrel mine."

The old man was about right. Six camels had yesterday been sent to Amadeb, a garrison town, for dhurra. We therefore had to divide their loads with the remaining camels. When most of the camels had their loads on, we told our men that we should want some of them to go with us. This (with the exception of about half-a-dozen) they flatly refused to do, saying that they were engaged as camel-drivers not to fight the Dembelas. They were evidently bent on retreating from the Abyssinian frontier whether we were or not. Suleiman, who knew these people pretty well, now stepped forward —

"What good you gentlemen go fight Dembelas? You only six or seven, the Dembelas hundreds. You do no good. Mahomet, he dead now, and the vultures eat him. If you go, these men go off with their camels. How, then, we get out of the country? The Basé and Abyssinians then turn round and kill us all."

This was good reasoning. Abdullah now brought my camel ready for starting, so—pending the settlement of "to be or not to be"—I spread my rug on the ground and lay down to read a book, with my rifle by my side. It was now about 11 o'clock. I had not been here above ten minutes when I saw everyone rushing across the camp, rifle in hand, shouting — "Hakeem," and "Doctor, doctor — quick!" I was up in an instant, rifle in hand, and darted across in the same direction as the others, naturally thinking—" The time has come at last. We are in for it now with the Dembelas."

It was not an attack at all, but a most pitiful sight. There was poor Mahomet, who had managed to crawl into camp, then sank exhausted on the ground. The poor fellow turned his large soft-looking eyes piteously on to me. He was supporting with his hands and tope as much viscera— covered with sand dried on it, and quite adherent— as would fill a good-sized washing-basin. My rifle was at once dropped for my dressing-case; water was obtained, the opening (made by a spear) slightly enlarged, the viscera washed, replaced in the cavity of the abdomen, and the opening secured by a suture or two. He was in a state of collapse, and death pretty certain. He had also a wound in the fleshy part of the arm, and two others in the muscles of the back, just by the spine. Whilst I attended to these, some extract of beef and brandy was obtained, a fire soon kindled, and a good supply of brandy and beef-tea, administered, which soon revived him. An angarep was then rigged up, and twelve of the Basé (six at a time) were told off at a dollar each to carry him on to the next camp. I followed close by, giving him brandy and beef-tea every half-hour; but all was of no avail, for he died at 9 o'clock next morning. He was a Mahomedan. A tope as a shroud, with some needles and thread, were given to the friends. They would not, however, use the needle and thread, preferring the shreds of the palm leaf. A grave was dug near the camp, and there the poor fellow was buried; Suleiman remarking, "These Basé, they soon have Mahomet up; they not leave that good tope there long." And I have no doubt he was right in his prediction.

Mahomet's account of the scrimmage, and his escape to camp, was this: He stated that when the Abyssinians, or Dembelas, said "aman" it meant "Put down your arms and take your lives; we are stronger than you, so you must give up all you have." He noticed that they were tremendously out-numbered, so thought it was the best thing to do. When he saw Mr. Phillipps trying to recover his rifle, another Abyssinian was about to strike him with the butt-end of a rifle; he rushed to his assistance, and it was then he received the fatal spear thrust in his abdomen, causing him to fall down on the sand, where he received two or three more, as detailed before. When everyone ran away, he tried to struggle on, succeeding ere night came on in getting pretty near to camp by alternately walking and resting awhile, until at last he sat under a tree quite exhausted. He says that he both saw and heard us when we were returning after our search for him, and that he cried out, but could not make us hear. The greater part of the way to camp next morning he accomplished by crawling on his hands and knees.

Who can imagine the sufferings of the poor fellow—out all night, sitting with his back to a tree? He said he felt the cold very much; and well he might, as, although the thermometer registered 101° F. in the shade at 1 p.m., it dropped to 37° by 11 p.m. He passed the night in constant expectation of a wild beast coming to tear him in pieces. We were very glad that we had him with us during his last few hours, where [he] received every attention that we could bestow.

February 13th.—Mahomet was buried, as I said before. Little was done to-day; one nellut and three gazelles were shot.

CHAPTER XIX.

MESSRS. JAMES AND PHILLIPPS START ON A VISIT TO BASA-LULU—CURIOUS WAY OF SHAVING CHILDREN'S HEADS—A DISGUSTING BASÉ—THE CAMEL-DRIVERS BECOME MUTINOUS—INTENDED ATTACK BY BASÉ—WE FIRE THE COUNTRY AND MAKE A ZAREEBA—ENCAMP AT WO-AMMA—TROUBLE AGAIN WITH CAMEL-MEN—LIONS DISTURB US—ARRIVAL AT HEIKOTA—A TALE OF BLOOD AND SLAVERY.

FEBRUARY 14TH.—Made a rather short march, and encamped at Aibara, on some table-land by the Mareb. Ere doing so we had to clear away a quantity of mimosa bushes and young palms; then construct a zareeba. Mr. Phillipps, at the request of one of the Basé, shot a monkey to-day. This was skinned and eaten by them in the evening, and was, no doubt, looked upon as a delicate morsel, probably as much so as grouse or partridge is with us.

February 15th.—This morning, at 9 a.m., Messrs. Phillipps and F. James went off to Amadeb, to complain to Rasalulu, a deputy of King John of Abyssinia, about our late attack, and endeavour to get their rifles back. Whether they ever succeeded in doing so I don't know; but I should think probably not.

To-day we lost another camel; this makes the sixth we have lost in the Basé country. A camel is a particularly stupid kind of animal, and does not seem to know what is good for him, or rather, what is bad for him, for he will frequently eat a very poisonous green-looking shrub, called "heikabeet." This appears to produce considerable pain, and, as far as I could make out, inflammation of the intestines. I brought some of it home with the intention of having it analysed, but somehow or other it has got lost.

February 16th.—The Basé women and children, when we first came here, were rather shy, and ran away from us as if we were monsters of iniquity; now they appear to be getting quite tame, and are continually hanging about the camp. The heads of the children are curiously trimmed, according to fancy, just as they are at Kassala. All kinds of fantastical devices are arranged, with the aid of a razor, just as a gardener operates on a box bush in

England. I have seen a child's head shaved completely, with the exception of a tuft of hair just over the right temple; another will have a tuft on each side, whilst a third will have those and one on the crown in addition; another will have several other little islands, and another a tuft running from the forehead to the back of the head, just for all the world like a clown in a circus, and so on.

Ali Bacheet to-day injured his foot with an axe. I bathed it, and whilst getting a bandage one of the Basé diligently employed himself in sucking it, then rinsed his mouth two or three times with the bloody water which had washed his foot. This I thought was a somewhat nasty proceeding, but I did not waste my breath in expostulating with these men of primitive habits.

Five tetél were shot to-day. In the evening our men with the dhurra from Amadeb returned.

February 17th.—Last night our camel-drivers, with their singing, and hyænas howling and laughing, much disturbed our slumbers. This morning the Basé here were very uneasy in their minds, being under the impression that we had sent to Amadeb for Turkish soldiers. However, I think we made them believe—what really was the case—that Messrs. James and Phillipps had gone to lay a complaint about the Dembelas.

Just after dinner, whilst we were sitting round the camp fire smoking the pipe of peace, the camelmen whom we had hired at Kassala came in a body to us, saying they wanted to return to Kassala, stating as a reason that they were afraid of the Basé and Abyssinians, they being so few in number. We gave them distinctly to understand that we were neither afraid of them nor the Basé; for the latter we had plenty of bullets if they interfered with us, and for our camel-drivers who did so we had the coorbatch, and so we dismissed them to chew the cud of reflection.

Two tetél shot to-day by Messrs. Colvin and A. James, and several beautiful birds by me. We are passing a very peaceful and calm existence at present, little to do except to amuse ourselves as fancy dictates. Some go out on horseback in search of antelopes or buffalos; I generally content myself just here with taking out a shot-gun after breakfast, prowling round in quest of some of the beautiful plumaged birds which are so numerous, and in the afternoon write up my diary and prepare letters for post. After that read one of the many interesting books which we have until 6 p.m., when we all have our evening bath, just before dinner, which was always ready at 7 p.m. After dinner we sit round the camp fire and chat over the social pipe, when some go to bed, and I skin and prepare my birds to bring home.

We had a capital library with us, and were never short of most interesting works, such as Macaulay's Essays, Sir Samuel Baker's "Nile Tributaries," Trollope's, Dicken's, Thackeray's, Disraeli's, and other works.

February 18th.—A young baboon and a small monkey were captured yesterday; this day they are quite tame, allowing us to stroke them without exhibiting any signs of fear. Unfortunately the young baboon had been injured in the thigh by a spear which severed the muscles, causing the wound to gape very much. The flies annoyed him so much that I determined to put him under chloroform, and bring the edges together by means of two or three silver sutures. I therefore put him on the table, where he lay as quietly and sensibly as any human being, looking up at me with his nice brown eyes in a very human-being like kind of way. He almost seemed to say, "I know it is for my good, doctor; don't hurt me more than you can help, and be quick about it." He took the chloroform very well, and when complete anæsthesia had been produced I relinquished the post of chloroformist to an assistant, with suitable instructions. He, however, was so intent in watching the operation that sufficient air was not admitted with the anæsthetic, the result being that just as I had finished putting in the last suture our poor little friend looked to all appearance dead. I at once set up artificial respiration, but to no purpose—the vital spark had fled.

Two Basé sheiks from Kokassie visited our camp to-day. They had a short pow-wow both on their arrival and departure. They kissed our hands profusely—overdid it, we thought; we were apt to look with suspicion on an excessive manifestation of friendship.

February 19th.—Just after breakfast I picked up my gun, intending to take a stroll in the neighbourhood, when Elongi, the Koolookoo Sheik, taking hold of my arm, led me to Beyrumfi, to whom he communicated some important information, which he in turn communicated to Suleiman in Arabic, and the latter to me thus —

"You not go out this morning, doctor. The Sheik, he say, 300 or 400 bad Basé have come about the mountains by us, and they come bym-bye to kill us all."

I regret to say that Suleiman's indignation caused him to indulge in profane language, and he expressed a strong wish to know "What the d—l dese black rascals meant. We find them plenty meat; we give plenty presents to them; we kind to them always, and now dey want to kill us all." Then, turning abruptly to Beyrumfi and a cluster of Basé, he opened a box full of rifle cartridges, and very angrily said, " Tell dese black d — s, and dey can tell de other Basé, that we will give them some of dese bullets, and that we kill one, two hundred of dem in five minutes."

Beyrumfi translated this pleasing intelligence to his hearers, who, in due time, I dare say, passed it on. Elongi and his men swore they would stick to us, and I believe they would; but for all that we did not allow any Basé to sleep within our zareeba. We had become rather lax in the matter of zareebas lately, and had not constructed one here; but I need hardly say that on hearing this all in camp were soon set in motion, I remarking what a fine field this would be for Mr. Gladstone to indulge in his tree-felling propensities. He would have found some ebony trees well worthy of his grand old arm.

We had a great deal of very fatiguing work for hours, not only in cutting down and dragging in a sufficient number of trees to form our zareeba, but also in felling young palm trees just round the camp. When all this had been completed the country was set on fire. This quickly spread for miles. In the midst of it all Messrs.

James and Phillipps returned from Amadeb much surprised at the activity in camp. We soon gave them all the news, and I cannot say that we were altogether surprised at the information we received in the morning, as we had observed a good many camp fires in the night—all over the hills—where no camp fires should be.

February 20th.—Last night we went to bed, leaving sentries posted round the camp, and well prepared to give a good account of ourselves should the Basé have conceived the idea of attacking us. Perhaps Suleiman's timely admonition and explanation respecting the penetrating power of our bullets deterred them; at all events we were not attacked, which was satisfactory both to us and the Basé. Had they done so, I computed that with our 22 rifles and guns, and about a dozen revolvers, protected by our strong zareeba, we could have polished off about 100 of these poor savages every five minutes, which would have been no satisfaction to them or us. Looking at the matter again in another light, had they come in sufficient numbers, or laid siege to the camp, we should inevitably have gone to the bad, which would have been a decided inconvenience to us, to say the least of it. Our comrades informed us that when they arrived at Amadeb they heard that our late disaster had been telegraphed to Kassala, Cairo, and, of course, to England. I then felt glad I had sent a true version of the affair to England, knowing full well that wild reports, of a most unreliable character, were more likely to get abroad than true ones. From my youth up I have remembered the story of the three black crows; also that David once made a very pungent remark, "I have said in my heart all men are liars," and Carlyle, "There are so many millions of people in the world mostly fools." However, respecting the latter remark, I should say that—speaking from experience—they are frequently not such fools as they look. The former remark was rather a sweeping one, not *quite* adapted to the present day.

To-day we moved on to Onogooloo, about two hours beyond Koolookoo. On passing the latter place Elongi and many of the Basé remained behind, but his father, a quiet, peaceable-looking old fellow, came on with us. This was a short march of about seven hours only.

February 22nd.—This day, after a march of about six hours, we arrived at our old camping placed, called by the festive name of Wo-amma, familiarly known as Whoa Emma. There we found that, within the past 12 hours, quite a drove of elephants had been past, and, of course, we were so unfortunate as to miss them. The Basé are thinning off, but Elongi has rejoined us to-day. To-day my rifle barrel was so hot at 5 p.m. that no one could grasp it.

February 23rd.—Breakfast at 7 a.m. On the march at 10, and encamp at Gebel-Moussa at 5.40 p.m. *En route* we observed a large tract of country on fire, and suddenly came upon a herd of buffalos, which raised a tremendous cloud of dust. Of course we gave chase for a short distance, and of course did not get near them, for they can go at a tremendous pace.

February 24th.—Life is more enjoyable, if we have some difficulties to overcome occasionally, and succeed in doing so; and if we do not, perhaps (speaking as a philosopher) it is better than having a quiet run of prosperity. To-day, like the past few days, has been warm, 95° in the shade. Our journey was short, namely, from 10 a.m. till 1.15 p.m., encamping at Abion. *En route* we came across many elephant tracks, a lion and lioness, and after that a lion, lioness, and three cubs, but did not succeed in bagging any of them, but three tetél, a nellut, gazelle, and two bustards were shot. The latter are remarkably fleshy, and very good eating. Seldom a day passed without tetél, nellut, gazelles, maarif, mehedehét or dick-dick being shot. The latter is a beautiful little antelope of the smallest kind. I shot many very small, beautifully plumaged sun-birds to-day—less than half the size of wrens—but only managed to bring two or three of them home, as the shot, small as it was, blew them all to pieces; they ought really to be shot with sand.

It became known in camp that we purpose to-morrow cutting across country for the river Settite, or Tacazze, amongst the Hamran or sword-hunting Arabs, *via* Sarcella. In consequence of this we were told (just before dinner) that after that meal we should receive a deputation of camel-drivers and horse-boys to enter a protest against this plan. Accordingly, just after dinner they came in a body, saying that nothing would induce them to pass the village of Sarcella, as the Basé there were bad people, and they had just heard that they had sworn to spear every man, woman, or child of the Beni-Amirs that they encountered, on account of the raid which Sheik Ahmed had made on them the other day, just after he left us on our march into their territory. This was the first news we had of his performances there. They said that after making "aman" with the Basé, he speared three or four hundred of the men and took all the women and children as slaves. We reproved them for their cowardice, saying that they were not old women or children, they had their spears and shields, whilst we had rifles and revolvers, and were strong enough to make a two days' march through their territory, instead of one day. Our arguments were fruitless; they were quite willing to go with us from Hiekota to the Settite, but they would not, on any account, pass by Sarcella. We, therefore, made a virtue of necessity, and gave up the idea.

February 25th.—To-day we encamped at Toodloak, having made a journey of seven and a half miles. I captured a chameleon on the road. Panthers rather disturbed us last night, and at 4 a.m. a hyæna close to my tent exercised his risible faculties so much that I, not seeing exactly where the laugh came in, got up and saluted him with a shower of stones. About 5 a.m. lions were heard; some of us got up and went in quest of them, came within about 40 yards of one, but he turned off into the jungle when he caught sight of us. However, during our stay in the Basé country 18 buffalos and about 60 antelopes, besides other game, were shot by members of the party. We could easily have secured elephants had we remained long enough and followed them up, and many more buffalos and antelopes had we remained longer in the country, and, of course, giraffes and ostriches. The only rhinoceros, or tracks of one, we did not find until we reached Abyssinia. I have not enlarged much on

R

hunting scenes, fearing that my book would become bulky, and that the *generality* of my readers would scarcely care to read a repetition of such scenes.

February 26th.—Heat getting great, 94° in shade to-day. Another 7½ hours brought us to Heikota. There we found quite a heap of letters, papers, and periodicals from England.

The contents of the letters were, of course, greedily devoured by us all, and as for the newspapers and periodicals, they furnished enough of news for days. Although many of them were fully two months old, the contents were new to us.

About an hour after our arrival Sheik Ahmed appeared and received us literally with open arms, at the same time kissing us on either cheek. This I could have put up with under different circumstances, but I must say this mode of salutation is not acceptable to me. We found from Herr Schumann that the wildest rumours respecting us had reached them—five had been killed by the Abyssinians, two taken prisoners and put in irons, all our men killed, whilst our camels and everything else had been annexed. The Sheik says that had he known of the attack in time he would willingly have put 1,400 men in the field at once to assist us. He gave us an account of his revenge on the Basé at Sarcella after he left us, but there were some unpleasant little details which he prudently omitted, thinking probably that they would shock our English susceptibilities. The particulars Herr Schumann furnished us with.

His tale was this—When the Sheik left us to join his men at Sarcella they had about 500 of the Basé in a cave; the Sheik arrived there quietly, beseiged them for about 10 days, of course cutting them off from water and food.

During this time they ate their goats and sheep raw, quenching their thirst with the blood of these animals. Finally the only course left open to the beseiged was to place themselves at the mercy of their merciless conquerors ; so, driven by hunger, thirst, and the smell of their dead, they crawled out, weakened by want, in threes and fours. All the men to the number of about 300, were speared on the spot, whilst about 200 women and children were taken into captivity and sold as slaves, realizing 30, 40, 50, 60, and 70 dollars each. About 30 remained unsold on our arrival; these I saw next day. All the cattle, sheep, goats, dhurra, and everything else the Beni-Amirs could lay their hands on were seized. Now we could understand why the idea of passing through or by Sarcella was so repugnant to our men. I have many patients to attend to, who literally appear to hunger and thirst after my pills and medicine.

CHAPTER XX.

PATIENTS ARRIVE FROM ALL PARTS—ROUGH JOURNEYS—ARRIVE AT THE HAMRAN SETTITE—MAHOMET SALI DECEIVES US—CROCODILES, TURTLE, AND FISH—WE MOVE ON TO BOORKATTAN, IN ABYSSINIA—NEXT DAY WE MOVE OFF, AS ABYSSINIANS APPROACH—WE CATCH ENORMOUS QUANTITIES OF FISH WITH THE NET—NARROW ESCAPE FROM A WOUNDED BUFFALO—THE COORBATCH ADMINISTERED—SCORPIONS AND SNAKES—HAMRANS VISIT US—HAMRAN MODE OF HUNTING AND SNARING—HAMRAN AND BASÉ—THE HAMRANS THREATEN TO FIRE ON US—AGAIN RETURN TO THE HAMRAN SETTITE—ENCAMP AT OMHAGGER.

FEBRUARY 27TH.—I was well employed at my medicine chest again this morning. Amongst some of my patients was a man who had followed us about for weeks from Kassala, but had always arrived too late to come up with us. Many others whom I had attended before we entered the Basé country also visited me, expressing their thanks for what I had done for them, and presenting me with a spear, a shield, an Arab knife, a gourd of wild honey, a sheep, and other things; indeed, I met with more gratitude amongst those poor Arabs than I have in much more favoured climes where people are well educated, and where the sentiment often is very scarce, as well as the money.

February 28th. — This morning, about seven o'clock, a great number of women and children came close to camp making a great noise with the accompaniment of the tom-toms and that peculiar trilling note to which I have before alluded. It seems that this was a complimentary serenade, and that they were rejoicing at our deliverance from the hands of the Philistines.

Yesterday was occupied a good deal in making arrangements with Sheik Ahmed for a march on to the Basé Settite. Mahomet Sali, who knows the country well, will be our principal guide there. We have not seen a flowing river since we left Kassala; we hope soon to do so, and are told that we shall find any number of nellut, gazelles, tetél, buffalos, giraffes, hippopotamus, lions, leopards, crocodiles, and plenty of fishing, besides monkeys, baboons, golden-crested and toke or fish eagles, paroquets, rollo-birds, and grouse, doves, guinea-fowl, partridges, king-fishers, &c., surely a sufficient assortment of sport to satisfy the most ardent sportsman.

A start was not effected until two. Sheik Ahmed, with some minor chiefs and a number of his people, accompanied us a part of the way, which was an uninteresting monotonous journey of about 10 miles over a dry, dusty plain, the only vegetation being a great number of mimosa bushes, not trees. The only game observed on the way was a few gazelles. Encamped at Falookoo, in Basé territory, at 5.30 p.m.

February 29th.—Marched from 10 to 4; encamping on a wretched plain, where the fine dust was about an inch thick, pitched our tents near to a deep well at Sogoda. Several Basé came to salute us. They do not seem *quite* so wild as those we have lately been amongst, and most of them wear a tope. This was not by any means an enjoyable journey, as the roads were bad and mountainous, and covered with intensely prickly trees, through which my camel rushed me, and which lacerated my poor face, legs, arms, clothes, and helmet in a dreadful manner. Needles and thread were in great request after dinner to repair the damage done to clothes.

March 1st.—This has been a long, tedious march from 10 a.m. to 11 p.m. All the discomforts and thorn-scratchings of yesterday intensified six fold; frequently men had to go on in front and cut down trees to enable the caravan to proceed. At 5 p.m. we arrived at a river-bed, dug a well, filled our barrels with water and resumed our journey. It was past 12 at midnight ere we dined, and 2 a.m. before we retired to our much-needed rest, which we had very little of, as we were up at 6 a.m.

March 2nd.—Feeling stiff, sore, and tired. A bath would have been most refreshing, but this morning we were obliged to deny ourselves the luxury because all the water obtainable was in our barrels. Although our clothes and flesh have not been so lacerated to-day, the march has been tedious and very monotonous. For nine successive hours our route lay through an immense forest of young mimosa trees; these and a quantity of dry, withered grass was all that we saw during the time, except a few wild hogs, one of which was chased and speared by a native. By 5 p.m. all our water was gone, and the thirst of every one was excessive, the heat being so great, 94° F. in the shade. After travelling 13 hours, we encamped at 9.30 p.m. by a broad, noble-looking river, the Tacazze or Settite which lay like a lake in front of our camp, either side being fringed with shrubs and trees of all kinds, amongst the branches of which brilliant plumaged birds unsuspiciously roosted, little thinking that I should be looking after them on the morrow.

This river was to us a most refreshing sight after travelling hundreds of miles over burning deserts and khors or dry river-courses, never seeing water except by digging for it. It was 12 o'clock this night ere we got our dinner. All are very angry with Mahomet Sali, our guide, who professed, and no doubt *does* know, the whole of this country and neighbourhood well, for he has brought us, not to the Basé, but the Hamran Settite, where there is not very much game, as the Hamrans, or sword-hunters, have destroyed it. This fellow told us on the way that he would take us to the Basé Settite, within two days or less of Abyssinia, where there would be plenty of game of all kinds, and here he brings us about three days out of the way. An unpleasant interview and discourse will ensue with Mahomet Sali on the morrow. Mr. F. L. James thinks, rightly or wrongly I don't know, that Sheik Ahmed has instructed Mahomet Sali and Beyrumfi not to take us to the Basé Settite, fearing we might get into trouble, either with them, or, what was more likely, with the Abyssinians. This place is called Geebau.

March 3rd.—Mahomet Sali was summoned before the council just after breakfast, and his delinquencies forcibly pointed out. What he said for himself I do not know, as I picked up a shot-gun and rifle, taking one of the boys with me to carry the rifle

THE AUTHOR ATTENDING TO ARAB AILMENTS.

and anything I shot. This river is full of crocodiles, turtle, and fish. I was not long out ere a crocodile received a bullet from my rifle. I also shot a sacred ibis, a crocodile bird, and a beautiful golden-crested eagle.

In the afternoon the big net was sent on a camel some considerable distance down the river, where it was rather deep, accompanied by most of our men and ourselves. The river was dragged, and about 100lbs. of fine fish were secured, some weighing 10 or 12 lbs. The addition of fish to our dinner was much appreciated.

March 4th.—The nights are now getting decidedly warm, so much so that I sleep now with simply a sheet covering me and both ends of my tent open. To-day it is 94° in the shade. Last night Sali saw a wild beast pass quite close to the camp just where he was sleeping. Presently he heard him washing himself, and indulge in a little vocal display. There was no mistaking his note—it was a lion. Sali at once called Mr. Phillipps, but could not get any intelligible reply from him, as he was so excessively sleepy, and knew nothing about it until next morning. Others, however, were much vexed with Sali for not letting them know.

Mahomet Sali was sent off this morning with five camels and two men to the Hamrans to procure dhurra. We at the same time, 10 a.m., strike our tents and start for the Basé Settite, to the great disgust of our men, who manifest a decided disinclination to visit that locality. We lunched at Khor-Maiateb on a nice piece of table-land overlooking a beautiful sheet of water, and shaded by tamarisk, tamarind, and other trees. This place simply swarmed with crocodiles. I saw a great many Marabou-storks and two Egyptian geese; one of the latter I managed to bag, and part of the skeleton of a hippopotamus—the carcase of which, I doubt not, had provided a rare feast for his slayers.

After lunch we pushed on, and very soon travelled over some vile country. First of all over very stony road, then down a very steep declivity, over rocks and big stones, next up a mountain side of the same character—no road, no pathway even; then along a mountainous pathway, through an awfully sterile country, covered with nothing but leafless trees, withered grass, and precipitous rocks, finally encamping at Boorkattan, above the most gigantic rocks of basalt, of great extent, these again overlooking the river. We can see, probably a day's march from here, an immense tall mountain in Abyssinia, on the summit of which is said to be a fortress. We found the large footprints of the hippopotamus in the sand by the river, and quite expect to have him in the morning.

We find before night that we are in Abyssinia, so that it is quite evident Mahomet Sali has not adhered strictly to the truth, as here we are positively in Abyssinia in one day's march. I indulged three times after our arrival in a bath in the river. I dare not dive into any of the pools, fearing that a crocodile might consider me a delicate morsel, but picked out a kind of cradle on the edge, where I could lie down comfortably.

March 5th.—We hear that there is an Abyssinian village about seven miles from here, and that our men are determined they will not proceed any further than this camp. They also think that our camp, pitched as it is on such elevated ground, can be plainly seen by Abyssinians, who they quite expect will make an attack on us to-day. Should they do so, we should come off badly, as there are no means of forming a zareeba. It is quite apparent that they did not feel easy in their minds last night, as a considerable number near my tent were chattering away half the night, instead of going to sleep or allowing me to do so.

After breakfast Beyrumfi was sent for. A great pow-wow ensued, he definitely stating that we can go no further without getting right among Abyssinians, that the country is so rocky, wild, and mountainous that hunting is impossible, and the camels cannot travel there. Accordingly orders are given to load up the camels and return to Khor-Maiateb, where we lunched yesterday.

I had just fixed my bag, rifle, &c., on my camel, when Mr. Aylmer came running to me, rifle in hand, saying, "Doctor, get your rifle and revolver ready. Some of our men say that they have seen a large body of Abyssinians coming down on us, some on horseback and some on foot; but at present they are a pretty good distance off." Our caravan was nearly ready to start. Of course we all armed ourselves pretty quickly; then saw some of our camel-drivers (one old fellow particularly) working themselves up into a frenzy of excitement, leaping about like lunatics, at the same time brandishing their spears in a most threatening manner, indicative of what would be the fate of the enemy should they appear. As we looked upon this performance as so much waste of time, we scruffed these fellows, boxed their ears, and told them to make haste and load up their camels, which they did with a will. As a rule they are generally a couple of hours loading, but now they were wonderfully quick, accomplishing the work in half the usual time. We got off in safety, and arrived at Khor-Maiateb in the afternoon. Temperature, 95° in the shade.

March 6th.—Crocodiles are rather too common here to be pleasant, and interfere with the luxury of the morning and evening bath. To avoid any unpleasant *contretemps*, I generally collected together several big stones by the side of a large pool, threw them in one after the other to frighten the crocodiles away, then threw myself in. This device proved eminently successful, enabling me to enjoy a plunge and a short swim. I need scarcely say I did not fool about long in the water, fearing they might return to see what white object was swimming about.

To-day we used the large net, and landed 210lbs. of different kinds of fish. Keeping sufficient for our dinner, the rest was divided between our men, who ate what they wanted, throwing the remainder into the bushes or anywhere round the camp, causing an insufferable stench next day, which we did not get rid of until the fish had been all gathered up and thrown into the river.

March 7th.—The little canvas boat is in great request, and enables us to go a good way up and down the river. The net was used to some purpose to-day, for we landed 360lbs. of fish and one turtle. At 12 a.m. about 20 Basé came to us with information that elephants are not far off, as they saw and heard them; also that on the 5th, near our last camp, whilst they were looking for wild honey, the

Abyssinians swooped down on them, killed several, including the Sheik's son, and stole three women and a few children. No doubt these were the very fellows who were coming down on us. When we discreetly and gracefully retired, they found us gone, and so seized the Basé. After lunch Messrs. A. and W. James and Colvin mounted their horses and went in search of the elephants. Temperature, 96° in the shade.

March 8th.—About 11 a.m. two or three Basé (who accompanied Messrs. James and Colvin yesterday) returned, saying that the latter had shot two buffalos, one of which was killed, the other wounded only, and that they had seen plenty of elephant tracks but no elephants. At 4 p.m. they all returned, having tracked and secured the wounded buffalo, and an ariel. A crocodile, fish-eagle, and an enormous horned-owl fell to my gun to-day. Temperature, 98° in shade.

March 9th.—Temperature, 100° F. dry bulb, wet bulb 71°, solar thermometer 156°. So far this is the hottest day I have ever experienced. Whilst bathing to-day I put my towel near the water's edge to stand on, as the stones were like hot coals to the feet. We have cleared many of our followers and men out of camp to-day. The Basé, Mahomet Sali, Beyrumfi, and all the Beni-Amirs have been discharged for misleading us. Messrs. F. James and

Phillipps have gone in quest of game, and Messrs. Colvin, A. and W. James have returned to the same place as before in search of elephants.

March 10th.—Last night seven or eight rifle reports from the other camp reached us. At 1 p.m. they were accounted for by Messrs. Colvin and company, who arrived in camp. They had shot at and wounded two buffalos (one a bull). Two or three lions had attacked one of the wounded, leaving very distinct marks of the struggle; still, the buffalo had managed to go on. They tracked him for some distance, but the heat became so great by mid-day—101° in the shade—that they had to desist. Another, wounded in the night, they followed up nearly to the jungle, when suddenly he darted on to them, charging most furiously in Mr. A. James' direction. He, however, saluted him with two eight-bore bullets in the chest, which had the effect of turning him from his purpose, and causing him to change his plan, for he turned and then charged Mr. Colvin, who, very fortunately for him, happened to give him a bullet in the fore leg at very close quarters, as the buffalo fell right against him with some violence, and sent him reeling on the ground. I should think this was about as close to an enraged wounded buffalo as Mr. Colvin or any other man in his senses could desire.

We could very frequently get a shot at a crocodile

when in the water, but seldom on land; they seem much too wary to be caught there. I have often seen them basking in the sun on the bank of the river, crept cautiously up, and whether they have seen me, smelt me, or I have trodden on a twig I know not, but before I could get near enough they have all disappeared in the water. They come up to the surface often. We see a dark spot in the middle of a quiet-looking pool, and take a pot-shot, but seldom get the reptile until next day, when we find him floating, but so mutilated that he is not worth securing. To-day, however, Mr. Aylmer shot one in the water near the camp, and was fortunate enough to secure him by the aid of a native, who dived into the pool with a rope, which he slipped over his upper jaw. I fancy crocodiles prefer white skins to black, for these black fellows plunge into the water and swim about where we would not dare to go.

Before the crocodile episode—in fact, just after breakfast—our court of justice sat. This consisted of ourselves, who were the judges, the jurors, and the counsel; and I venture to say that strict justice was dealt out with an even hand. The culprit was a fine, strapping, rather good-looking fellow of about six feet, a camel-driver. He had been troublesome on two or three previous occasions, but last night he passed the bounds of discretion. His brother roused him up in the night to take his turn at sentry-duty; in return for this he warned his brother that he would make him suffer in the morning—which he certainly did, as he got him under some trees and there chastised him severely with a stick. When we heard of this, the culprit, prosecutor, and witnesses had to appear before the tribunal. The charge was proved, and the culprit was ordered 20 lashes of the coorbatch, to be administered by Suleiman, four camel-men to hold him down. He at once dispensed with the assistance of the camel-men, and without making any bother at all, laid down on the sand, face downwards, whilst Suleiman went in search of the coorbatch. The castigation was duly administered, the fellow taking it without flinching an atom. When finished he got up, brushed the dust from his tope, and walked off in his usual manner. He seemed not to bear the least malice, for some time afterwards he was as busy as anyone helping to land the crocodile.

March 11th.—Two bull buffalos, a tetél, and nellut were shot to-day. Scorpions are too plentiful here; we are continually finding them in our tents, but so far none of us have received any of their dreadful stings. They belong to the class *Arachnida*. A scorpion has what looks like a claw in his long tail, through which the poison, which lies in a bag at the bottom of it, is projected. This tail, preparatory to taking the offensive, lies curled up on his back, not unlike a squirrel. He can at will bring this down with considerable force, but only in a straight line—he cannot twist it to strike.

Whilst strolling up the river-bed with my gun in the afternoon I came upon Mr. W. D. James, who had just met with a rather curious, and not altogether agreeable, adventure. He had brought his photographic apparatus with him, and planted it within a convenient distance from a pool, intending to photograph gazelles when they came to drink. He was successful in obtaining a good picture of two—one drinking, the other looking straight at the camera. Whilst waiting patiently for them, seated on some rocks under a large baobob tree, he heard a hissing noise behind him. On turning his head, he saw a snake waving about in an erect position, with tongue out, looking as if he was about to strike. Mr. W. D. James did not sit on the stone any longer, but seized a stick, and was lucky enough to kill it ere he was able to bite.

About a week ago we set some mustard and cress; to-day we had a good quantity for luncheon, and found it a very agreeable addition.

March 12th.—A few Hamrans called to-day, and

are very anxious to persuade us to go towards Abyssinia, saying they are friendly with the Abyssinians, and can show us hippos. The offer is not accepted. I find these fellows do not by any means confine their hunting tendencies to simply the use of the sword, as I have often found very ingeniously constructed snares plentifully placed in runs leading to the river. Doubtless when the animals are thus ensnared they are despatched with the sword or spear.

I will try and describe the kind of snare: They get a strong branch of a tree that will bend, not break, into a circle; this they firmly secure. They have a number of strips of wood, broad at the base, and gradually getting narrow, converging until they meet in the middle of the circle bent downwards on one side; these again are firmly secured to the circle. A hole, perhaps a foot deep, and half a foot or a foot in diameter, is dug in the ground where the run is. On the top of this hole is placed the snare, covered with earth, attached by a strong rope to a great log, or the trunk of a tree. The unsuspecting animal comes to drink, puts his foot on this, and it slips in. He cannot pull his leg out, for the harder he pulls the more firmly is he secured, as the sharp spokes stick into his flesh. It is, in fact, just like a wheel: the tire is the outer circle, and the axle represents the hole through which his leg goes.

The reason the Hamrans are called sword-hunters is this—I am quite sure that neither I nor any of our party can speak from experience, as we never saw the feat performed, but Sir Samuel Baker has: Whilst hunting the elephant, or giraffe, a Hamran on horseback gallops in front of an enraged elephant armed with a sword, whilst one behind, similarly armed, gallops after him. The elephant may elect to turn round and chase the one behind—in any case, he is between two evils, for eventually the one behind, whilst the horse is going at full gallop, will, when he is near enough, jump off and with great dexterity hamstring the elephant with his long two-edged sword; then, of course, he can easily be despatched. His tusks are cut off and sold, and his carcase provides a good feast.

Two Basé who had remained in our camp slipped off to the mountains on seeing the Hamrans in our camp, returning again after their departure. It is quite evident they do not regard them as friends.

March 13th.—This morning several Hamrans, with the late Sheik's son, interviewed us, and seem very desirous of acting as pioneers in this part of the country. We declined their services. This seems displeasing information to them, and they also express anger at our having two Basé in camp. On leaving us they went towards the Basé country. Suleiman explained this by saying, "The two Basé in our camp, they go soon as they see these Hamrans. Now he go after the Basé; they kill his father long time ago. Now he kill all the Basé he find if he strong enough and have plenty of mens with him." This was really the case, and the Hamrans were now hunting the Basé just as we would wild animals. However, they had a good start, and probably made the best of their way to their country.

Our camels were now being loaded, as we had resolved to move our camp. Whilst we were preparing, a Hamran came, saying he was sent to tell us that we had given the Heikota sheik a number of presents, but they had nothing to do with him. We were now in the Hamran's country, or soon would be, and they were not willing for us to kill their game without permission from their Sheik, adding that if we advanced they would fire on us. Our reply was, "Tell your friends that our camels are loaded, and so are we. We are coming your way in less than half-an-hour, and strongly advise them to save their powder, as that is a game that two can play at. Threats don't alarm us in the least. If they are ready to commence hostilities so are we." I suppose they thought better of it. Shortly afterwards we started without hindrance until we got just beyond our old camping ground, by the Settite, where our tents were then pitched. There were two hippopotami in the river just here, one of which we saw. The river was dragged, but they slipped under the net.

March 14th.—Marched from 8.30 a.m. until 2.30 p.m., encamping on a high, flat table-land overlooking a beautiful sheet of water plentifully bordered on the bank by trees and bushes in which could be found any number of beautiful birds and doves. At the back of our camp was a large wood on perfectly level ground, which gave shelter to myriads of guinea fowls, doves, and other birds, also vast numbers of baboons. The occupants of the water were crocodiles, turtle, and very numerous different kinds of fish. The shore, a little way from camp, was frequented by Marabou storks, flamingoes, ibis, cranes, storks, Egyptian geese, herons, crocodile-birds, &c., &c.

This was the most enjoyable camping ground we had yet come to. It was also the hottest place we had hitherto found, for the temperature at 2 p.m. to-day was 105° Fah. in the shade. During such hot weather a bath was of course a most delicious thing to indulge in, but I must say I did so with some trepidation, as the pool in front of us was frequented by some good-sized crocodiles whom it was as well not to trifle with. I therefore contented myself, as a rule, with lying down in the water on the edge where it was shallow. When feeling inclined for a plunge and swim I invariably adopted the preliminary caution of hurling in several big stones; on these occasions I was sufficiently discreet not to remain long in the water, having conceived a very wholesome objection to furnishing any of these scaly monsters with such a repast as a Williams. The water was quite tepid, of course from the great heat. This place is called Omhagger, not far from the village of Ombrager.

CHAPTER XXI.

A BOA-CONSTRICTOR VISITS US—THE BURTON BOAT—MOUSSA'S BEHAVIOUR ENTAILS A THRASHING AND HIS DISCHARGE—GREAT HEAT—A FINE HIPPOPOTAMUS KILLED—HAMRAN FEAST — THE WHITE ANTS—ANOTHER HIPPOPOTAMUS KILLED — MAHOMET SALI BRINGS SUPPLIES — NATIVE MUSIC IN THE NIGHT—DELICATE HINTS CONVEYED TO THE PERFORMER—A REMARKABLY FINE NELLUT SHOT—ARAB AND EGYPTIAN TAXATION—BABOONS—A HAMRAN STORY—ALI BITTEN BY A SCORPION—ON THE MARCH ONCE MORE—ROUGH JOURNEYS.

In the evening, whilst George and Anselmia, our two European servants, were dining by their tent, George called out, " A snake, a snake." A little terrier, named " Tartar " (which Mr. W. D. James had brought from England) began barking furiously, whilst we sallied forth with anything we could lay our hands on—Mr. Phillipps and I each with a spear, Mr. Colvin with an Abyssinian sword—darted off, just in time to see a great boa-constrictor gliding through the grass and into some thorny bushes where we could not pursue him.

George said, "I heard something hissing," and said to Anselmia, "What the devil is that?" looked round and saw an enormous snake about a yard off in the tree behind me, hissing away, with head up. I was off in quick sticks. Last night a lion came so close to my tent, and made such a noise that he woke us all up, and produced quite a stampede amongst the horses and camels. Some of the natives sleeping just outside my tent threw firebrands at him. Unfortunately the moonlight was wanting at the time or we might, perhaps, have bagged him.

Two tetél, four ariel, and several birds were shot to-day.

March 15th.—Hyænas were rather noisy last night, but I have never known them so troublesome anywhere as at Kassala. The heat to-day was 106° in the shade,—so far the hottest day I ever experienced. Of course the Burton boat is in frequent use now. To-day, whilst quietly punting about near the bushes with my gun laid across the seat, I observed some beautiful and strange birds. I quietly seized my gun, and found the barrel so excessively hot that I positively could not hold it until I wrapped my pocket-handkerchief round it. I succeeded in bagging two fine spotted giant kingfishers. This morning Moussa, a mischievous young rascal, whom we had brought with us from Kassala, was severely thrashed with the coorbatch, then sent away with our head camel-man (who was going for dhurra) to the Sheik at Ombrager, to be forwarded on to Kassala. It seems that he had quarrelled with Idrees, a native servant from Keren; then, whilst struggling together, he whipped out a pair of scissors and with it snipped out several bits of flesh from his arms and chest. This was not his first offence, for on the 13th he received 20 lashes of the coorbatch. Then he laid himself down at once, face downwards, and took it without flinching; to-day he got it severely, and yelled most vigorously. His offence on the former occasion was this: Whilst Sali was running to camp, rifle in hand, this impudent young scamp struggled with him for the possession of it (this was just after dark). In the struggle the rifle went off, and might have lodged a bullet in Sali or anyone in camp. Unfortunately the coorbatch is the only remedy for these natives—the only way of keeping up discipline. If treated with kindness and forbearance they think we are getting lax and easy, will at once take advantage of it, skulk about and do nothing, but the coorbatch at once brings them to reason.

Mr. A. James found a man's skull to-day, also a gigantic tortoise shell. Mr. Phillipps angled and caught an enormous gamout, weighing 31 lbs. Two ariel, a nellut, and calf buffalo were shot.

March 16th.—Temperature 105°, wet bulb 71°, solor 160°. Last night hyænas and wild cats exercised a disturbing influence on our slumbers. Soon after breakfast a Hamran Sheik, with attendants, called, presenting us with a good quantity of milk and a sheep. During the day a crocodile was shot, also a very fine hippopotamus. The latter was observed poking his head above water in a large pool a little way from camp, little thinking of the danger awaiting him. He had no sooner done so than crash went a hardened bullet into his skull. Down he went, but could not stay long, for he must come up to breathe. On his reappearance he received another leaden messenger in his skull. On his coming to the surface a third time he spouted up a quantity of blood and water, and received one more bullet, after which he disappeared mortally wounded. The next time he came to the surface a floating corpse. A few hours afterwards ropes were obtained and fastened round him by some Arabs, who dived, and he was dragged to shore amid universal rejoicing, they knowing right well that a feast was in store.

We find the white ants very troublesome here. Should anyone be careless enough to leave his satchel or portmanteau on the bare ground he would regret it in the morning. Anyone who has visited Central Africa will come away with very distinct recollections of the white ants. They are really wonderful little creatures, and the structures they erect are often on a colossal scale. Quite near to our dining place here is one of their buildings. As a rule they are built of a conical or sugar-loaf form, but I have seen them of the form of turrets. They are worked up from the soil of the country by the ants, and are of the consistency of stone, and so strong that a buffalo or leopard has been known to take up its position on the top for the purpose of observation. During one portion of our journey, on emerging from a wood, I saw what I at first took to be a village on a large plane; the habitations resembled huts, in some cases 15 feet high, and proportionately large at the base. They were only a colony of white ants, and I dare say their village consisted of 200 of these ant hills. The white ants (*Termes bellicosus*) are not true ants; that is, they do not belong to the order *Hymenoptera*, which embraces the industrious bee and the crafty ichneumon, but belong to the order *Neuroptera*, which embraces the brilliant, though voracious dragon-fly, the ephemeral may-fly, and the wily ant-lion. They are called ants because they are similar to them in their habits and in the constitution of their colonies. Their antennæ are larger than the head, their mandibles are well-developed, and the inferior pair of wings is generally as large as the superior.

There are four classes found in the colony of the white ant—the king and queen, who live together in a central chamber near the ground, after having lost their wings; the workers, who build and nurse their young; the soldiers, who never build or nurse, whose duty consists in defending the nest when attacked. Neither the workers nor the soldiers have wings. The largest worker is supposed to be a fifth of an inch long. The soldiers, which have an enormous head and formidable mandibles, are at least twice as long, and are said to weigh as much as thirty workers, attaining the length of nearly four-fifths of an inch, while the female, when she has become a queen, and about to form an extensive colony, attains the length of six inches, and lays eggs at the rate of sixty a minute, or more than eighty thousand a day. The white ants are most destructive to houses, furniture, clothes, and books;

they will, in fact, destroy anything but stone and metal. Anything that is reducible to powder will, where they have located themselves, fall to certain destruction. They work unseen. I have often noticed twigs, leaves, branches of trees, and so on, destroyed by them. They plaster them over with mud, and underneath this cover they work. Wooden pillars and beams are continually made perfect shells by their operations, and the safety of houses is frequently affected, though externally they would appear strong and good. The library at the Faurah Bay Church Missionary College, Sierra Leone, was in a great measure destroyed by their instrumentality.

In 1879 the Bishop of Sierra Leone appealed for funds in order to repair the churches, which, he said, "are ant-eaten." Now, although the white ants are so annoying that hardly anything is proof against their attacks, they are a great blessing in tropical climes, their office being, in the economy of nature in these hot countries, to hasten the decomposition of the woody and decaying parts of vegetation, which, without their intervention, would render these regions uninhabitable by breeding a pestilence. The remains of the white ant in the Coal Measures is an evidence that it was, to a certain extent, through their destructive agency that the tropical vegetable matter was accumulated which went to form our coal. The white ant, by hastening the decomposition of vegetable substances, has ever proved a friend to man; the true ants also have proved themselves a boon to the inhabitants of tropical climes by destroying what are popularly classed as vermin.

March 17th.—I am happy to say that the temperature has dropped to 97°, and that is quite as hot as one cares about. Whilst breakfasting, about 6 a.m., a native came, saying "Assint effendi," at the same time jerking his thumb towards the river. This meant a hippopotamus. He was accordingly sought for, found and killed before 8 a.m., not far from camp. To see the Arabs then cutting up the carcase, wallowing in gore, and stuffing lumps of meat or fat into their mouths, and rubbing the latter on their heads was a most disgusting sight, almost as bad as the Basé. Festoons of meat soon ornamented every tree in the neighbourhood of the camp. The natives themselves looked like a number of dips melting in the sun. Every head to-day is dripping with fat, which melts and drops about all over the shoulders. Feeling a little Mark Twainish, I cannot help remarking that this plastering of the head with fat is, no doubt, a very ancient custom, in which Aaron, his friends, and contemporaries were accustomed to indulge to a great extent. Do we not read? "And they annointed his head with oil, which ran down even unto his beard." This was probably the fat obtained from hippopotamus, buffaloes, &c., and clearly indicates that these old gentlemen were, more or less, affected with sporting proclivities; but it is more than probable that they were not at that time in possession of eight-bore rifles and hardened bullets.

During the greater part of this day we have observed a peculiar hazy appearance on the other side of the river—extending for miles—resembling mist in appearance. It was really a very fine dust. In the evening this was followed by a good deal of wind, which much increased towards night.

March 18th.—Last night and this morning was cooler than any for weeks past. Temperature at 1.30 p.m. 92° in the shade. Mahomet Sali put in an appearance to-day with a camel-load of flour and bread from Kassala. He also brought the skin of a very fine boa-constrictor, which one of our party was not long in annexing. It really was intended for George, but the annexer gave the owner two dollars for it, and so it became his pretty quickly. The bread we have is like the Cairo bread we brought with us. It is baked hard in squares, resembling dog-biscuits. When wanted at meal-times they are dipped in water and then put over the fire for a few minutes, when they become spongy and eatable.

Two or three little matters conspired to ruffle me rather last night. When retiring for the night my first business was to kill two scorpions and some gigantic spiders which I found in my tent. Having accomplished these murders to my entire satisfaction, I undressed, lastly taking off my socks. I had no sooner put my feet on the matting than the soles of my feet felt as if they were pin-cushions, receiving a thousand prickling sensations—sometimes not unlike those produced by a galvanic battery. I found on inspection of the matting swarms of large black ants. This was not all. I got into bed, but was not allowed to sleep without the accompaniment of a stringed instrument, somewhat resembling a banjo, which a wretched Arab had constructed out of an empty preserved meat tin. He had stretched a piece of skin tightly across this, attached a bridge, three strings, a finger-board, and all the rest of it, then strummed and fingered away close to my tent, producing the most monotonous sounds for an hour or two after I was in bed, evidently as much in love with his instrument as someone else would be with his violoncello. I had not done anything deserving such torture as this wretch thought

T

proper to inflict on me, so would not stand it any longer. I therefore got up and delicately conveyed a hint (in the shape of a boot which I hurled at him) that this mode of serenading in the middle of the night was not only unappreciated by me, but decidedly objectionable. The stringed instrument ceased for a while until I was just going to sleep, when this demon in human form again started. I immediately threw out three more rather forcible hints. They were another boot and two empty claret bottles; and I rather think the last two hints appealed forcibly to his feelings, as the light guitar was then laid aside, and I was allowed to sink into a calm sleep.

During the day Mr. W. D. James shot a magnificent buck nellut, which had the finest head we have yet seen. His horns, taking the direct length, measured $39\frac{1}{2}$ inches; taking the curves, 53 inches. An enormous tortoise was brought to camp this morning alive (abugeddir, as they called him). Two stout men can stand on his back, and he walks away with them as if they were two straws.

March 19th.—Temperature, 92° in shade. The hazy appearance noticed during the last two days has passed away; the wind also has subsided. I think we may expect a hot day again.

This morning a son of the Hamran Sheik came to

camp, demanding a tax of eight dollars on our guide. The latter is to receive 25 dollars per month, out of which the Heikota Sheik wants eight dollars. To begin at the fountain-head, the Egyptian Government have a head-tax—every young person on reaching a certain age is taxed. The owner of every date palm-tree has to pay a tax, the same with the owner of a " sageer," or sakia (a water-wheel); in fact, I believe everybody and everything is taxed. The Government look to the Governor-General of the Soudan for a good round sum; he, in turn, looks to the Mudir, or governor of a district. He squeezes the necessary out of the sheiks of the various tribes, and they in turn (to use a metaphor, suck the orange dry) screw out of the poor Arabs of the tribe what they require. If the sheik fails to produce the sum required of him by the Mudir, the latter swoops down on his camels, flocks, and herds and sells a sufficient number of them to produce the required sum; but if the sheik has no camels, &c., he himself is seized and put in durance vile until the tribe find the necessary number of dollars.

> Some worms there are who feed on men;
> Others there are who feed on them.
> These lesser worms have worms to bite 'em;
> Thus worm eats worm *ad infinitum*.

How can Egypt ever prosper under such a

system? What inducement have these poor Arabs to accumulate anything more than is sufficient for their daily wants? None. When we engaged servants at Heikota, at, say, 12 dollars per month, the first thing the sheik did was to take two dollars from each man, and very probably as much, or more, at the termination of their services. The beasts, the ants, the reptiles, and birds prey on one another; crocodiles on big fish, and big fish on little ones. There is no Salvation Army there, and if there were (I don't want to be ironical, but *Byron*-ical) I do not think there exists a more preying community.

Two nellut and a maarif shot to-day.

March 20th.—This morning, just after breakfast, I took up my gun and went about 100 yards from camp, with the intention of shooting a baboon. But my heart smote me—they looked so awfully human—and I desisted; but I sat down and derived much amusement from watching enormous baboons and little monkeys gambolling by the water's edge.

On returning to camp I found Suleiman conversing with a man wearing a belt full of cartridges (a rather uncommon spectacle). The conversation lasted some time. I was told afterwards that when he learned from Suleiman that we had been again by or in Abyssinian territory, he exclaimed, "You have to thank the good God that you came away when you did. Had the Abyssinians seen your tents and all those boxes they would certainly have come down on you and killed everyone of you for the sake of the tents alone, to say nothing of the boxes." He also informed him that about a month ago they killed a party of Hamrans, who went up there hunting from this neighbourhood, just for the sake of a gun or two, and whatever else they could lay their hands on.

A buck nellut, two wild boars, killed; two buffalos wounded. Temperature, 97° F. in shade.

March 21st.—Temperature, 100°. Nothing of interest to-day. A tetél, two nellut, and mehedehét shot; maariff wounded, but not secured. To-morrow we turn our faces to the Red Sea coast, and expect to reach Massawa in about three weeks time.

March 22nd.—Last night, just as I was about to retire for the night, I was sent for to Ali, the cook, who had just been stung on the thigh by a scorpion. He was evidently suffering great pain. I gave him a strong dose of ammonia and some brandy, at the same time advising him to poultice the wound after I had cauterised it. Suleiman having more faith in a more heroic mode of treatment, obtained a razor, and with it made a series of little gashes, remarking at the same time, "There, now Ali better after that;

the bad blood come from him now." Of course I did not interfere, but allowed them both to have their own way, to their mutual satisfaction.

As we were now about to take our farewell of the river, I indulged in a swim at 6 a.m., not forgetting at the time to hurl in several large stones preparatory to my dive, as a warning to all crocodiles to vanish for a time.

At 10 a.m. the hamlah was on the move. Our journey this day was pursued under very unpleasant conditions, as we travelled frequently through large bushes of mimosa and kittars, tearing our helmets and clothes to pieces, and inflicting not a few scratches on our bodies. At 7 p.m. we encamped at Khor-Maiatah, about five miles from our old camp. The day's sport was a crocodile and buffalo.

CHAPTER XXII.

ENCAMP AT LAKATAKOORA WITHOUT THE CARAVAN—DESCRIPTION OF VILLAGE—BASÉ LADIES VISIT ME ERE I GET OUT OF BED—THEY RECEIVE PRESENTS AND ARE VERY AMUSING—ENORMOUS NUMBERS OF DOVES AND SAND-GROUSE—ABOOSALAL TO SOGODA—BOA-CONSTRICTOR KILLED—AN UNPLEASANT JOURNEY, WE ALL GET SEPARATED—ARRIVE AT HEIKOTA AGAIN.

MARCH 23RD.—Leaving Khor-Maiatah at 8.45 a.m., we had an exceptionally unpleasant day of it. We had seen the last of that fine river, the Tacazze; now if water was wanted it could only be obtained by digging a few feet in the sandy river-beds. We travelled over mountains, plains, valleys, river-beds, and nearly all day through a forest of those horrid mimosas, finally arriving at Lakatakoora, in the Basé country, at 7 p.m., *without* the caravan. At about 11 p.m. Cheriff, with the canteen, Ali the cook, and a few only of the camels arrived.

As we had not tasted food since about 1 p.m., Cheriff's canteen was soon surrounded by us, and the contents of it cleared out in a very short time. Our dinner (which was a scanty one this time) did not appear until 12.30 a.m. Whilst this was being prepared by Ali we fired off rifles, burnt blue lights, and lighted a beacon fire for Suleiman with the hamlah to see where we were; but all to no purpose—they had lost their way. The moon retired for the night, and so many trees had to cut be down to enable them to come on, that at last they gave up the idea of attempting to find us, so slept out.

We also had rather a hard time of it. There was no choice of a camping-ground—there was but one. This was a large open space devoid of vegetation, but covered with a thick layer of impalpable dust, about an inch or so in thickness, infested with white ants. Fortunately our tents and bedding arrived. I did not wait for my tent to be pitched, but placed my bedding on the canvas covering of my tent on the ground, and there I managed to get through the night in a rather unsatisfactory manner. The other members of the party elected to remain up until their tents were pitched.

March 24th.—I passed a somewhat uncomfortable night amongst the white ants, lulled to sleep by the music of hyænas, some of whom seem to have been intensely amused at our situation, if one may judge from the bursts of merriment issuing from *their* camp, as they were evidently excited by uncontrollable fits of laughter, making the woods in the immediate neighbourhood resound by the exercise of their risible faculties.

I awoke about 6.30 a.m., but did not arise until 7. Quite near to our camp I observed on a precipitous mountain side enormous basalt rocks, some *single* rocks as big as a good-sized house. This was the village of Lakatakoora; and amongst these rocks, concealed from view, lived some Basé. I had not been awake long ere many of the Basé ladies, covered with beads, their eyelids and lips stained with kohl, rings in their noses and ears, and a strip of cloth around their waists, came and shook hands with me, murmuring "Mida" (good-day). Both men and women came in such increasing numbers that I decided to get up, and had to perform my toilet in their presence. They watched the whole performance with evident interest. Such a contrivance as a tooth-brush and tooth-powder elicited expressions of wonder and admiration, but a hair-brush and comb pleased them still more. Water was scarce. I therefore had to wash *à la* Turk. Mahoom stood by me with a salmon tin full of water, pouring out little driblets of water into my hands, finally douching my head with the remaining drop, about two ounces.

Our guide had been sent off at 6 a.m. in search of the lost portion of the caravan. He found it, and piloted it into our camp at 8.30 a.m. The Basé were very friendly and obliging in the way of water, for they brought us this invaluable liquid in very beautifully worked baskets, so closely woven that not a drop escaped, slung on the shoulder, like a pair of scales. They also brought us several gourds of wild honey, which we bought. Many beads and small looking-glasses were given to the ladies, who appeared highly delighted and amused when they saw their own faces reflected from a looking-glass for the first time in their lives. They crowded round the fortunate recipient of one of these reflectors, peeping over one another's shoulders, giggling and laughing at their own reflection in a most amusing manner.

All being packed up by 10 a.m., we moved off a short distance, halting at Aboosalal at 12.30 p.m. on the sandy bed of a khor, surrounded on either side by lofty, precipitous rocks, along which scampered hundreds of enormous baboons and monkeys. Both men and camels seemed completely knocked up. A little way from camp was a little pool of water in this khor; and in the neighbourhood, without exaggeration, were thousands upon thousands of doves and sand-grouse. I took my gun down there in the evening when they came to drink, and stationed myself behind a huge rock. In less than half-an-hour I bagged about 15 brace of sand-grouse and five brace of doves.

The day before we arrived here the natives had killed an elephant. They and the vultures had picked his bones pretty clean, as nothing but his skeleton remained when I saw it. His tusks, of course, had been taken away. Later on they were offered to me by a Sheik's son; but as they were damaged, small, and the price excessive, I was not a purchaser.

March 25.—Made a long march from Aboosalal to Sogoda, where water could be found. We started soon after 8 a.m., and long before we reached our destination darkness came on. This was a most unpleasant journey through prickly trees, again tearing our patched-up clothes and helmets. In one place we all got separated, each one selecting the way he thought best. I lost my way in a forest of kittar and mimosa bushes. I was obliged to dismount my camel, and presently got in such a fix that I could scarcely move either backwards or forwards. Noises became indistinct, and finally, I could not hear a sound. Others were, apparently, in the same position as myself, for shots and revolvers resounded on all sides. Eventually we reached the camping ground in detachments at 8, 9, and 10 o'clock, dining at 11 p.m., bed at 12.30. In the evening, before dark, we came across the trail of a boa-constrictor, followed it up, and successfully despatched the reptile, which measured 12 feet in length. The next day we pitched our tents at Fahncoub, on very good ground, surrounded by fine trees. Sogoda was a horrid place, the ground being covered with fine dust.

March 26th.—Starting from Fahncoub at 8.30 a.m., we once more reached Heikota at 11.30, having travelled a distance of 10 miles only. We found Herr Schumann, the animal collector, had gone, calling at Kassala, and taking all the animals with him to Souâkin: I take the opportunity of sending a letter on to Kassala by Alki, who has been a very good trustworthy fellow, but who is now leaving us, as he has a bad whitlow.

CHAPTER XXIII.

AN ABYSSINIAN IMPROVISATORE AND HIS LITTLE SLAVE—PREPARE FOR A MARCH TO MASSAWA—A STRANGE BASÉ BREAKFAST—PATIENTS—ARRIVE AT TOODLOAK—BENI-AMIES ENCAMPED ON THE GASH—LIONS AND LEOPARDS ARE SHOT—OUR MONKEYS IN CAMP—BABOON MODE OF ATTACKING LEOPARDS—CRAFTY BABOONS—LIONS ABOUND—HYÆNA METHOD OF ATTACKING A LION—HYÆNA INTERVIEWS MR. COLVIN—ARRIVAL AT AMADEB—DEPARTURE FROM AMADEB—BAREAS ATTEMPT AN ATTACK ON THE CARAVAN—BENI-AMIES WATERING THEIR FLOCKS AND HERDS—WE MEET WITH A YOUNG ELEPHANT—LEOPARD AND HYÆNA SHOT AT KHOR-BARAKER.

MARCH 27TH.—A great part of the morning was occupied with sorting out the heads of antelopes, buffalos, &c. I was particularly engaged in attending to about 50 patients in the morning, and perhaps 20 or so in the evening. Many of them had come from long distances to see the " Hakeem."

In the afternoon a little Abyssinian boy, about 12 years of age (an improvisatore), made his appearance, accompanied by his slave (a small black boy), perhaps seven or eight years of age, carrying a rude native instrument with three or four strings on it, something like a banjo. He favoured us with a song, in which the word "Ingelese, Ingelese" occurred very frequently. The interpretation of the whole song I do not know, but it referred principally to the prowess of the English in the Abyssinian war. On being asked if he would sell this instrument, he replied —

"No, I cannot do that; it is my father and my mother."

The young rascal had saved up all his money and bought the little black boy as his slave. He was delighted on seeing a scrap-book and a small musical box. These Mr. James presented him with, also a dollar, which the youngster handed over to his slave with quite the air of a superior.

March 28th.—To-morrow we hope to be on the march once more. To-day we are much engaged in securing fresh camels and camel-men for the march to Massawa. I was employed for fully two hours in the morning, and again in the evening, in relieving the several necessities and tribulations of my Arab friends.

March 29th.—Physic again greedily sought for by Hamrans, Beni-Amirs, Shukeriyahs, and Hadendowahs. I was engaged in dispensing from breakfast time until near luncheon time, and again all the evening until dark. If we do not move away from Heikota the medicine chest will soon be empty, for these people seem to positively enjoy mixtures and pills. In the evening, after dinner, all our late camel-men and horse-boys were paid off, each one receiving five dollars backsheesh, and a good knife and a razor, which are much prized. I have already spoken of the wonderful digestive powers of the Basé people, but they exceeded my wildest expectations, for on the 26th a circumstance occurred whilst we were on the march that convinced me they could digest anything from a boot to a pair of trousers, even with a man inside of them. Had anyone recounted the anecdote to me I daresay I might have been somewhat incredulous, and I cannot blame anyone, who does not know me, for being the same. However, they can please themselves as to whether they believe what I am going to state or not. I can vouch for the fact as I saw it myself.

In front of my camel, whilst on the march, were two Basé. One of them found that a portion of his sandal (made of buffalo hide) had worn away and came off; he was a careful Basé and wasted nothing. Feeling rather hungry, the owner of the sandal pounded the bit of seceding sandal between two pieces of stone, and having done so began to masticate it. The other Basé man, who had secured a bit of the toothsome morsel, evidently thought this a superfluous proceeding on the part of his comrade, so incontinently proceeded to masticate it without this preliminary precaution. Their teeth certainly are good, even beautiful, and would be envied by any drawing-room belle, and I am sure their digestive powers would also be envied by any individual living—no need of Richardson's Peptacolos here. I would recommend the party who wrote about "The Stomach and Its Trials" to peruse the above instructive anecdote.

March 30th.—This morning, after breakfast, my tent was surrounded again with the patients, who had arrived from all parts, far and near, on camels, on donkeys, and on foot. Amongst them was one old man who, after the approved native fashion, squatted on his haunches, holding out a little squeaking chicken, about a week or two old, at arm's length, calling out "Hakeem howaga" (doctor, sir). This he continued at intervals for about a quarter of an hour, until I had got rid of many patients. What he intended this diminutive chicken for, unless as a present, I was at a loss to understand; but when, at last, his turn came, I soon discovered through Mahoom why the old man was so importunate. Yesterday he came complaining of his eyes. I then told him he must procure a small bottle for some lotion. "And now," said Mahoom, laughing till he could hardly stand, "he bring you dis little chicken." What he thought I was going to do with the chicken I don't know, unless he expected me to smash it up, and with it make a lotion for his eyes. On my previous visit I gouged out some diseased bone from a boy's foot, straightened the leg of another boy who had suffered from a contracted knee, and so on. My fame spread; hence the influx of patients suffering from all kinds of diseases, curable and incurable. At 11.30 a.m. we left Heikota, reaching Toodloak at 7 p.m., where we encamped on very dusty ground.

March 31st.—Here we found a very large village of Beni-Amirs encamped on the Gash, who may be likened to locusts, as they remained at Heikota until the animals had eaten up everything there; then they moved away to pastures new. Toodloak is quite a lion neighbourhood. An immense zareeba had been constructed on the river-bed in a large circle. Within this was an inner circle formed by the huts of the tribe, and into that inner circle

W

many hundreds of camels, sheep, cattle, and goats are every night driven in for protection from the wild beasts; yet, notwithstanding this, a lion will sometimes leap the barrier and bound off with a sheep or a goat. Temp. 100° F. in the shade. The nights are now much warmer than they were three weeks ago.

April 1st.—Last night two lions, a lioness, and two leopards were shot, and all secured except one lion. We saw no less than seven or eight last night. The lion was a very fine fellow, measuring nine feet two inches from nose to tip of his tail. Sali cut a bit of the lion's liver, to make him brave, as he said—a quite unnecessary proceeding, for he once was plucky enough to enter the jungle in search of a wounded lion, and that is what few would care to do.

April 2nd.—Lions are plentiful here. Last night they made a great noise round the camp, probably attracted thither by the sheep and goats. The Arabs had to mount guard over these, walking round in couples with spears and shield, and shouting to keep them away. Last night the party went out in couples at considerable distances apart. Each couple was ensconced in a small zareeba, in front of which was a goat or sheep, tethered to a stake driven in the ground, to tempt a lion. Opposite Mr. Colvin's zareeba, whilst he was patiently waiting inside for a lion to make his appearance, he had the mortification to see one leap on to his sheep, seize him, and bound off again with the sheep, pegs and rope ere he could get a fair shot at him; he discharged his rifle, but missed his lion. The heat is so great to-day that it is quite uncomfortable to walk across the river-bed in slippers—104° F. in the shade. To-morrow we shall probably start afresh, and pitch our moving tents a day's march nearer home.

April 3rd.—All astir this morning preparing for the march to Amadeb, where we expect to find letters and newspapers from England. We have some tame monkeys and baboons in camp, which are very amusing and playful. When we are at breakfast some of them come and watch us, thankfully receiving any crumbs of comfort we choose to throw them. Although their movements are quite unfettered, they make no attempt to leave us and join their comrades who have not been civilized. Baboons, which are very large and strong, will sometimes form themselves into a limited liability company for the purpose of attacking a leopard, relieving one another at intervals; then, at last, when they think a favourable opportunity has arrived, all suddenly swoop down on him at once.

They will often lay in wait for the goats and sheep going to water, then go and suck them whilst they are drinking; after which refreshing performance these robbers, not liking to return to their mountain fastnesses empty-handed, will take the liberty of borrowing a kid from the flock. Last night, about 10 o'clock, we heard lions near camp. One came pretty close to the horses, causing quite a stampede amongst them; at the same time all the camels got up, showing signs of great uneasiness. Lions are very numerous here, hyænas few. When hyænas predominate they will often attack a lion, and in a very systematic way, too. A number will get in front of him, and act as designing persons in England sometimes do. They throw dust in his eyes, then the whole pack will fall upon and make an end of him. At such times both the lion and hyænas make a great uproar. We heard them one night, and Sali, who is an excellent tracker, told us that hyænas were then attacking a lion. We hear that Sheik Ahmed, with a number of the Beni-Amirs, have made arrangements with the Basé for a shooting expedition in their country, intending to go as far as Maiambasar, then cross from there to the Settite. They have a curious way of making themselves agreeable out there. To make themselves acceptable, they will take wives from amongst the Basé;

then when they leave the country they leave them behind, at the same time presenting them with a piece of cloth, some dhurra, and, perhaps, a few dollars.

April 4th.—Marched about nine hours to-day, encamping in a very mountainous region. Whilst the tents were being pitched, Mr. Colvin picked up a book, went about a hundred yards from camp, and sat down under a tree to read. He had not been there long ere he heard something breathing near him; looked round, and saw a hyæna within a *very* easy distance. He naturally got up and made tracks for camp, as he had no rifle with him. His unwelcome interviewer followed him pretty closely until he approached the camp. Soon after this, very near to camp, one of them made for Dra, who drew his sword and shouted. George saw him, and at once gave him the contents of his rifle.

April 5th.—Marched from 8 a.m., reaching Amadeb, a garrison town, at 8.30 p.m. We travelled a very mountainous region to-day — in one part, for the distance of a mile or two, over large boulders of marble on the roadway. On arriving at Amadeb, all were soon busy in reading their letters from England. The Bey here treated us with great consideration and kindness, providing us with tea, sugar, milk, biscuits, and cigarettes whilst our tents were being pitched and we were reading our letters. I had almost forgotten to mention one very exciting incident during our journey to-day, and it was this—All our party, except Mr. Colvin and myself, had gone on considerably in advance of the caravan (we were travelling along a dry river-bed, consequently on very open ground), when Suleiman came up in great haste, saying, "Doctor, have you got your rifle ready? The caravan is going to be attacked in the rear;" and off he went to inform the others. Colvin and I soon got our rifles and revolvers in readiness, and trotted back to the rear, where we found our men in a great state of excitement, leaping about, brandishing their spears, and insanely yelling, "Whoop! whoop!" which, of course, was no use, but an inconsiderate way of spending time and ventilating their feelings. Facing them were, perhaps, 80 or 100 Bareas (akin to the Basé), indulging in the same lunatic kind of performance. Our reinforcements arrived, in the shape of George, Anselmia, and the rest of the party. The Bareas, seeing our strength, then vanished like chaff before the wind. This was destined to be our last scare. From the information we could gather, it seems that the Bareas thought our numerous boxes were filled with dollars, and (according to Dra and Girgas) began pointing their spears towards them as if on hostile intentions bent. They retaliated by pointing rifles at them, which had the effect of inciting these fellows into a kind of war-like dance, accompanied by a significant brandishing of spears; and there is very little doubt that blood would have been spilt had we not promptly appeared on the scene.

April 6th.—Amadeb appears to be a tolerably large place. The houses are made of mud bricks baked in the sun, and are thatched. The whole town is surrounded by a mud wall. As we did not start until 3 p.m., I had many patients to attend. At 5 p.m. we encamped on pretty good ground, surrounded by trees, in which were thousands of doves, about 16 brace of which Mr. F. James and I soon knocked over, thus providing luncheon for the next day or two. We found water here.

April 7th.—We marched from 8 a.m. until 8 p.m., a distance of about 30 miles. At noon we passed a place where some thousands of camel, cattle, sheep, and goats were being watered. Of course, at this time of the year, all the river-courses are dry, and the water has to be drawn up from deep wells. The Beni-Amirs, and other neighbouring tribes, are a pastoral people, and owners of enormous herds, on which they wholly subsist. They produce nothing, and seem to require nothing, except a few yards of cotton. Their mode of watering the herds is a very laborious one. On this sandy river-bed I observed about 20 very large but shallow mud-basins, and close to each basin a well. At the top of each well is an Arab, provided with a large antelope skin (dressed), fastened around the sides, and attached to a long rope. This skin he drops into the well, and hauls up, hand-over-hand, full of water, which he tips into the mud-basin until it is full. With such insufficient means, of course, a long time is occupied in filling the basins.

In the afternoon George, who had gone on ahead, came back much excited, saying there was a young elephant in a wood which could be easily shot, adding that if he had had an elephant rifle with him he should have been tempted to let fly. It was fortunate that he had not, for presently we met the owner of this captured elephant, accompanied by a number of natives. They had halted for a short time, and had secured the elephant to a tree by a rope round the neck and leg. He had been captured at Forfar. His tusks were just protruding. Just as I approached him a native ran up, saying, "Batal, batal howaga" (bad, bad, sir). The man was right, for this infant had already wounded five men severely. I, therefore, kept a respectful distance. The country through which we travelled to-day was very mountainous, and here and there big plains covered with bushes; still nothing like so bad as the road before we got to Amadeb.

April 8th.—Marched from 8 a.m. until 1 p.m., encamping at Gargee, situated on Khor-Baraker. We stay here to-night, hoping to secure another lion. Just after dinner we heard jackals barking very much like dogs.

CHAPTER XXIV.

A LION NEAR THE CAMP—THE MONKS OF CHARDAMBA—WE MEET ALI DHEEN PASHA, GOVERNOR-GENERAL OF THE SOUDAN—ARRIVAL AT KEREN, OR SANHÎT—THE PRIESTS AT KEREN—ACCOUNT OF KEREN—MERISSA—DRA, A DOMESTIC SLAVE, MADE FREE—DESCENT FROM SANHÎT TO THE ANSEBA VALLEY—THE BIRDS THERE—ALONG THE RIVER-BED OF THE LABAK—A BIG MARCH— MASSAWA—FAREWELL TO CAMELS—MASSAWA TO SOUÂKIN —TAKE IN CARGO—FAREWELL TO THE SOUDAN—ARRIVAL AT SUEZ.

APRIL 9TH.—About 9 o'clock we were off again, halting at 5.30 p.m. at Adatur, on the River Bogoo. A fine leopard and hyæna were shot last night. About 9 p.m., whilst I was writing my diary, alone in camp, the others having gone out in search of lions, a native came up to me, whispering, "Asset, asset, howaga" (a lion, a lion, sir). It was a lovely moonlight night, so light that I could see to read or write distinctly. I looked on to the river-bed in the direction indicated by the Arab, and there, 40 yards off, I plainly saw a noble-looking lion. I was not long in obtaining a rifle from my tent, and following him up the river-bed; but to no purpose, as he was too far off to risk a shot at him. Finally he turned off into a large palm grove on the opposite side, where, of course, I did not follow him. I am told that about 14 years ago all this neighbourhood belonged to Abyssinia, but now belongs to Egypt. From this spot, not very far off, we noticed a most precipitous mountain, called Chardamba, in Abyssinia; it is almost inaccessible, and can only be ascended by taking off one's shoes and stockings, on account of the smoothness of the stones, at least, so Mr. Phillipps says. He and some of his party had the curiosity to climb it last year, and nearly got killed by stones being rolled down on them, for on the very summit of this mountain dwell some monks who have quite eschewed the pomps and vanities of this world. Many of them are withered, shrivelled old fellows who have lived there without once coming down for the space of 30 or 40 years, and, to all appearance, are one or two hundred years old. They possess a deep well, a chapel, each one a separate apartment or den, and they grow a little dhurra.

The next day we marched from 7.30 a.m. until

5.30 p.m., encamping at Ashdera. On the road we met, about 1 p.m., Ali Dheen Pasha, the Governor-General of the Soudan (who succeeded Ali Riza Pasha, a most unpopular governor). He was coming from Massawa, and, I believe, going on to Kassala. We had a very long pow-wow with him. He informed us that our Abyssinian affair had created quite a sensation in Cairo, that the Minister of the Interior had telegraphed to him asking if we were safe, and that the Mudir of Kassala had been dismissed for not sending soldiers with us, which, by the way, was not his fault, for we would not have them. The palace at Massawa was built by Gordon Pasha when Governor of the Soudan. This Ali Dheen kindly placed at our disposal, until a boat could take us to Suez.

On the 10th April a march of about 10 miles only brought us to Keren, or Sanhît. Soon after our arrival Réschid Pasha sent an officer, whom Ali Dheen Pasha had sent on, to inquire if we had arrived safe, and were comfortable. From here we sent telegrams to Massawa respecting boats to Suez. Although our journey was a short distance, it took us a considerable time to accomplish it. I should think, for about the distance of a mile, we traversed a most precipitous ascent in a zig-zag fashion; this was not far from Keren. On reaching the summit we found ourselves in quite a different kind of country. We soon paid a visit to the priests at Keren, who have an excellent garden. They kindly sent us some fine cabbages leeks, carrots, potatoes, and lettuce. As we had not seen anything of this kind for months they were, of course, a great luxury for dinner in the evening. In the afternoon the army doctor (who could speak French tolerably well) called on me, and as I had almost finished my campaign I gave him the greater part of the contents of my medicine chest. In the afternoon the tom-toms were set going, accompanied by the peculiar trilling note of the women, to express their joy at our arrival. They had heard that we had all been killed by the Abyssinians, our men also, many of whom came from here—Ali Bacheet, Dra, Girgas, and Mahomet Zanzimeer. The latter was thus called because he generally attended to our zanzimeers when we arrived in or started from camp. Pere Picard and another priest dined with us in the evening. After dinner about 60 children, well clothed, nice and clean, from their schools, came to witness the mysteries of the magic lantern; not only they, but Réschid Pasha, with a number of officers, came also, and were much pleased. When they took their departure rockets, together with red and blue fires, were let off.

Keren, or Sanhît, is the capital and only town of Bogos. It is 4,469 feet above the level of the sea, on the edge of the highlands of Abyssinia, and on one side of a table-land, about four miles long by two broad, surrounded by hills. Being situated in such a high position, it is healthy at all times of the year.

This elevated plateau has for its southern boundary the Abyssinian mountains, which come down to within about two miles of the town, which is built just outside the gates of the fort, and consists of two short, broad streets of very poor Greek stores, and some clusters of Abyssinian houses and Arab huts.

About a mile distant across the plateau is the French monastery. With the exception of the Pasha's residence, the monastery and its adjacent buildings are the only respectable-looking habitations there. They have an Amharic printing press for publishing Bibles in the native tongue, schools for educating Abyssinian boys for the priesthood, also for the education of girls. When I was there, about four priests and a few sisters fed, clothed, lodged, and educated upwards of 80 boys and 50 girls. They had a good schoolroom, chapel, dormitories, pharmacy, and harmonium, which latter one of the sisters play. The children, who looked very clean and orderly, sang very nicely a hymn in French for our especial benefit. These priests print, bind books, have carpenter's and blacksmith's shops, a dairy, vegetable garden, and appear to be a very useful community, exercising, I should say, a great deal of self-denial by residing in such a place as they do. They cannot certainly have a very festive time of it, for the Egyptian authorities regard them as spies, while, on the other hand, the Abyssinians, who distrust them, will not allow them into their country. I must speak of these priests as I found them. None of us were Roman Catholics, but they behaved with very great kindness to us; and we must award them a great degree of credit for the civilizing influence they exercised amongst these waifs and strays. The thought that occurred to me was that if Roman Catholic priests could be doing all this good, why not English missionaries also? There is generally a garrison of about 1,000 soldiers at Keren. There is scarcely any trade, as merchants will not risk their lives and goods, knowing the hostility of the Abyssinians, who are anxious for the recovery of Keren and the lost province of Bogos, added to which the Egyptian policy is to isolate Abyssinia, thereby preventing the importation of arms and ammunition for King John's army. The Beni-Amirs and other neighbouring tribes, who are all owners of large herds, on which they wholly subsist, are the Egyptian subjects. Fuel is scarce, as it has to be brought from the Anseba valley, four miles distant. Water also has to be brought from a distance, but there is a well inside the fort which supplies the garrison. Dhurra is dear, as the continual dread of Abyssinian raids prevents people from cultivating, also from building decent houses. There are no camels, and very few horses and mules.

I once tasted at Kassala a kind of beer made from dhurra, called merissa, and thought it exceptionally nasty. It is probably the same as that mentioned by Herodotus, and is in common use in the Soudan and Upper Egypt. I was again induced by a native, who thought he would be attentive to me for some little professional attendance I had given to taste this vile liquid. Thinking, perhaps, it might not be so nauseous as my last dose, I drank some, and acted like a stoic and philosopher, for I did not exhibit any outward and visible sign of the rebellious feelings taking place within. But "no matter;" I mentally resolved that in whatever part of the Soudan I might at some future time find myself, I would never again degrade my esophagus by allowing any merissa to glide down it, for I would just as soon have taken

MOUNTAIN PASS NEAR KEREN OR SANHÉT

one of my own vile black draughts, and infinitely have preferred a bottle of Bass's pale ale. I have no hesitation in saying that if merissa—a very euphonious name, so much like Nerissa—was the usual beverage in England, the Blue Ribbon Army would find in me a very ardent supporter, as it is more unpalatable, thick stuff than schliva (a Bosnian drink, made from the juice of prunes, possessing a strong asafœtida flavour). Merissa is made from dhurra, which is allowed to germinate in the sun, then reduced to flour by hand-mills. This, again, is converted into dough, boiled, and left to ferment. I hope that if I ever again pollute my lips with merissa—not Nerissa—I may be served in the same way, that is, that I may germinate in the sun, be ground into powder, made into a pulp, boiled, and allowed to ferment.

To-day a circumstance occurred in camp, illustrative of a curious custom existing in the Soudan. Dra, who has been with us as a native servant ever since we left Kassala, is, we find, a slave. Some altercation took place this morning between Dra and another native, when the latter called him a slave. This excited Dra's anger to such an extent that he talked about knifeing his accuser. However, Messrs. James and Co. enquired into the matter, and found that he was what they call a

x

slave—what we should call a domestic slave or bondsman—and that it came about in this way— Dra's father had, some time ago, "pinched" a cow, *i.e.*, purloined it. He was ordered to pay back two within a month; failed to do so. The fine was then doubled every month, until he owed about a hundred cows. As there was just about as much probability of his being able to pay his fines as there would be of my paying the National Debt, he and all his children and children's children became bondsmen and bondswomen of the creditor. Should Dra, who was single, desire to marry, he would find it difficult, under such circumstances, to obtain a wife; but should he succeed in doing so, and children be born to him, all the males would be slaves, and the females *compelled* to become public women. This little matter was talked over in the evening at the dinner table, when it was ascertained that his freedom could be secured by the payment of 35 dollars, which my colleagues gave to the priests to effect his freedom with. They say that papers will have to be made out and signed by the Pasha at Keren, and that on payment of the 35 dollars he will be free. A man then goes round the town with a trumpet, and proclaims the fact in all directions. This, I am told, is quite typical of the system in vogue here.

On the 11th of April, at 11 a.m., we were once more on the road to Massawa, encamping at 5 p.m. at Gubana. Ere we left Keren a donation in aid of the schools was given by the party, and the priests very kindly sent us a sack of potatoes, carrots, and parsnips. As we had been without fresh vegetables so long, these were really quite a treat. We descended from Sanhît into the Anseba valley. About a mile from the town, in the lowlands, were the gardens of the priests, full of vegetables, growing in the most luxuriant manner. The trees, too, flourished, and were covered with beautiful green foliage. Here, on reaching the river-bed, we found a little water actually on the surface.

April 12th.—To-day we travelled 10 hours through quite a different kind of country to what we have lately been accustomed. A great variety of lovely plumaged birds are abundant in the Anseba valley. Even the doves here are tinged with bright yellow, green and blue. I managed to secure some specimens of them, the brilliant plumaged rollo-birds, paroquets, and a fine eagle. Soon after starting our route lay up the side of a frightfully precipitous mountain. The ascent was made by a most tortuous pathway, where in very many places the camels walked on the brink of a fearful abyss. Having at last reached the summit of this mountain in safety, our descent was made by an equally horrible pathway, after which we travelled for the greater part of our journey along a dry river-bed, surrounded on each side by steep, precipitous mountains covered with large cactus trees in full bloom, and gaunt, leafless, but enormous baobob trees, and, of course, the never-to-be-forgotten prickly mimosas, but I saw much less gum arabic exuding from them there than I did in the Basé country. Large tamarisk trees, also, were numerous. The branches of all kinds of trees lay scattered about in the greatest profusion, the natives having chopped them off for the goats, sheep, and cows to feed on.

On the 13th April, another 10 hours' march brought us to Kalamet, where we pitched our tents for the night, having travelled through very wild and picturesque scenery, the greater part of the distance being along the river-bed of the Labak. Water was very near to, and in some places on, the surface. For a distance of about two miles we journeyed along a very deep pass; on either side of us extremely rugged, lofty, precipitous crags, clothed with cactus trees and other bushes, through which we occasionally discerned jackals and wild goats peeping at us with astonishment. Scarcely any birds of any description were seen this day. The pass, I believe, is called El Ain; a representation of it appeared some months ago in the *Graphic*. Our camping and marching, like Bedouin Arabs, is now nearly at an end, for in another day or two we expect to reach Massawa, once more set our eyes on the Red Sea, and a steamer, don decent apparel, and return to civilized life.

Our next day, April 14th, was occupied in marching to near Kamfar, a distance of about 27 miles. This was an easy road for the camels, as the greater part of the distance was along level ground, covered with mimosas, more like the desert near Souâkin. We came across a few jackals, ariels, gazelles, falcons, and extremely beautiful diminutive sunbirds, so small that they ought to be shot with sand.

April 16th.—At 7.30 a.m. we once more, and for the last time, mounted our camels, and made a good march of about 32 miles, arriving at Massawa at 8.30 p.m. Some of our Arabs had never before had an opportunity of seeing the Red Sea; now that they did, their delight seemed great. We should not have made such a long march to-day but that a messenger had been sent from Massawa, to meet us with the information that an Italian steamer (Rubattino line) would be leaving on the morrow, and that if we missed that we might, perhaps, have to wait two or three weeks ere we should get another. However, we did not intend to wait, for we should have chartered a stambouk from there to Aden, there catching a P. and O. boat for Suez.

Massawa, the principal seaport of Abyssinia, is on a small barren coral island in the Red Sea, about a mile long, by 400 yards broad, at the northern extremity of the Bay of Arkeeko. It is connected with the mainland by a causeway a mile in length, built across the shallow water. There are barracks and huts for about 1,000 soldiers. It is badly off for water. This has to be carried two miles to the town. The town is built partly of stone and coral, but most of the houses are constructed of poles and bent grass, and surrounded by a reed fence. The most considerable buildings are the mosques, the houses of the traders, and a few warehouses, which are built of coral, and the bazaar.

The surrounding country is little cultivated, and industry paralysed by fear of raids by the Abyssinians. But little trade is done with the Soudan; formerly a brisk trade was done with slaves, and that seems likely to be the case again. Most of the imports come from Abyssinia. They are grain, gold, cotton, manufactures, glass-wares, spices, arms, cutlery, hides, butter, wines and spirits. Principal exports, rhinoceros-horns, gold, ivory, honey and wax.

As usual, vexatious export and import duties are imposed by Egypt. No guns or powder are allowed to be imported. There are very few camels, and horses and mules are scarce and dear. The population has been estimated at about 4,000. The island is dependent on Egypt, and is ruled by a governor appointed by the Khedive. The chief inhabitants of Massawa are a few Greeks and Italians, an Italian and French Consul, one Englishman, and a small colony of Banians, through whose hands almost all the trade passes.

On arriving at Massawa I took my leave of camel riding, and cannot say I was sorry, having ridden, probably about 2,000 miles on caravan camels, which roared at me when I mounted them, roared when I dismounted, roared if I passed them, and roared if I looked at them. My knickerbockers were just about done for, and I should not like to say how many hours I had spent in repairing them, on two occasions, with a girba cut up. The Bey soon put in an appearance; had a bit of a pow-wow; gave us coffee and cigarettes, then showed us to the palace, where we had our camp-beds once more unfolded.

April 17th.—So much had to be done to-day—paying servants, selling camels, and tents, &c., that we found it impossible to get away. Word to this effect was sent to the Italian steamer, so the Captain has postponed his departure until to-morrow. Abdullah, a negro, who had always seen to getting my camel ready, helping to pitch and take down my tent, and otherwise proved a faithful henchman, presented me with his spear, and kissed my hand. I rewarded him with a small pin-fire revolver, 50 cartridges, a good knife, a razor, two dollars, and my knickerbockers. His delight was unbounded, possibly at receiving the last-named unmentionables. I am told that at an island near here a considerable pearl fishery is carried on, and that at another island close by large quantities of fine melons are grown.

At 8.15 a.m. the next morning we took our leave of the Soudan. The Bey had received orders to pay us every attention. He accordingly sent a gunboat, manned by sailors of the navy, with an officer, and we were at once rowed off to our

THE CAUSEWAY AT MASSAWAH.

steamer, bound for Suez. In the evening of the next day, at 5.30 p.m., we anchored at Souâkin. I and two others went ashore and spent the evening with Mr. Bulay (who was always most kind and obliging), returning to the ship at 10.30 p.m. All sorts of dreadful reports about the attack of the Dembelas on us had reached him, which, fortunately, were not true. Other startling news he gave us, such as that the Queen had been again shot at; that Arabi Pasha was getting a power in the State, and that the Khedive was likely to be dethroned, and Arabi substituted.

About an hour before we dropped anchor at Souâkin some of our boxes arrived from Kassala. We are likely to remain here two or three days taking in cargo. The day before we left Souâkin a French Consul and two American gentlemen (a doctor and missionary, who were at Shepheard's Hotel in November last at the same time that we were), came on board. They had been to the White Nile. We have quite a menagerie on board—parrots, paroquets, tiger-cats, jackals, monkeys, baboons, extraordinary looking geese, two enormous tortoises, and other animals. We took on board a good many cattle for Suez, and left the Soudan for good at 9 a.m. next day, April 22nd, arriving, after a very pleasant, but warm voyage, at Suez about 3 a.m. At 8 we went ashore and breakfasted at the Suez Hotel. Of course Mr. Clarke, the excellent and obliging manager of this hotel, related the usual tale of our horrible massacre, &c.

CHAPTER XXV.

SUEZ TO CAIRO—ALEXANDRIA—ON BOARD THE "MONGOLIA"—PASSENGERS ON BOARD—HIBERNIAN HUMOUR—VENICE—THE PIAZZA OF ST. MARK—THE CAMPANILE—THE PIAZZETTA—THE ZECCA, OR MINT—THE PALACE OF THE DOGES—ST. MARK'S—THE ARSENAL.

APRIL 27TH.—Heads and skins had to be sorted out, turpentined, packed and sent by sea from Suez, together with Mahoom and Girgas, the latter an Abyssinian whom Mr. Phillipps is taking home with him as a servant. On the 28th we left Suez for Cairo, arriving there at about 5 p.m., where I found several letters awaiting me—some of rather old dates. Of course the wildest reports of our massacre had reached Cairo, and been the topic of the day at the time. Our stay in Cairo was of short duration this time, as we found the Peninsular and Oriental Company's steamboat *Mongolia* would be leaving Alexandria on the 4th May. Messrs. Colvin and Aylmer went on to India, but the rest of us started for England.

Leaving Alexandria on the 4th, with a goodly number of passengers, about 120, we had a pleasant voyage to Venice, passing on the 5th the Morea, Navarino, and Caudia, on the 6th Xante and Cephalonia, and on the 7th arrived at Brindisi, viewing Montenegro and Corfu in the distance. There we got rid of the mails, and fully half the passengers, and at 6 p.m. on the 8th steamed up the grand canal, and soon arrived at Venice, the Queen of the Adriatic, the home of poetry and song. How pleasant it was to find myself, after all this Arab life, comfortably housed at the Hotel d'Italie, amongst civilized people, I will leave the reader to judge. There were a great many notables on board, amongst them several ladies connected with officials in Cairo. We knew that matters were a little unsettled in Egypt at this time, and so drew our own conclusions. These ladies were being sent out of the way, and within 3 or 4 weeks after I had seen the last of the great square in Alexandria it was in ruins. There were on board big men and little men, both in stature and in their own estimation. There were fat men and thin men, agreeable and chatty men, disagreeable and morose men, humble and meek men, busy and sleepy men, easy-going looking men, one or two of the " Ah ! I see, thanks, I'll not twouble you" kind of fellows, Colonels, Lieut.-Colonels, and other officers, Governors and Judges returning home on leave of absence, and genial, good-hearted, jolly sort of fellows. I acted here, as I always do at home, avoided the starchy " Ah ! I see—not-twouble-you kind of fellows," full of their own importance, whose brains are concentrated in their nicely-polished boots, &c., and fraternised with the sociable, sensible, good-hearted kind. Amongst them was one of my own profession, brimful of Hibernian humour and mirth. He was a brigade-surgeon in the 68th in India, where he had been for 25 years, and was now on leave of absence. Dr. Kilkelly and I conceived a mutual regard for one another. He and I, with a Judge from Cawnpore, a Colonel and Lieut.-Colonel, generally got together on the deck, enjoying ourselves very comfortably until we parted. I cannot remember all the jokes and witticisms of our friend, Dr. Kilkelly, but I do remember one circumstance that amused us all immensely, and caused great laughter, as much in the way of saying it as the thing that was said. We had been having a great talk about the Soudan. When I happened to say " Two of our party are going on from Cairo to India, and will not be in England until this time next year," the doctor exclaimed, "Sure, ye don't say they are going on there now? I could not have thought a man in his senses would be going to India now. Do ye know what it is like this time of the year?"

"Hot, I suppose," said I, whilst the others smoked their pipes and looked amused, evidently expecting some "rale Irish joke."

"Well, then, I'll tell ye," said our humorous friend, with a merry twinkle in his eye, and a really comic aspect; "d'ye know, docthor, when I have been in India this time of the year I have often made the natives dig a grave for me to lie in, half fill it with grass and pour buckets of cold wather on me to keep me from melting. I'll tell ye another thing—cholera is so bad at this time of the year, that, by the Viceroy's orders, coffins of all sizes are kept ready at the railway stations, and when the ticket-collector goes round, saying, 'Yere tickets, plase,' he finds a poor divil in the corner who does not respond; looks at him, finds him dead, pulls him out, finds a coffin the right size, puts him in, and by St. Pathrick he's buried before the sun sets. Now what d'ye think of that? That's what India's like this time of the year."

Of course we all roared with laughter at the

voluble and comical way in which this was said, and I mentally made a note that I should not start for India in May for my first visit.

Amongst our passengers were two sons of Sir Salar Jung, the Prime Minister of the Nizam of Hyderabad, on a visit to England. The elder one, though young, was a very Colossus, and an extremely intelligent, agreeable fellow, who spoke English fairly well, and was very chatty. He invited me, if I visited India, to visit him, and promised I should have some tiger-hunting. Whether I shall ever do so, or he would remember his promise, I don't know—probably not. Dr. Kilkelly and I put up at the same hotel (the Hôtel d'Italie), and spent a few days very pleasantly. I cannot say I should like to live in a place where, if I enter my front door, I must step out of a gondola, or if I want to visit a friend I must cross the street in a gondola; but it is a charming place to pay a visit to for a few days, especially for a person with a romantic and poetic turn of mind, and although romance has, to a great extent been knocked out of me, I still have sufficient of the poetic temperament to have been highly pleased with my visit to Venice, short though it was.

Pursuing the course I have hitherto adopted, I will not leave Venice without a brief sketch of it and my visits to various places of great interest, although, perhaps, repeating an oft-told tale. The man who ventures on a description of a visit to Venice ought to be thoroughly imbued with romance and poetry ere he can do justice to his subject. Under such circumstances I cannot hope to rival many another; but, as the Yankees say, "I'll do my level best." On the evening of my arrival, I met, by appointment, one of the officers of the *Mongolia*, whom I accompanied to St. Mark's Place. The side of the Piazza facing St. Mark is a line of modern building erected by the French, somewhat in the style of the Palais Royal at Paris, but yet having some sort of keeping with the edifices on the south side. They are termed the Procuratie Nuove, and form the south side, the Procuratie Vecchie the north side. The end is composed of a French façade uniting the two. Near the east end of the Procuratie Nuove, just by the point where it makes an angle with the Piazetta, stands the Campanile of St. Mark. It is, in fact, the belfry of the Cathedral, although it stands some considerable distance from it. The separation of the belfry from the church is very common in Italy, and there are a few instances of it in our own country. On the summit of the Campanile is a large open belfry to which you ascend in the inside by means of a series of inclined planes. The sides of the belfry are formed by sixteen arches, four facing each quarter of the heavens. A gallery with a parapet runs round the outside. I was told that the First Napoleon ascended the inclined plane by means of a donkey. I, however, had to walk it, and was well recompensed for my trouble by the magnificent view obtained from the summit. Southward lies the noble Adriatic, with the Pyrenees to the right; northward the Tyrolese Alps; immediately spreading round this singular post of observation lies the city of Venice, map-like, with its canals and neighbouring isles; and just under the eye, to the east, is St. Mark's Church, considerably below, with its fine domes, its four bronze horses, its numerous pinnacles, and in front of it its three tall, red standards.

It is impossible to describe the effect produced on the mind, on a summer's evening, as the sun is going down in his glory over the mainland beyond the lagoons, lighting them up with his parting rays, while the murmurs of the crowd assembled in St. Mark's Place ascend like the hum of bees around the hive door, and the graceful gondolas are seen noiselessly gliding along the canals. Traversing the Piazza, we find ourselves in the Piazetta running down from the east end of the great one by St. Mark's Church to the water-side, where the eye ranges over the lagoons and isles. The next side of this open space contains a continuation of the walk under arcades, which surround St. Mark's Place. The upper part exhibits a specimen of the Italian style, designed by Sansovino. The whole belonged to the royal palace, or Palace of the Doges, which extends along the south and west sides of the Piazza. Turning round the west corner of the Piazetta, on the Mole, with the canal in front, we see another of Sansovino's works, called the Zecca, or Mint, from which the gold coin of the Republic derived the name of Zecchino. In front of the open space and landing steps of the Piazetta are two lofty columns, which appear so prominently in the pictures of that part of Venice. They are of granite, and came from Constantinople—trophies of Venetian victories in the Turkish wars. The right hand column, looking towards the sea, is surmounted by a figure of St. Mark, standing on a crocodile. The left hand is surmounted by the lion of St. Mark. The west front of the ducal palace forms the east side of the Piazetta; the south front runs along the whole, and looks out upon the sea. They are its most ancient portions. The front, overlooking the Piazetta, is composed of two rows of arcades, one above the other; the lower a colonnade, the upper a gallery, surmounted by a very large and lofty surface of wall of a reddish marble, pierced by fine large windows. One gentleman says of it, "The ducal palace is even more ugly than anything I have previously mentioned."

Mr. Ruskin, on the other hand, says that, "Though in many respects imperfect, it is a piece of rich and fantastic colour, as lovely a dream as ever filled the imagination, and the proportioning of the columns and walls of the lofty story is so lovely and so varied that it would need pages of description before it could be fully understood."

Having done the Campanile, and strolled round the Piazza and Piazetta, we took our seats in the Piazza. On the west and south sides, as well as the north, the lower part of the buildings under the arcades is appropriated to shops or cafés. The latter are particularly celebrated. Towards sunset the area of St. Mark's Place is overspread with tables and chairs, where ladies and gentlemen are seated at their ease, as if in a drawing-room, taking refreshments. A space in the middle is left for promenaders, and when the military band is playing, which it does two or three times a week, the concourse is immense, and the scene very lively and charming, enabling one to realise the saying of Bonaparte, "The Place of St. Mark is a saloon of which the sky is worthy to serve as a ceiling."

Having enjoyed the sweet strains discoursed by the military band to our heart's content, we took our departure, my companion to his ship, and I to my hotel.

The following day was occupied in various ways by Dr. Kilkelly and myself. In the first place we, of course, paid a visit to the Palace of the Doges. If those walls could speak, how many tales of horror and cruelty they could unfold! Our visit to some portions of the Palace enabled us to vividly imagine some of them. Of course, in many of the trials here, whatever may be thought of the sentence inflicted, guilt, and that of a heavy kind, was proved against the accused. The place was not always a slaughter-house for innocence, a butchery for men guilty of light offence. Grave crimes against the State were here disclosed, and the memory especially dwells on that night in the April of 1855, when Marino Faliero, a traitor to the Government of which he was the head, was arraigned before his old companions in office, and when the sword of justice, covered with crape, was placed on the throne which he had been wont to fill. A very minute inspection of the Doge's Palace was not practicable, for two reasons; one was want of time, the other the impatience of my friend. Whilst in the Council Chamber of the Senate, and for a minute or so looking at the largest painting I ever saw in my life, "The Day of Judgment," my hasty friend seized me by the arm, exclaiming, "Come along, do;" and soon afterwards, when I was deeply engaged in the futile endeavour *apparently* of dislocating my neck by looking at the painted ceilings, and getting up the requisite enthusiasm for the marvellous productions of some of the masterpieces of Titian, Paulo Veronese, and Tintoretto, I was told to "Come along, docthor. Sure ye'll have a crick in yer neck, and not be able to eat yer dinner at all, at all, if ye stand looking at the ceiling in that kind of way;" and so I allowed my volatile friend to rush me through the Palace of the Doges, coming away with a hazy recollection of thousands of books, wondrous paintings, the Council Chamber of the Senate, before whom an undefended prisoner had formerly appeared; the Council of Ten, where he generally got deeper in the mire; the Council of Three, whose decrees were like the laws of the Medes and Persians; and, finally, the dungeon, or condemned cell, just by one end of the Bridge of Sighs, where he was strangled within, I think, three days of his condemnation. I was also shown a dungeon, but not so low down as the condemned cell, where no ray of light could be admitted, but where the poor wretch had a stone slab, such as we have in our cellars, to lie upon, and let into the wall was an opening through which the Grand Inquisitor could calmly gaze on the torturing process produced by the rack and thumb-screw, and other ingenious but painful arrangements constructed for blood-letting. Some of the blood of deceased victims was shown to me on the walls, possibly like the blood of Rizzio on the floor in Holyrood Palace, renewed once a year. Of course there were many objects of great interest in the Doge's Palace that I should have, no doubt, made many notes of had I been by myself, but mental notes were all I was permitted to take. Many people give a free rein to their fancy, and argue much on the origin of species. This is a free country, and I may form my own idea of the General Post-Office. Suppose I were to say that it originated from the Doge's Palace? but fortunately for us, with a more agreeable class of men as letter-carriers. I remember to have seen a lion, griffin, or "goblin damned," at the head of one staircase, with open mouth, whose sole object was to receive accusations, true and false, against citizens of the State, and woe betide him if he came before the Council of Three, from whom there was no appeal. Here our accusers have to prove us guilty, there the accused had to prove himself innocent; and I doubt not that, in those dark ages of cruelty, such a mode had its inconveniences, necessitating a considerable amount of trouble for nothing on the part of the accused.

We passed on from the Doge's Palace to St. Mark's. This church is very ancient; it was begun in the year 829, and after a fire rebuilt in the year 976. It was ornamented with mosaics and marble in 1071. Its form is of Eastern origin, and it is said its architects, who were ordered by the Republic to spare no expense, and to erect an edifice superior in size and splendour to anything else, took Santa Sophia, in Constantinople, for their model, and seem to have imitated its form, its domes, and its bad taste. But if riches can compensate the absence of beauty, the Church of St. Mark possesses a sufficient share to supply the deficiency, as it is ornamented with the spoils of Constantinople, and displays a profusion of the finest marbles, of alabaster, onyx, emerald, and of all the splendid jewellery of the East. The celebrated bronze horses stand on the portico facing the Piazza. These horses are supposed to be the work of Lysippus; they ornamented successively different triumphal arches at Rome, were transported by Constantine to his new city, and conveyed thence by Venetians, when they took and plundered it in 1206. They were erected on marble pedestals over the portico of St. Mark, where they stood nearly six hundred years, a trophy of the power of the Republic, until they were removed to Paris by Napoleon in the year 1797, and placed on stone pedestals behind the Palace of the Tuileries, where they remained some time, until they were again restored to Venice. In St. Mark's I was shown two pillars of alabaster, two of jasper, and two of verde antique, said to have been brought from King Solomon's temple, also two magnificent doors, inlaid with figures of gold and silver, and a very large crucifix of gold and silver, brought from Santa Sophia. I was also shown the tomb of St. Mark the Evangelist. How true all this is I cannot say, but perhaps many of my readers would like to know why St. Mark should be so much thought of in Venice, so much so as to become the patron saint, and have his name given to the most celebrated and splendid of its churches. Over a thousand years ago—to be precise, in the year eight hundred and twenty-nine—two Venetian merchants, named Bano and Rustico, then at Alexandria, contrived, either by bribery or by stratagem, to purloin the body of St. Mark, at that time in the possession of Mussulmen, and to convey it to Venice. On its arrival it was transported to the Ducal Palace, and deposited, by the then Doge, in his own chapel. St. Mark was shortly after declared the patron and protector of the Republic; and the lion, which, in the mystic vision of Ezekiel, is supposed to represent this evangelist, was emblazoned on its standards and elevated on its towers. The Church of St. Mark was erected immediately after this event, and the saint has ever since retained his honours. But the reader will learn with surprise that notwithstanding these honours the body of the Evangelist was, in a very short space of time, either lost or *privately sold* by a tribune of the name of Carozo, who had usurped the dukedom, and to support himself against the legitimate Doge, is supposed to have plundered the treasury and to have alienated some of the most valuable articles. Since that period the existence of the body of St. Mark has never been publicly ascertained, though the Venetians firmly maintain that it is still in their possession, and, as I said before, positively show the tomb which, they say, covers him.

Our next visit was to the arsenal. This occupies an entire island, and is fortified, not only by its ramparts, but by the surrounding sea; it is spacious, commodious, and magnificent.

Before the gate stand two vast pillars, one on each side, and two immense lions of marble, which formerly adorned the Piræus of Athens. They are attended by two others of smaller size, all, as the inscription informs us, "Triumphali manu Piræo direpta" ("Torn from the Piræus by the hand of Victory"). The staircase in the principal building is of white marble, down which the French (who invaded Venice) rolled cannon balls, an act of wanton mischief quite inexcusable, at the same time they dismantled the Bucentaur, the famous State galley of the Republic—a very Vandal-like act.

Venice, when in the zenith of its fame, might justly be said to bear a striking resemblance to Rome. The same spirit of liberty, the same patriot passion, the same firmness, and the same wisdom that characterized the ancient Romans seemed to pervade every member of the rising State, and at that time it might truly be said of Venice —

> Italia's empress! queen of land and sea!
> Rival of Rome, and Roman majesty!
> Thy citizens are kings; to thee we owe
> Freedom, the choicest gift of Heaven below.
> By thee barbaric gloom was chased away,
> And dawn'd on all our lands a brighter day.

But *tempora mutantur*.

CHAPTER XXVI.

WE HEAR OF THE MURDER OF LORD FREDERICK CAVENDISH AND MR. BURKE—A GRAND SERENADE ON THE GRAND CANAL—MY JOURNEY FROM VENICE TO ENGLAND.

EVERY evening during our stay in Venice, just about the time we finished dining in the evening, a gondola full of serenaders would take up their position just beneath our open window, and sing some of their charming Italian ballads in a very pleasing style, undisturbed by the rattling of cabs and omnibuses. Indeed, it seemed very strange, as we wandered about this town of waterways, spanned by about 360 bridges, never to see a vehicle or living thing except human beings. Of course, the quietude that reigned all round was very favourable to the serenaders. One very favourite song, both with the serenaders and visitors, was called " Santa Lucia." This, I think, we had every night, for, if they left this out of their programme, someone at the hotel would be certain to ask for it. Venice, as all the world knows, is noted for its glass manufactories. To one of these, owned by Dr. Salviati, my friend and I wended our steps. We were much interested on going over the place, and much burdened on coming out of it, as each of us emerged with an armful of purchases. It was fortunate for me that my stay was of short duration, as each time I returned to my hotel after a stroll, I generally did so with an armful of purchases of some description or other.

Dr. Kilkelly, whose residence was in Dublin, had arranged with me that we should return to England by a different route to that by which I had come by. We intended to travel through the Brenner Pass to Munich, then to Bingen on the Rhine, down that river to Cologne, and on to England, but as we were to have a grand serenade on the Grand Canal at night, we postponed the journey until the morrow. Soon after this, whilst walking along, a large poster of the *Standard* newspaper attracted our attention, announcing "The Murder of Lord Frederick Cavendish." A paper was soon procured, and there we read the account of his murder and that of Mr. Burke's, dastardly deeds that all respectable Irishmen blush to think of, and which excited the indignation of my friend to boiling-point. This at once altered his plans entirely. Said he, "I must start home to-morrow. As head of the family I must get to Dublin at once; perhaps the place will be under martial law." I then relinquished the idea of taking our route, not caring to go by myself, and resolved to spend another day or so in Venice, returning *viâ* Turin.

In the evening the doctor, Mrs. and Miss P., and myself made our way to the water-side, with the intention of engaging a gondola to witness this grand aquatic *fête*. How we should have got on with the gondolier I don't know, as he could only speak his own language; but, fortunately, I knew just sufficient Italian to pull us out of the difficulty. In whatever country I remain a few days, my first business is to know the value of the coins and be able to count in the language of the country. This I have always found extremely useful, particularly in Turkey, where the coinage is very confusing to a stranger. A piaster is worth about 2d. There they have silver, copper, metallic, and paper piasters; and unless one knows all about the rate of exchanging a Medjidie, the trusting individual may possibly and probably be the victim of misplaced confidence.

Having secured our gondola, we pulled up opposite Danielli's Hotel, a little way above the Doge's

Palace. Here we found a large floating stage, occupied by those who were to take part in the seranade. It was profusely and very prettily decorated with festoons of flowers and evergreens, among which were interlaced a vast number of variegated lamps (the centre piece forming quite a tree of these little lamps). Under this stood the conductor, whilst around him was the orchestra and singers. This great stage started from opposite Danielli's Hotel, drawn by two boats. Following it were hundreds of gondolas jostling one another on the Grand Canal, each one trying to get as near as possible to the stage. Those on shore took as much interest in the proceedings as those on the canals, for at every stoppage—and these occurred very frequently—a performance took place. Opposite each stoppage there was a grand pyrotechnic display by those on shore. Our first halt was opposite the Palace of the Doges and the Piazetta of St. Mark, where numberless Roman candles, Bengal lights, rockets, &c., were let off, brilliantly illuminating the far-famed old Palace, Piazza, Campanile, St. Mark's, and all the surroundings, and so on past the hotels (once gorgeous marble palaces); the Church of Santa Maria della Salute, on the opposite shore; the Palazzo Foscari, the Academy of Arts, and other palaces, winding up with a grand scene at the Ponte Rialto. The time occupied was about three hours, from 9 until 12 p.m. No amount of word-painting can convey to the reader an adequate description of the scene, which was most enjoyable throughout. It was a beautiful summer's night—no moon, not a cloud; the blue sky studded with bright twinkling stars, the stage adorned with flowers, evergreens, and hundreds of variegated lamps; no sound but the splash of the gondoliers' oar and jostling of the gondolas; a stop, then sweet strains of music arising from stringed and wind instruments and two or three dozen well-trained male and female voices; and every now and then the banks on either side lighting up, by the illuminations, the grand old churches and fine old marble palaces of the old Venetian nobility, to each of which is attached a history. It was a scene which I shall always remember, but which I feel quite unable to describe as I should wish. Our hotel was soon reached when all was over, and I went to bed, lulled to sleep by the sweet Italian music of gondoliers which came floating on the midnight air as they returned home after this grand serenade.

On the following day my friend, the doctor, started for England. Soon after his departure Mr. P. and I hired a gondola, and paid a visit to the

Academy of Arts, some of the principal churches, palaces, and various places of interest, and saw some grand old sculpture, the tombs of Canova and Titian, and paintings by Rubens, Titian, Tintorello, Paulo Veronese and others. I had resolved on the morrow to forsake this dreamland under the clear blue sky of Italy, and once more rouse myself to the stern realities of life. Accordingly, I found myself in the train next day at 9 a.m., with a ticket for Paris. Passing Verona, Padua, and other interesting places, I arrived in Paris at 5.30 p.m. on the evening of the next day. A day's rest there, and I was on my way to dear old England, which I reached in due time. A trip abroad is mentally and bodily beneficial, but after wanderings in various countries, I have come to the conclusion that the most comfortable place to *permanently* reside in, provided one is not absolutely devoid of the "almighty dollar"—as the Americans would say—is "perfidious Albion."

I have travelled through the waving forests of Austria, miles of charming vineclad slopes in Hungary, acres of maize, rice, and tobacco fields near Salonica, the beautiful cypress groves of Scutari, near Constantinople, roamed over the wild mountains of Bosnia and Montenegro, through classic Greece and Italy, and traversed the burning sands of Africa; but, go where I will, nowhere is the general appearance of the country so beautiful as in old England, where we find the little cottage of the rustic so prettily embowered amidst fruit trees, shrubs and flowers, whilst all around are undulating green fields, rippling brooks, and winding rivers. Nowhere else is there anything to compare to our pretty country lanes and variegated hedgerows, covered with sweet-smelling hawthorn, the wild rose, honeysuckle, and the red berries of the ash, whilst the banks are adorned with foxgloves and beautiful ferns, or white with primroses, cowslips, and a thousand other wild flowers which surround fields of waving golden ears of corn and the well-wooded estates of the landed gentry, that in turn give shelter to the fox, who will afford sport in the winter, and to the hares, rabbits, partridges, and pheasants, who will assist in satiating our gastronomic propensities.

It is an Englishman's privilege to grumble, and whilst living here we often find a great deal to grumble about, in politics particularly; but I don't think there are many who, having travelled abroad continuously for six, twelve, or eighteen months, will not say with me, on returning home once more, "England, with all thy faults, I love thee still."

"A plain unvarnished tale I have unfolded," and

as such, at this particular time, I trust it will meet with the approbation of the *majority* of my readers.

Many faults, I am sure, may be picked out, as I have not only written, but revised the book myself, instead of employing (as some do) a skilled and experienced reader. Even had I done so I should still be able to say—

> " Whoever thinks a faultless piece to see,
> Thinks what ne'er was, nor is, nor e'er shall be."

FINIS.

www.ingramcontent.com/pod-product-compliance
Lightning Source LLC
Chambersburg PA
CBHW031428230426
43668CB00007B/478